MIDDLE SCHOOL/ JUNIOR HIGH PRINCIPAL'S HANDBOOK

A Practical Guide for Developing Better Schools

MIDDLE SCHOOL/ JUNIOR HIGH PRINCIPAL'S HANDBOOK

A Practical Guide for Developing Better Schools

Allan A. Glatthorn
University of Pennsylvania

Norman K. Spencer
School District of Philadelphia

Prentice-Hall, Inc.
Englewood Cliffs, New Jersey

Prentice-Hall International, Inc., *London*
Prentice-Hall of Australia, Pty. Ltd., *Sydney*
Prentice-Hall Canada, Inc., *Toronto*
Prentice-Hall of India Private Ltd., *New Delhi*
Prentice-Hall of Japan, Inc., *Tokyo*
Prentice-Hall of Southeast Asia Pte. Ltd., *Singapore*
Whitehall Books, Ltd., *Wellington, New Zealand*
Editora Prentice-Hall do Brasil Ltda., *Rio de Janeiro*
Prentice-Hall Hispanoamericana, S.A., *Mexico*

© 1986 *by*

PRENTICE-HALL, INC.
Englewood Cliffs, New Jersey

Library of Congress Cataloging-in-Publication Data

Glatthorn, Allan A.
  Middle school/junior high principal's handbook.

  Includes index.
    1. Junior high schools—United States.
2. Middle schools—United States.   3. School improvement programs—United States.   4. Junior high school
principles—United States.   I. Spencer, Norman K.
II. Title.
LB1623.G55   1986   373.2′36   86-5006

ISBN 0-13-582008-1

We dedicate this book to our mothers and our wives:
Anna G. Glatthorn and Barbara P. Glatthorn, and
Estelle S. Thomas and Rosemary Welch Spencer.

About the Authors

Allan A. Glatthorn, Ed.D., is professor of education at the Graduate School of Education, University of Pennsylvania. Involved in education for more than thirty years, he has been a classroom teacher and subject-matter supervisor, as well as principal of a grades 9–10 school that achieved national recognition. The author of several professional books and the senior author of more than forty school textbooks, Dr. Glatthorn has served as a consultant to more than 200 school districts to help them improve curriculum, climate, and instruction.

Norman K. Spencer, Ed.D., principal of the Benjamin Franklin High School in Philadelphia, has had more than twenty-five years' experience in the school system as a teacher, counselor, inter-group specialist, assistant principal, and assistant to the district superintendent. Having earned a reputation as a principal who knows how to "turn schools around," Dr. Spencer was appointed principal of an inner-city junior high school that suffered from several critical problems—a high absence rate, poor discipline, and low achievement. Within just a few years, he made a positive difference: The school became one of the most effective junior highs in the city. He has used those same processes in his present role as principal of a large urban high school.

About This Book

Middle School/Junior High Principal's Handbook is for all administrators who are interested in better schools for young adolescents and who want to know how to make those improvements. The *Handbook* is concerned primarily with field-tested, research-based methods for improving middle and junior high schools. However, the book does not offer single prescriptions; instead, it suggests many routes to better, more effective schools for young adolescents.

Effective schools for young adolescents can be called middle schools or junior high schools. For the sake of simplicity, the former term is used here to identify any school that has two or more of the grades between 5 and 9; but effective schools for young adolescents can encompass several types of grade-level organization.

The *Handbook* begins with Part One, "The Factors Affecting All Middle Schools" and provides a foundation for the rest of the book:

- Chapter 1 identifies the important features of effective middle schools, as established through recent research.
- Chapter 2 examines the major societal factors that influence young adolescents and their schools.
- Chapter 3 reviews the key features of adolescent development that must be kept in mind by middle-school educators.

Part Two, "Goals for Effective Middle Schools," is concerned with goals, since they influence the entire school-improvement process:

- Chapter 4 explains a process for achieving a consensus on goals among administrators, teachers, and parents.
- Chapter 5 shows how to bring school goals and school programs into alignment, as in too many schools there are wide discrepancies between the goals stated and the programs implemented.

Part Three, "Programs for Effective Middle Schools," focuses on the specifics of the educational program:

- Chapter 6 offers specific suggestions for ensuring that the curriculum reflects educational goals.

- Chapter 7 provides some practical help for the administrator who wants to improve the school's curriculum.
- Chapter 8 offers some tested methods for improving curriculum delivery through more effective supervision.
- Chapters 9 and 10 are concerned with how to improve the activity and the guidance programs for young adolescents, the other two key aspects of the educational program.

Part Four, "The Proper Environment for Effective Middle Schools," is concerned with school atmosphere:

- Chapter 11 offers guidelines for improving the school climate, the environment in which learning takes place.
- Chapter 12 is concerned with the school's organizational structure—that is, organizing the time, space, and personnel in the school for educational purposes.
- Chapter 13 describes the importance of developing good parent and community relationships for school improvement.

The *Handbook* concludes with Part Five, "Achieving Excellence in Middle Schools":

- Chapters 14 through 16 focus on the primary means for achieving excellence in middle schools—through careful assessment, through effective staff development, and through forward-looking leadership.

Each chapter follows a similar pattern, beginning with a highlighting of the "indicators of excellence," which are the desirable characteristics for achieving that component, based on the analyses of students, society, and schools. These general indicators are fully described and made more specific so that you are given a set of criteria for school improvement. The chapter then suggests processes to use in translating those criteria into specific improvement strategies. At the end of each chapter are ready-to-use samples of surveys, forms, and instructional plans to help you improve your school's effectiveness.

Appendices at the end of the book offer several real-life examples of middle schools that have been successful in developing specific programs that follow the strategies recommended in the *Handbook*. Thus, *Middle School/Junior High Principal's Handbook* achieves a useful synthesis of research and practice.

Allan A. Glatthorn
Norman K. Spencer

Acknowledgments

We wish to acknowledge a special indebtedness to all those middle/junior high school leaders who responded so professionally to our search for exemplary practices. We received many more replies than space would allow us to use—and we wish to express our special appreciation to all those who helped. We know that as leaders of excellent schools they are inundated with requests for information— and we deeply appreciate their willingness to assist the profession by describing in detail how they developed their own processes for effectiveness.

Contents

**PART TWO
GOALS FOR EFFECTIVE MIDDLE SCHOOLS**

PART THREE
PROGRAMS FOR EFFECTIVE MIDDLE SCHOOLS

PART FOUR
THE PROPER ENVIRONMENT FOR EFFECTIVE MIDDLE SCHOOLS

Chapter 11: Improving School Climate 130

PART FIVE
ACHIEVING EXCELLENCE IN MIDDLE SCHOOLS

PART ONE

THE FACTORS AFFECTING ALL MIDDLE SCHOOLS

1

What Is an Effective Middle School?

Characteristics of an Effective Middle School

1. Clearly articulated goals, supported by all involved.
2. A balanced curriculum, responsive to the needs of adolescents.
3. Varied modes of teaching emphasizing concept development and achievement motivation.
4. A balanced and diversified activities program.
5. A strong student-centered guidance program.
6. An organic organizational structure featuring smaller "houses" and team teaching.
7. A school climate with a strong academic emphasis.
8. Supportive community relationships.
9. Continuing evaluation of all programs.
10. Systematic staff development.
11. A strong leadership team.

The experts have been debating the nature of effective middle schools for years. In too many instances they seem to be exchanging their biases. Rather than presenting one more subjective answer, it makes more sense to resolve this debate by drawing from the research on adolescents and effective middle schools.[1] The analysis of that research yields the guidelines shown in Figure 1-1; those guidelines will be examined briefly in this first chapter and then used in the related chapters that follow.

THE GOALS AND PURPOSES OF AN EFFECTIVE MIDDLE SCHOOL

First, in more effective schools, goals and purposes are clearly stated. They are presented in written statements and discussed fully in faculty and parent meetings. In less effective schools, there is a sense of vagueness about the purposes of education; faculty and parents are unsure as to what the school stands for and tries to achieve. And in more effective schools, there is general support for those goals and purposes. Although there will inevitably be disagreements about the methods employed to achieve those goals, there are no divisive arguments about the general outcomes intended. In less effective schools there are factional disputes, for example, between those who value effective goals and those who disparage such goals.

THE CURRICULUM OF AN EFFECTIVE MIDDLE SCHOOL

Effective middle schools have a quality program that stresses both the basics and the higher-order skills. Earlier studies of effective schools noted the central importance of reading and computational skills, but more recent studies note that quality curricula must also be concerned with critical thinking and problem solving. Less effective schools seem unable to achieve either goal: Their curricula focus neither on teaching the basics nor on developing higher-order thinking skills; courses seem diffuse in purpose and ineffective in implementation.

The curriculum of an effective school is also marked by relevance and diversity. Successful middle schools have found ways of making the course work seem meaningful and relevant to adolescents, who perceive the importance of what they are learning. And the courses are sufficiently diverse that they appeal to a wide range of interests and reward several talents.

THE ORGANIZATIONAL STRUCTURE OF AN EFFECTIVE MIDDLE SCHOOL

Organizational structure is critical to an effective middle school. First, there is an evolving structure. Unlike some schools that become frozen into one particular organizational pattern, the more successful middle schools identified in recent research continue to modify their structure, based upon teachers' perceptions of student needs. These schools differed in many of the particulars of schedule and staffing, but in each instance these decisions were perceived as organic, rather than fixed. Second, they used some type of "house" structure by which the larger school was subdivided into semi-autonomous units. And these houses were staffed by teams of teachers, in a way that minimized the influence of subject departments and maximized the opportunities for teacher–student interaction.

The decision-making process is also important. In the more successful schools, the teaching teams have a large measure of influence over both school-wide matters, such as grading systems and assembly schedules, and instructional issues like curriculum content and pedagogical method. This involvement of teachers in decision making tends to create in them a sense of power and efficacy, making them in general more satisfied with their work environment. In less effective schools, teachers report that they feel disenfranchised and powerless, feelings that lead to low morale and disinclination to make special efforts to improve the school.

THE CLIMATE OF AN EFFECTIVE MIDDLE SCHOOL

School climate is another major area where there are sharp distinctions between more effective and less effective schools. First, successful schools seem characterized by an academic ambience—the degree to which environmental forces press for student achievement on a school-wide basis. In general the research suggests that an effective school has developed school policies that promote academic press or ambience; these policies in turn influence certain classroom practices that affect student academic norms, student self-concept of academic ability, and student sense of academic efficacy.

Second, staff expectations about student achievement are crucial. In successful schools, both administrators and teachers have high expectations for students and communicate such expectations clearly and forcefully: "We believe that you can achieve—and we will do all we can to help you achieve." And the leaders and teachers use every opportunity to proclaim those expectations: In assemblies, in the morning announcements, in the corridors, and in the classrooms, students are challenged to achieve their best. In less effective schools, administrators and teachers too often project to the students a contrary set of expectations: "You're disadvantaged—and we don't expect too much from you." Those low expectations often become a self-fulfilling prophecy.

Finally, in effective schools there is a sense of good discipline. There are a few reasonable rules designed to produce a positive learning environment, and those rules are systematically emphasized and consistently enforced. Everyone feels responsible for good discipline; it is not solely the job of the disciplinarian. In less effective schools, disorder seems rampant. Students roam the corridors, arrive late for class, and scoff at adult authority.

COMMUNITY RELATIONS AND AN EFFECTIVE MIDDLE SCHOOL

Successful schools also have strong community relations programs. However, those programs are built not upon propaganda and hype but rather are based on substance. They have solid community support because they are successful. And the administrators and teachers know how to keep parents informed and involved; parents have frequent contact with the school and consider themselves well informed about school affairs. Finally, both administrators and teachers in effective middle schools know how to stay within the limits of community tolerance; for example, they do not try radical ideas in conservative communities.

EVALUATION IN AN EFFECTIVE MIDDLE SCHOOL

In successful schools there is an effective assessment program. Administrators and teachers use standardized and criterion-referenced test scores to diagnose problems and assess progress. Administrators and supervisors provide constructive classroom supervision that focuses on the critical aspects of successful teaching. And the curriculum is monitored—to ensure that the "written" curriculum is actually being implemented and that there is a close fit between what is taught and what is tested.

STAFF DEVELOPMENT IN AN EFFECTIVE MIDDLE SCHOOL

In the best middle schools, the school's leaders—with much teacher input—have developed and implemented an effective school-wide staff development program. That staff development program is based upon a careful assessment of needs, deals with problems and issues important to teachers, and makes extensive use of teacher-centered activities. In less effective schools, staff development is a hit-or-miss operation: A consultant gives a speech about a topic the principal considers important. There is desultory discussion, but no follow-up.

LEADERSHIP IN AN EFFECTIVE MIDDLE SCHOOL

In successful schools, the principal and key members of the leadership team play an active role in ensuring curricular articulation, in emphasizing mastery of essential skills and concepts, in supervising teachers, and in monitoring the curriculum. Leadership efforts focus on the improvement of instruction, not simply on the maintenance of the organization. In less effective schools, teachers are left to their own devices: no one seems to care about what happens instructionally.

SUMMING UP

The best way to use these guidelines to is review them carefully with your faculty, rather than simply adopting them mindlessly. The guidelines have been derived from sound research and will be most useful if you and your faculty analyze them carefully to determine the specific ways your school can improve.

Note

1. The guidelines have been drawn from several reviews of research on effective schools. Two sources were especially useful: Joan Lipsitz, *Successful Schools for Young Adolescents* (New Brunswick, NJ: Transaction, 1984), and John I. Goodlad, *A Place Called School: Prospects for the Future* (New York: McGraw-Hill, 1984).

FIGURE 1-1. Guidelines for middle-school effectiveness

GOALS

- The goals and purposes of the school are clearly articulated.

- There is a strong consensus among administrators, teachers, and parents about those goals and purposes.

CURRICULUM

- The curriculum reflects and is developed from the goals of the school.

- The curriculum facilitates the mastery of essential learning and inquiry skills.

- The curriculum facilitates the learning of the important skills and concepts of the basic academic subjects.

- The curriculum fosters the physical and emotional development of the students through a sound program in health and physical education.

- The curriculum enhances the ability of the students to think creatively and express themselves in creative forms.

- The curriculum contributes to the development of personal and interpersonal skills and attitudes, giving specific attention to those skills and attitudes especially important for adolescents in our society.

- The curriculum is perceived as relevant by students and responds to diverse student needs.

continued

FIGURE 1-1.   (cont.)

TEACHING AND LEARNING

- Teachers give special attention to assessing cognitive readiness.

- Teachers use the computer and television to improve instructional efficiency.

- Teachers alternate modes and methods of learning.

- Teachers emphasize concept development by full explication, detailed ex-emplification, and guided discussion.

- Teachers strengthen achievement motivation of young adolescents by helping them set reasonable goals, acquire needed skills, and implement plans for achieving those goals.

- Teachers attempt to develop learner autonomy by making appropriate provisions for independent learning.

- Teachers make appropriate provisions for cooperative group learning.

ACTIVITY PROGRAM

- The activity program includes diverse activities that develop and reward multiple talents.

- The activity program includes activities that will encourage healthy heterosexual interactions, without compulsory dating and dancing.

- The activity program includes activities that enable adolescents to develop social and interpersonal skills.

continued

FIGURE 1-1. (cont.)

GUIDANCE PROGRAM

- The school provides continued guidance for students trying to make wise choices from among many options.

- The guidance program provides all adolescents with the help they need to achieve developmental tasks: to cope with their feelings, develop perspective about problems, and find needed resources.

- The school provides special support and services to those encountering more serious problems.

ORGANIZATIONAL STRUCTURE

- The organizational structure of the school is an organic one, evolving in response to teacher perceptions of student needs.

- The school creates a sense of smallness by using a "house" system staffed with teams of teachers.

- Teaching teams have a great deal of influence over school-wide matters and classroom issues.

- The school schedule allows for periods of both activity and relaxation.

- The school makes provisions for flexible grouping, so that students can for at least part of the time be with peers at similar stages of development.

continued

FIGURE 1-1. (cont.)

SCHOOL CLIMATE

- The school is characterized by an academic ambience; there is a shared concern for academic achievement.

- Administrators and teachers have high expectations for students.

- There is a clear sense of order about the school: There are a few rules, which are clear, reasonable, and enforced.

- Administrators and teachers stress the importance of school discipline as a means of maintaining the school as a social order, developing a respect for authority and an appreciation of the need for rules.

- The school provides a stable and predictable environment for adolescents experiencing instability and uncertainty.

COMMUNITY

- There are supportive community relationships, based upon the success of the school and frequent parent contact.

EVALUATION

- There is a continuing assessment of all the major components of the school's program, in order to provide administrators and teachers with the data needed for systematic school improvement.

- Particular attention is given to the evaluation and monitoring of the curriculum, to ensure that curricular goals are being achieved.

continued

FIGURE 1-1. (cont.)

STAFF DEVELOPMENT

- There is a systematic and continuing staff development program in which the principal and the teachers work together to improve the school and solve emerging school problems.

- The staff development program helps administrators and teachers respond effectively to the special developing needs of the adolescents.

LEADERSHIP

- There is a strong and active leadership team, headed by the principal, that focuses on the improvement of instruction.

2

How Social Trends Affect Middle Schools

Societal Changes and an Effective Middle School

1. Greater ethnic diversity of the population, requiring new emphases and approaches.

2. Highly mobile families, resulting in some instability for the young.

3. The growth of the information age, which requires a new approach to curriculum and instruction.

4. The continuing importance of television as a shaper of values and attitudes.

5. An era of overchoice for the young: too many options with too few structures.

6. Changing patterns of career decision making: new careers, with many career changes.

The middle schools of today are educating adolescents who will be young adults in the year 2000. The nature of that society in the near future should influence the kind of education provided by the school of today.

THE EFFECTS OF ETHNIC DIVERSITY

The United States has always known tides of immigration, but we are in the middle of a new wave that seems to be gathering increasing force. The influx of thousands of Hispanics and Asians offers the nation both new resources and new challenges. These new immigrants represent a fresh source of human talent that is already infusing fresh energy into our culture and injecting new vigor into the economy. But those immigrants also create new strains and make additional demands: They must be educated; they need jobs; they require places to live. And for a while, at least, they will seem to be competing for scarce resources with working-class blacks and whites who see them as interlopers and outsiders.

The schools, of course, feel the effects of such strains. Consider, for example, the history of one large urban high school in the middle of Philadelphia. When it first opened, its planners hoped that it would keep middle-class white families from fleeing to the suburbs. For a few years there were serious clashes between the white and black students who acted out in the school the tensions that had developed in the neighborhood. Then for many years the school seemed free of racial clashes, largely because it had become almost entirely black in its ethnic makeup; the white middle-class families had moved out of the decaying neighborhood. Now it is again experiencing serious ethnic tensions, but this time the combatants are black and Asian. Once again the school has become a battleground on which neighborhood conflicts erupt.

THE DISRUPTIONS CAUSED
BY THE MOBILE FAMILY

Ours has always been a mobile nation. From the time of the first settlers who moved westward in search of a better life, we have been a restless people. Recent census figures indicate that the average American will move thirteen or fourteen times in the course of a lifetime. And most experts who study such trends predict that mobility will continue to be an important feature of American life: As companies seek more favorable business climates and more profitable markets, young adults will follow, going where the jobs are. For the most part, the movement will be from north to south and from east to west. According to Census Bureau estimates, 90 percent of the population growth of the early 1980s occurred in southern and western states.

One principal of a large urban middle school put this picture of a mobile society in even more dramatic terms. He reports that in a given year, his school experiences a 50 percent turnover:

Our Puerto Rican children leave for the islands in the winter. The district offices announce new plans for integrating the schools and send us students with the desired skin color. Unemployed parents move to Houston and take their children with them. And I play with other principals the game of "swap your worst apples." Somehow in the midst of all this madness I'm supposed to be educating kids.

Although most other middle schools do not experience such extreme disruption, the problems this principal confronts are present in almost every middle school in large metropolitan areas.

THE LIMITATIONS OF THE INFORMATION AGE

We live in a period of time that some have dubbed the "information age." It is an age when the development, transmission, and application of new knowledge have become the primary activities of a large sector of the economy and when one's access to information is the major determiner of power. Consider the evidence:

- One government economist estimates that the "information economy" (that part of the economy that produces and distributes information goods and services) now accounts for close to two-thirds of the Gross National Product.[1]
- The attainment of scientific and technical information doubles every five to six years.
- Close to a million personal computers are being sold each year; some experts predict that the market will grow by about 40 percent annually.
- According to the most reliable analyses, about two-thirds of the economic growth occurring between 1948 and 1973 came about from the increased education of the labor force.
- Many colleges now require students to own their own computers.
- The Houston Independent School District plans to have 30,000 computers in its schools within a few years.[2]

A few decades ago the farmer was the typical American worker. Just a few years back the assembly line worker seemed to be the representative figure. Now it is the information specialist—someone who knows how to locate and process information—who is paramount.

Many educators have responded to this radical shift in our society by requiring a "computer literacy" course for all students. In fact, several districts have now developed a K-12 sequence in computer literacy. Others question the value of such approaches. They point out that the computer is only a tool and that there is no need to understand how that tool works in order to use it effectively. With a few hours of self-instruction, any reasonably intelligent person can learn to operate most personal computers. And computers and their languages are developing so rapidly that some believe that programming will soon be an obsolete profession.

The limitations of emphasizing "computer literacy" are even more obvious at the middle-school level. Consider this obvious problem: The students who are now in middle schools studying "computer literacy" will be applying for jobs and to professional schools about ten years from now, but by that time computers will have changed so radically that the information they are acquiring now will be totally obsolete.

It seems more useful for middle schools to respond to the information age in two related ways: Teach problem-solving and information-processing skills; and use computers to improve instructional efficiency by freeing teachers to do what only humans can do.

THE INFLUENCE OF TELEVISION

Most experts have concluded that middle-school youngsters are spending more time watching television than they are sitting in classrooms. And it seems reasonable to predict that watching television will continue to account for one-third of the waking hours of adolescents. TV sets with high-quality stereo sound will show programs that feature popular music with visual dramatizations. Video tape recorders will enable youngsters to watch their favorite shows again and again. And satellite transmission systems will give them a choice of programs especially designed to appeal to their tastes.

What are the effects of so much television watching? The answers are not yet clear. Television broadcasters point out its advantages: Television informs, broadens horizons, creates shared experiences, and entertains. Alarmists see television as addicting and perceive its effects as pernicious: It makes children more violent and turns them into mindless zombies. A more reasoned position that emerges from an analysis of the best evidence reaches these tentative conclusions about the effects of television:

- It can be a useful instructional medium. Most research concludes that instructional television is just as effective as the live teacher in imparting information and teaching basic skills. It obviously enriches the learning experience by providing visual images where they are most essential.
- There is some tentative evidence that watching too much television has subtle effects on one's learning style. TV "addicts" seem to read less, have a somewhat diminished fantasy life, and tend to become more passive in their learning styles.
- There is persuasive evidence that commercial television influences the values of the viewer. The commercials, the soap operas, the popular series,

and even the news tend to perpetuate stereotypes about age groups, sexes, ethnic groups, and other nations. And television has a demonstrable effect on the political process: It influences which candidates are nominated, how they are presented to the public, and who is elected.

THE PROBLEMS CAUSED BY OVERCHOICE

This also seems to be a period of time when adolescents are faced with too many options to consider and too many decisions to make. It was not always thus. In years gone by, life was simpler, and the options were fewer. If you were young, your mind was untroubled by choices. You would probably live your adult life in the same town in which you had been born. Boys knew that they would follow their father's occupation; girls knew that they would be mothers and homemakers. And there was no uncertainty about right or wrong. Alcohol and sex were reserved for adults and rarely discussed in the presence of the young. Drugs were only whispered about, strange substances consumed by artists and criminals. Class lines were clear and difficult to cross. It must have seemed idyllic—at least, to those who had wealth and power.

Now consider the changes confronting many young adolescents and the questions troubling them, if they are at all reflective:

- "Our family is moving. How can I make new friends?"
- "My parents are getting divorced. Which one will I live with?"
- "One of my friends is pregnant. Should she get an abortion?"
- "Some of my friends are drinking. Should I try it?"
- "Some of the boys and girls in my class say they have slept together. Should I start having sexual intercourse?"
- "Both of my parents are working. How am I supposed to take care of my younger sister?"
- "My father's job is now being done by a robot, and he is out of work. Will there be a job for me?"
- "People keep talking about a nuclear war. What can I do about it besides worry?"
- "My grandfather is terminally ill. Should my parents let the doctors withdraw life-support systems?"

Living in a world of too many choices can be troubling for adolescents. Middle schools can help them through both the counseling program and the curriculum. As explained more fully in Chapter 10, an effective counseling program can help these youngsters cope with conditions they cannot change and make wise choices when they have clear options.

A TIME OF CAREER INSTABILITY

It is likely that the decades ahead will be marked by two related developments in career patterns. First, there will be significant shifts in the job market. There will be less need for workers in production industries. One study estimated that only 5 percent of the new jobs created in the 1970s were in manufacturing; almost 90 percent were in the knowledge or service areas. There will be an increased need for managers and skilled technicians—a shift dramatically illustrated in a recent report on current job trends. The five occupational groups growing most rapidly at the present time are data processing machine mechanics, paralegal personnel, computer systems analysts, computer operators, and office machine services. It is significant that the four groups growing most rapidly involve occupations that did not even exist thirty years ago.

The second change grows out of the first: Young people and adults are changing in their job values and career orientation. Years ago a man prepared for a single career, worked for one company, and identified closely with the job: "I'm a teacher." Now all that has changed. Men and women move from career to career—from teacher to lawyer, from bank clerk to travel agent, from factory worker to computer repairer. They work for several companies and are much less concerned about "loyalty to the firm." And they tend to see the job as a means to an end, not an end in itself.

SUMMING UP

The trends described here—the international village, the mobile family, the information age, television time, an era of overchoice, and a time of career instability—will clearly affect adolescents and their schools. In the best middle schools, administrators and teachers will be sensitive to those changes and make the necessary modifications in programs and resources. Figure 2-1 summarizes the kinds of modifications that seem indicated by the preceding analyses.

Notes

1. Marc Porat, *Information Economy: Definition and Measurement* (U.S. Department of Commerce, May 1977).
2. John Naisbitt, *Megatrends* (New York: Warner, 1982).

FIGURE 2-1. Social trends and effective middle schools

CURRICULUM The curriculum should:

- Help students develop a global perspective, becoming especially sensitive to the nature of developing nations.
- Include interdisciplinary units that focus on the development of intercultural understanding.
- Include the systematic study of a foreign language.
- Stress problem solving and information processing.
- Help students make wise use of television.
- Include interdisciplinary units that help students understand societal changes.
- Develop the skills needed for career selection and preparation.
- Help students make sound moral choices.

TEACHING AND LEARNING Teaching and learning activities should:

- Emphasize the importance of diagnostic assessment.
- Use the computer and television to improve instructional efficiency.

continued

FIGURE 2-1. (cont.)

GUIDANCE PROGRAM The guidance program should:

● Provide continued guidance for students trying to make wise choices from among many options.

ORGANIZATIONAL STRUCTURE The organizational structure should:

● Make it possible for a team of teachers to work with a smaller number of students so that the team can provide continued guidance and support during difficult times.

SCHOOL CLIMATE The school climate should:

● Provide a stable and predictable environment for adolescents experiencing instability and uncertainty.

3

How Young
Adolescents Develop

Characteristics of Young Adolescents

Physical
1. Rapid and uneven growth.

2. Glandular and metabolic imbalances.

3. Many nutritional abnormalities.

Cognitive
1. Most are at the stage of semi-formal operations; some at the concrete and some at the formal stages.

2. Most continue to develop in general intelligence; some uncertainty about the rate of development.

3. Marked changes in political thinking.

Moral
1. Most are at the conventional "good-boy–good-girl" stage; some at a more authority-oriented stage.

2. Most consider social conformity the major reason for following rules, have a high level of empathic distress, and are capable of experiencing guilt feelings.

3. Most are changing in their views toward convention.

Pyscho-social

1. Most begin to loosen childhood ties while still feeling positive about parents.

2. They begin to act more autonomously and assertively within the family.

3. Dating begins, but heterosexual relationships are superficial.

4. Crowds and cliques become important.

5. There is a growing orientation toward achievement and commitment.

6. Identity formation becomes the social issue: The peer group is used to explore the self, test new identities, and get feedback.

Before analyzing the research on early adolescence, it might be useful to point out two cautions. First, statements about adolescent development do not apply to all young people. Adolescents are especially varied in their development and cannot be categorized simply. Second, educators especially should understand that adolescents are subtly but deeply influenced by such external factors as school experiences, family interactions, peers, and general societal trends. They live in a complex world and to a great extent are shaped by that world.

Given those cautions, what can be said about the significant features of early adolescence? The following discussion reviews the most important characteristics of their physical, cognitive, moral, and psycho-social development identified by the most current research and details their implications for schools.

PHYSICAL DEVELOPMENT OF THE ADOLESCENT

The general picture of the physical development of the young adolescent has five distinguishing features, which are summarized in Figure 3-1. First, the period is one of rapid growth. The "adolescent growth spurt" for girls begins at a mean age of 9.6 and reaches peak velocity at 11.8; for boys the growth spurt occurs about two years later. For the teenagers involved, of course, the spurt is a mixed blessing. The young teenager discovers that clothing no longer fits and classroom desks are uncomfortable. Teachers and parents call attention to the accelerating growth in ways that the youngster finds embarrassing. At the same time, however, there is a sense of pride in the realization that childhood is being left behind.

A Period of Uneven Growth

Growth within the individual is uneven. Bones grow faster than muscles, resulting in the physical awkwardness and lack of coordination typical of many adolescents. Legs and arms develop proportionately faster than the trunk—and hands and feet develop faster than legs and arms. And there is some evidence of slower brain growth between ages twelve and fourteen.[1] The research on brain growth indicates that for many at this age there is almost no increase in brain size or mass. It should be noted, however, that many experts do not believe that this slowing of brain growth has any significant impact on the development of intelligence.

This is also a time of important changes in sexual development. Secondary sex characteristics appear. The boy's voice grows deeper, and facial hair starts to grow. The girl's breasts and hips increase in size. On both boys and girls, pubic hair appears. Girls begin to menstruate at a mean age of 12.9—and boys experience their first ejaculation about two years later. One of the controversies among scientists studying adolescence is whether the onset of puberty will continue to occur at an earlier age. Several studies indicate that the adolescent growth spurt and the onset of puberty have been occurring four months earlier each decade—but at least one study has indicated that the trend toward earlier onset has already ended.[2]

Developmental Differences within Same-Age Groups

There are also dramatic differences between adolescents of the same age. During both the junior and senior high period, a group of adolescents of the same chronological age will usually have a range of at least six years in maturational age.[3] In one major study, early-maturing boys exceeded late maturers physically by an average of eight inches and thirty-four pounds. The greatest differences in size, weight, and performance will occur in girls at ages twelve to fourteen and for boys between ages fourteen and sixteen. Such differences have an obvious impact on the perceptions of others, as noted in several studies.[4] Adults considered the early maturers above average in attractiveness. Peers consider the early maturers more grown-up, more likely to have older friends, more attractive, and more deserving of being elected to office.

Finally, it is a time when major imbalances in the glandular system and recurring nutritional deficiencies can cause health problems, although adolescents are usually free of major illnesses. Changes in the thymus and thyroid glands can result in changes in metabolism, blood pressure, and pulse rate, often producing reactions that the teenager cannot understand. Glandular imbalances can result in skin problems and allergic reactions. Nutritional problems can become acute. A government survey concluded that youth between the ages of ten and sixteen had the least satisfactory nutritional status, resulting in problems of underweight, overweight, iron-deficiency anemia, and dental caries.[5]

These significant physical characteristics should not be perceived as problems. Too many adults view the distinguishing traits of adolescence as causes for concern, making the teenager feel deficient. Instead, these traits should be looked on as common adolescent features, a knowledge of which should help both educators and parents understand and respond to young people with greater sensitivity and awareness.

COGNITIVE DEVELOPMENT OF THE ADOLESCENT

What is known about the cognitive development of adolescents? Figure 3-2 summarizes the current research. To grasp the significance of several of those generalizations, it will be useful to define the three stages of cognitive development that have been identified by Jean Piaget and other contemporary cognitive psychologists as important during the middle-school years:[6]

- *Concrete operations:* occurs usually between ages seven and eleven; characterized by the ability to think logically in solving concrete problems.
- *Semi-formal operations:* occurs between ages ten and twelve and is an important transition stage. The child's mental capacity is developing, and the child is able to perform some abstract thinking.
- *Formal operations:* occurs between ages eleven and fifteen and is the stage in which maximal qualitative growth occurs. At this stage, ideas can be manipulated without the need to refer to concrete operations, and logic can be applied to the solution of problems.

Let's take a closer look at each stage.

Stage of Concrete Operations

Many adolescents are still in the stage of concrete operations. This stage marks a series of important developments in young learners. They can imagine events and processes as reversible, understanding for the first time that addition and subtraction, for example, are essentially the same operation. They have mastered the conservation task, a test that assesses their ability to understand that a given mass is the same even though its shape has changed. They can handle classification systems, can order events along a continuum, and can order objects along some abstract dimension, such as size or weight. They can reason simultaneously about parts and wholes. In short, they can think relationally. But their cognitive operations are severely limited. Their thought is attached to concrete reality: They are not able to deal with more than two classes at one time, because they lack the cognitive structures to handle such relationships.

Stage of Semi-Formal Operations

Most adolescents, however, have by the age of twelve moved to the stage of semi-formal operations. They can perform the following mental operations:

- develop and use conscious memorization strategies
- make inferences
- use circumstantial judgment and are able to explain events in reference to the attendant circumstances
- differentiate between words somewhat related in meaning
- explain metaphors
- understand humor with greater sophistication
- have deeper understanding of such logical connectors as *or* and *although*
- develop metacognitive and metalinguistic abilities and are able to reflect about their own thinking and use of language

Accordingly, this period of adolescence is a very crucial one as far as school is concerned. Adolescents need opportunities to enjoy their subjective experiences while developing the capacity to examine those experiences from an objective perspective.

Stage of Formal Operations

Some adolescents by the time they have finished middle school are functioning at the most advanced level of formal operations. This stage is marked by four significant advances in thinking: approaching problems by generating hypotheses and thinking deductively, conceptualizing and testing the relationships between logical propositions, combining inverse and reciprocal relationships, and adopting strategies for retrieving and organizing information.

Another significant feature of this move to formal operations is that adolescents are becoming less egocentric in their thinking. The younger adolescent is markedly egocentric, feeling always on stage, seeing the world only through the lens of the self, lacking the ability to differentiate personal concerns from the concerns of others. However, many of those who have achieved the stage of formal operations are able to move from this obsession with the self, to entertain the viewpoints of others, and to see the world as others might see it.

INTELLECTUAL DEVELOPMENT

Does intellectual development begin to slow down in early adolescence? The experts differ here. Several scientists argue that general intelligence (as measured by IQ scores) continues to develop regularly throughout adolescence, with the rate of increase slowing down only during young adulthood. After reviewing all the longitudinal studies on intelligence, one researcher reached this conclusion: "Based on a growing body of longitudinal studies of development, it appears that overall mental ability increases rapidly throughout the years of childhood and adolescence...."[7]

However, Epstein and Toepfer take a contrary position. They argue that there are two quite different periods of brain growth between the ages of ten and fourteen. Between ten and twelve the brain seems to grow rapidly, but during the next two years it seems to grow more slowly—if at all. They conclude that during this period the learner will have difficulty initiating new cognitive skills and will learn better when instruction focuses on consolidating cognitive skills developed during the preceding period of rapid growth.[8]

This argument has had a strong influence on many middle-school educators, but many psychologists are not convinced. One expert believes that their theory is "intriguing... [but] still very general and conjectural."[9] And in a review of the research on brain growth and cognition, two other experts conclude that there is no strong link between brain development and cognitive development; the research findings, they note, do not support the belief that children cannot learn new skills when their brains are growing slowly.[10]

POLITICAL THINKING

Finally, there is evidence of a very important shift in the political thinking of adolescents. After interviewing more than 750 youngsters from ages eleven to eighteen in the United States, England, and Germany, two researchers concluded that this dramatic change in political perspective occurs between the ages of thirteen and fifteen.[11]

Before that period, children have great difficulty reasoning abstractly about issues of government and politics and are limited to rather concrete perceptions. After that period they seem able to think in more abstract and less egocentric terms about such concepts as community. Before that period, their view of justice is both primitive and punitive; after that period, they project a deeper understanding of the law and a more humane view of punishment. The younger adolescent also seems to lack the capacity to make use of moral and political principles; the older student can use principles in making social and political judgments. A fourth difference is in their perception of human psychology. Before the shift they project a rather shallow and somewhat simplistic understanding of human motivation; by age fifteen or sixteen they seem to have a richer and more sophisticated insight. Finally, they change in their understanding of political and social institutions: Younger adolescents have only an incomplete and superficial understanding of political parties and other social institutions; after age fourteen or fifteen, their perceptions become more accurate and their analyses less superficial.

MORAL DEVELOPMENT OF THE
YOUNG ADOLESCENT

Moral development is a third important area of adolescent growth because young adolescents are faced with many moral choices. Understanding of how they make those choices can help middle-school educators develop more appropriate climates for learning and more relevant curricula.

Kohlberg's Stages of Moral Development

The most important research on moral development has been done by Lawrence Kohlberg, whose work provides a framework for the discussion that follows.[12] There are six stages of moral development, grouped into three levels: pre-conventional, conventional, and post-conventional. These stages are defined briefly as follows, using for the most part Kohlberg's own wording:

Stage 1: (Pre-conventional) Right action is that which avoids punishment and shows unquestioning deference to superior power.

Stage 2: (Pre-conventional) Right action consists of that which satisfies one's needs—and at times the needs of others.

Stage 3: (Conventional) Good behavior is that which pleases or helps others and is approved by them—the "good-boy–good-girl" orientation.

Stage 4: (Conventional) Right behavior consists of doing one's duty, showing respect for authority, and maintaining the social order.

Stage 5: (Post-conventional) Right action is defined either in terms of general rights or internal decisions of conscience, without universal principles.

Stage 6: (Post-conventional) Right action is determined by reference to ethical principles based on universality and consistency.

Most psychologists who have examined the issue conclude that these stages are closely related to Piaget's stages of cognitive development. Only when the child has achieved concrete operational thinking can he or she even begin to think at a pre-conventional level: Before the time when concrete operational thinking has been achieved, children equate the good with what they want. During the stage of concrete operations, the child begins to make moral decisions at the pre-conventional level, first concerned primarily with punishment, then with a "marketplace" orientation of reciprocity. Only when the adolescent achieves the formal operations stage can he or she move beyond the level of conventional morality.

Adolescent Moral Development

At age thirteen, most of the boys whom Kohlberg studied are at Stage 3. They are concerned with doing what others believe is right, with securing the approval of significant others, and with conforming to rather stereotyped images of good and bad. For the first time, behavior is often judged by intentions and is even overused as a means of evaluating the morality of actions: "But he meant well."

Many, however, have moved to Stage 4. They are concerned with doing their duty, with showing respect for authority, and with maintaining the social order for its own sake. Their moral statements reflect what might be termed a "law and order" orientation, even though they may not always act according to that understanding of morality. Only a few—if any—have begun to develop an orientation toward the internalized conscience.

However, as Figure 3-3 notes, there are some findings that indicate a difference between adolescent girls and boys. One researcher discovered that middle-class adolescent girls in grades 5–7 seemed to have more internalized moral orientations than did their male counterparts; the girls seemed to rely more on their own sense of conscience.[13]

How do young adolescents analyze the need for rules? The most important findings show that more than half of the middle-school students surveyed believed that rules should be followed in order to conform to societal norms. The next-largest group cited rational, utilitarian principles.[14]

Adolescents and Convention

These general findings on moral development are supplemented by some useful studies concerned with the attitude of young adolescents toward convention. Social conventions are determined by the social system in which they are formed; they are based on accepted usage and operate to maintain the social organization. Thus, the student who conforms to a school's dress code is following the conventions of the school. Such decisions need to be distinguished from moral choices, which are concerned with the intrinsic rightness and wrongness of actions. Some important changes in attitudes about conventions take place between the ages of ten and sixteen.[15] These changes are:

- Ages ten to eleven. Convention is seen as arbitrary and changeable; adherence to convention is based on concrete rules and authoritative expectations.
- Ages twelve to thirteen. Conventions are seen only as social expectations; the evaluation of rules is coordinated with evaluation of the consequent act.

● Ages fourteen to sixteen. There are the beginnings of a systematic concept of social structure; convention is seen as a normative regulation.

Obviously, teachers and administrators should be sensitive to the distinction between conventions and morality. If a youngster violates convention by calling the teacher by the first name, the teacher should treat it as a violation of convention and respond to the young person accordingly, not react as if it were a violation of moral principle.

Young adolescents also are able to empathize with distress and to feel a sense of guilt. The young adolescent is able to empathize with the distress feelings of others, gaining an understanding of the other's sorrow and being able to respond with genuine feeling about that sorrow. Unlike younger children, the young adolescent is also able to act upon this sense of empathic distress. One psychologist notes that young adolescents are capable of experiencing feelings of guilt after acts of both omission and commission, and their feelings of guilt are usually followed by an attempt to make reparations.[16]

PSYCHO-SOCIAL DEVELOPMENT
OF THE YOUNG ADOLESCENT

One useful framework for understanding psycho-social development proposes that young adolescents experience six kinds of changes: in attachment, autonomy, sexuality, intimacy, achievement, and identity.[17] Figure 3-4 summarizes the most important features of those six types, which are explained here in detail.

Attachment to Peers

Early adolescence is a time of increasing attachment to the peer group and disengagement from the family. However, the research data reject the stereotyped view of early adolescence as a time of family conflict and total reliance upon the peer group. The picture is much more complex and ambiguous than the stereotype suggests.

Some research indicates, in fact, that parental influence is strongest at sixth grade and only gradually declines to a low point at grade twelve. As young adolescents strive to attach themselves to significant peers, they still desire and need the support of the family structure. For example, a nationwide study of church-related families revealed that only 12 percent of the youth surveyed say that "my parents and I disagree on what is important in life."[18] The general picture that emerges from several studies is one of a young adolescent who is able to live in and understand the norms of two worlds—family and peers.

The Desire for Autonomy

While leaning on peers and family for support and guidance, young adolescents continue the struggle toward autonomy. They want to hold on to others even as they try to walk alone. They speak often of the need to be independent, all the while checking on how others perceive that independence. They become more assertive and autonomous within the family, usually with the encouragement of parents who urge them to think for themselves. At home and in school, with adults and with peers, they test their ability to stand alone, often in ways that disconcert others. Some studies suggest that in early adolescence, boys seem to be more autonomous than girls; this finding may be related to the fact that friendship ties are more important for girls.

The Beginning of Sexuality

Early adolescence is a time of marked sexual development; predictably, therefore, it is also a period when sexual activity with others becomes important. The survey of church-related youth referred to previously indicates that 12 percent of the fifth-graders and 17 percent of the eighth-graders surveyed reported that they had experienced sexual intercourse. Other studies report that girls begin to date at age fourteen, and boys just a bit later, between fourteen and fifteen. Experts studying adolescence believe that the sexual feelings of young adolescent girls are closely related to feelings of tenderness, self-disclosure, and intimacy—whereas those of boys seem more focused on erotic arousal and satisfaction. Hill notes another important difference: Girls' first intense sexual experiences appear to occur in the context of dating; boys' experiences, when they are alone.

The Formation of Intimate Groups

Adolescent achievement of intimacy tends to occur in three settings: the crowd, the clique, and individual friendships. The crowd is the larger group and the most inclusive, composed of adolescents with similar interests and values. Each crowd usually is composed of cliques, which are about one-third the size of crowds: Smaller in size, the clique permits much greater intimacy. Early adolescence is a pre-crowd stage, with isolated unisexual cliques.[19] The crowd becomes more important, with unisexual cliques in group-to-group interaction—and then heterosexual cliques develop. It is not until later adolescence that the crowd is fully developed, with heterosexual cliques in close association. Within this crowd-clique structure, individual friendships become very important, for girls especially. For girls, friendship means mutual self-disclosure, a process by which girls educate one another about how to handle anxiety-producing experiences. For boys, friendship is companionship based on similarity of interest and involving common activities, with very little self-disclosure and intimacy.

Other-Oriented Achievement

Early adolescence is a time when achievement becomes more future oriented and career choices become more realistic. With this sense of developing achievement, the adolescent also becomes more committed—to family, peers, and the social order. One rather important aspect of this increase in other-oriented achievement is what Hill calls "differential socialization by gender." It is during this period that scores on aptitude tests begin to vary: Girls score higher on tests of verbal ability; boys, on tests of mathematical ability. Girls begin to act on the assumption that high scholastic achievement and popularity with boys are somewhat incompatible.

The Formation of an Identity

According to Erikson, identity formation is the key issue for adolescents—the development of a conscious sense of uniqueness, for continuity of experience, and for an identification with the group's ideals.[20] There is obviously a paradox here. The person needs to develop a strong sense of self, but that self is firmly fixed in a context of others. For the young adolescent especially, the peer group becomes vital in the formation of such an identity: The young person uses the peer group to explore the sense of self, to try out new roles and identities, and to get feedback from the group. Thus, early adolescence is a time when the question "Who am I?" is more than rhetorical and is answered partly with input from peers.

IMPLICATIONS FOR MIDDLE SCHOOLS

This, then, is in general the composite picture of early adolescence—a time of significant change in physical growth, cognitive ability, moral awareness, and psycho-social development. And those young adolescents need middle schools whose staff and programs are sensitive to those changes. But being sensitive to the special needs of young adolescents does not necessarily imply making total accommodation to them. In fact, growth comes about only when there is sufficient tension between the individual and the environment. Accordingly, the staff and the programs of excellent middle schools should also challenge the young. In sum, an excellent middle school is one that responds to the special developmental needs of young adolescents, while at the same time providing sufficient challenge and tension for growth to occur.

Figure 3-5 summarizes the specific ways in which effective middle schools can both respond to adolescents' needs and challenge them to grow. Each of those recommendations is derived from the analysis of adolescent development presented in this chapter.

Notes

1. Herman Epstein, "A Neuroscience Framework for Re-structuring Middle School Curricula," *Transcesence* 5 (1977), 6–11.

2. Joan Lipsitz, *Growing Up Forgotten: A Review of Research and Programs Concerning Early Adolescence* (New Brunswick, NJ: Transaction, 1980).

3. Dorothy H. Eichorn, "Variations in Growth Rate," *Childhood Education* (1968), 286–91.

4. J. A. Clausen, "The Social Meaning of Differential Physical and Sexual Maturation," in *Adolescence in the Life Cycle: Psychological Change and Social Context,* eds. S. E. Dragaston and G. H. Elder, Jr. (New York: Wiley, 1975), 25–47.

5. United States Congress and Senate Select Committee on Nutrition and Human Needs, *To Save the Children: Nutritional Intervention through Supplemental Feeding* (Washington: U.S. Government Printing Office, 1974).

6. Jean Piaget, *The Psychology of Intelligence* (Totowa, NJ: Littlefield Adams, 1966); Morris Eson and Sean A. Walmsley, "Promoting Cognitive and Psycholinguistic Development," in *Toward Adolescence: The Middle School Years,* ed. Mauritz Johnson (Chicago: University of Chicago Press, 1980), 204–26.

7. John J. Conger, *Adolescence and Youth: Psychological Development in a Changing World* (New York: Harper & Row, 1977), 152–53.

8. Herman T. Epstein and Conrad F. Toepfer, Jr., "A Neuroscience Basis for Reorganizing Middle Grades Education," *Educational Leadership,* 35 (1978), 665–60.

9. David Elkind, "Investigating Intelligence in Early Adolescence," in *Toward Adolescence: The Middle School Years,* ed. Mauritz Johnson (Chicago: University of Chicago Press, 1980), 282–94.

10. Kurt W. Fischer and Arlyne Lazerson, *Human Development* (New York: W. H. Freeman, 1984).

11. Joseph Adelson, "The Growth of Thought in Adolescence," in *The Development of Adolescent Thinking,* ed. Barbara Presseisen (Philadelphia: Research for Better Schools, 1983), 6–22.

12. L. Kohlberg and C. Gilligan, "The Adult as a Philosopher: The Discovery of the Self in a Post-Conventional World," *Daedalus,* 79 (1971), 1051–86.

13. Martin L. Hoffman, "Sex Differences in Moral Internalization and Values," *Journal of Personality and Social Psychology,* 32 (1975), 720–29.

14. J. L. Tapp and F. J. Levine, "Compliance from Kindergarten to College," *Journal of Youth and Adolescence*, 1 (1972), 233–49.

15. Larry P. Nucci, "Conceptual Development in the Moral and Conventional Domains: Implications for Values Education," *Review of Educational Research*, 52 (1982), 93–122.

16. Martin L. Hoffman, "Fostering Moral Development," in *Toward Adolescence: The Middle School Years*, ed. Mauritz Johnson (Chicago: University of Chicago Press, 1980) 161–85.

17. John P. Hill, *Understanding Early Adolescence: A Framework* (Chapel Hill, NC: Center for Early Adolescence, 1980).

18. Peter L. Benson, Phillip K. Wood, and Arthur L. Johnson, "Findings of Early Adolescents and Their Parents: Highlights from the National Study," *Momentum* 15 (1984), 8–11.

19. D. C. Dunphy, "The Social Structure of Urban Adolescent Peer Groups," *Sociometry* 26 (1963), 230–46.

20. Erik H. Erikson, *Identity: Youth and Crisis* (New York: Norton, 1968).

FIGURE 3-1.   Physical development of the adolescent

RAPID GROWTH

- pronounced and accelerated physical development of height, body breadth, organ capacity, and muscular strength

UNEVEN GROWTH WITHIN THE INDIVIDUAL

- bones grow faster than muscles
- legs and arms grow faster than trunk
- hands and feet grow faster than arms and legs
- some evidence for slower brain growth

UNEVEN GROWTH BETWEEN GROUPS AND INDIVIDUALS

- girls are usually taller and proportionately heavier than boys
- menstruation usually begins at age twelve or thirteen
- first ejaculation usually occurs at age thirteen or fourteen
- boys tend to be a year or two behind girls in the growth cycle
- much variability occurs between individuals

ADOLESCENT

GLANDULAR AND METABOLIC IMBALANCES

- glandular imbalances may result in skin problems and allergies
- basic metabolic irregularities may produce restlessness or listlessness

NUTRITIONAL ABNORMALITIES

- although health is generally good, some nutrition-related problems (overweight, underweight, iron-deficiency anemia, and dental caries) may develop

FIGURE 3-2.   Cognitive development of the adolescent

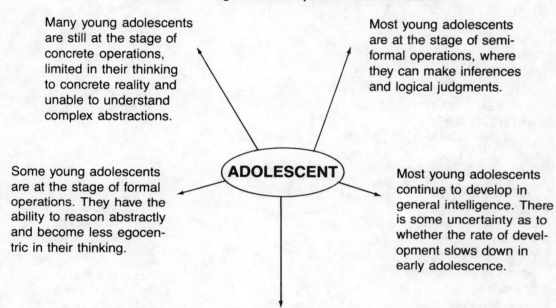

Many young adolescents are still at the stage of concrete operations, limited in their thinking to concrete reality and unable to understand complex abstractions.

Most young adolescents are at the stage of semi-formal operations, where they can make inferences and logical judgments.

Some young adolescents are at the stage of formal operations. They have the ability to reason abstractly and become less egocentric in their thinking.

Most young adolescents continue to develop in general intelligence. There is some uncertainty as to whether the rate of development slows down in early adolescence.

The young adolescence is experiencing some marked changes in political thinking, beginning to reason about political issues in a more conceptual and principled manner.

FIGURE 3-3. Moral development of the adolescent

Most young adolescents are at a conventional "good-boy–good-girl" orientation.

Some young adolescents are at a more advanced conventional level of being oriented toward authority, doing their duty, and maintaining the social order.

Only a few young adolescents have developed autonomous moral principles and an orientation toward internal decisions of conscience.

Young adolescent girls seem to have a stronger orientation toward internalized moral principles and a more humanistic moral orientation.

ADOLESCENT

Most young adolescents consider social conformity the major reason for following rules.

Young adolescents change in their views toward convention: The youngest see convention as an affirmation of a rule system; the older see it as mediated by the social system.

Young adolescents have a high level of empathic distress and are able to respond to such feelings with appropriate action.

Young adolescents are capable of experiencing guilt feelings following both acts of commission and omission.

FIGURE 3-4.   Psycho-social development of the adolescent

ATTACHMENT

- While maintaining positive feelings toward parents, the young adolescent begins to loosen childhood ties in order to disengage from parents.
- The young adolescent is able to conceive of two parallel social worlds (family and peers) and distinguish the norms and conventions of both.

IDENTITY

- Identity formation becomes the central issue of adolescence, as bodily changes and new social roles require new conceptions of self.
- The peer group is used to explore self, test new identities, and get feedback.
- In the search for identity, there is increasing conformity to peer influences and to gender-related stereotypes.

INTIMACY

- Crowds and cliques become important as young adolescents develop the capacity to sustain emotional relationships and to transform acquaintanceships into friendships.
- Friendships between girls seem to be more intense and involve more self-disclosure than do those between boys.

ADOLESCENT

SEXUALITY

- Gender identity is transformed in order to incorporate sexual activity with others.
- Dating begins, but heterosxual relationships often have a superficial and game-like quality.

AUTONOMY

- The young adolescent extends the self-initiated activity begun at an earlier age into wider realms, often with the approval of parents.
- The young adolescent begins to act more autonomously and assertively within the family, while continuing to value the support of the family.

ACHIEVEMENT

- There is a growing orientation toward achievement and a concomitant commitment to self, friends, and the social order.
- Achievement ambitions seem to become more future-oriented and realistic.
- Differential socialization by gender seems to intensify. Many girls opt out of "boys' subjects." Gender differences on tests of mathematical and verbal skills begin to appear.

FIGURE 3-5. Adolescent development and effective middle schools

CURRICULUM The curriculum should:

- Include units of study that help young adolescents understand, accept, and foster their physical development.

- Include units of study designed to facilitate the moral development of young adolescents.

- Include units of study that help young adolescents understand themselves and the developmental tasks they face.

- Place the development of thinking at the center: build upon concrete operations, develop semi-formal operations, and explore formal operations.

- Include units of study designed to challenge gender stereotyping and emphasize the importance of mathematics and science for all students.

- Help students develop the ability to analyze the mass media critically.

TEACHING AND LEARNING Teaching and learning activities should:

- Begin with an assessment of learner's present level of cognitive development.

- Alternate modes and methods of learning.

- Emphasize concept development by full explication, detailed exemplification, and guided discussion.

- Strengthen achievement motivation of young adolescents by helping them set reasonable goals, acquire needed skills, and implement plans for achieving those goals.

- Develop autonomy by making appropriate provisions for independent learning.

- Develop attachment by making appropriate provisions for cooperative group learning.

continued

FIGURE 3-5. (cont.)

ACTIVITY PROGRAM The activity program should:

● Offer diverse activities that develop and reward multiple talents.

● Offer activities that will encourage healthy heterosexual interactions, without compulsory dating and dancing.

● Offer activities that will enable young adolescents to develop needed social and interpersonal skills.

GUIDANCE PROGRAM The guidance program should:

● Provide all young adolescents with the help they need to achieve developmental tasks: help them discern feelings, develop perspective about problems, and find needed resources.

● Provide special support and services to those encountering more serious problems.

ORGANIZATIONAL STRUCTURE The organizational structure should:

● Include a school schedule that allows for periods of both activity and relaxation.

● Provide for flexible grouping, so that students can for at least part of the time be with peers at similar stages of development.

continued

FIGURE 3-5. (cont.)

SCHOOL CLIMATE The school climate should:

- Stress the maintenance of the school as a social order.
- Stress the importance of authority and the need for rules.

STAFF DEVELOPMENT The staff development program should:

- Help staff understand key features of physical development of young adolescents and how the school can best respond to such features.
- Teach staff how to assess and make special provisions for cognitive development of learners, paying special attention to the development of thinking skills.
- Aid staff in developing and facilitating the moral growth of young adolescents and in structuring a school environment that will support such growth.
- Sensitize the staff to the psycho-social development of young adolescents.
- Help staff provide learning environments that will help students achieve developmental tasks, giving appropriate attention to individual and group learning approaches.

PART TWO

GOALS
FOR
EFFECTIVE
MIDDLE SCHOOLS

4

Developing a Consensus
on School Goals

Setting Goals for an Effective Middle School

1. The goals and purposes of the school are clearly articulated.

2. There is a strong consensus among administrators, teachers, and parents about those goals and purposes.

The guidelines for middle-school effectiveness indicate that the goals of the school should be both clearly stated and generally supported by everyone involved. This chapter will describe some processes that can be used in both articulating those goals and achieving the desired consensus.

DEVELOPING A TENTATIVE
GOAL STATEMENT

The first step in the process is to develop a tentative statement of middle-school goals. If your middle school already has a statement of its goals, then you can consider that statement as the tentative version in the process described here. If your middle school does not have such a statement of its goals, then you can either begin to develop your own using the following procedures or modify the one that is used in the survey shown in Figure 4-1.

1. Collect goal statements from several sources, including such sources as the state department of education, the school district, other middle schools, and professional books. One of the best sources is John I. Goodlad's book *A Place Called School: Prospects for the Future* (New York: McGraw-Hill, 1984), which includes a comprehensive list of goals for all schools, developed by systematically studying major goal statements of the past and goal statements in current use by state departments of education.

2. Review all those goal statements, paying special attention to the general categories used, and decide which general categories you will use in your own goal statement. This is a rather important step, since the way you conceptualize and organize the goal statements will have important implications for the rest of the process.

    It is especially important to develop a goal structure that will simplify the curriculum development process. We therefore begin by identifying the essential learning skills and the basic academic subjects. We are influenced here by a major curriculum document from the College Board, *Academic Preparation for College,* which identifies what it calls "basic academic competencies" (the learning skills) and "basic academic subjects."[1] We should note here that we agree with that report in seeing the arts as one of the basic academic subjects.

    It also seems useful to emphasize the importance of creative thinking and creative expression in all fields of human endeavor—and to do so in a way that will minimize some of the artificial distinctions implicit in a subject-centered curriculum. Writing a poem, designing a bookcase, and decorating a room are all expressions of the creative spirit; it is not important whether they take place in a subject called *English, industrial arts,* or *home economics.* The categories therefore reflect this perspective.

    It is desirable from a curricular point of view to separate wherever feasible the three domains of objectives—the cognitive, the affective, and the psycho-motor. Note, therefore, that the "personal" and "interpersonal" categories place primary emphasis on attitudes and values and that "health and physical education" outcomes are treated separately.

3. Once you have specified the general categories, identify for each the specific outcomes you think are important. There are two cautions here. First, restrict those specific statements to outcomes; do not include methods or procedures. Here are some examples of items from several middle-school goal statements that are actually methods, not outcomes: to individualize instruction, to personalize learning, to adapt instruction to preferred learning styles. Mixing methods and outcomes will only confuse the program

development process. The second caution is to limit the number of specific statements to a manageable number—perhaps no more than forty. Using longer lists makes it more difficult to achieve a consensus and to plan a program.

Those three steps will result in the production of your tentative or draft version of the goal statement.

REFINING THE PRELIMINARY STATEMENT

The next stage in the goal-setting process involves refining the preliminary statement in order to ensure that it is both clear and comprehensive. The simplest and most effective way of refining the statement is to ask the faculty to meet in small groups—by teams or departments—to discuss the draft version. Make it clear that you will later be assessing priorities and attempting to build a consensus and that you want their input at this stage only to improve the draft version. Ask them to focus on three questions: Which statements are unclear and need to be reworded? Which specific goals should be added? Which specific goals seem inappropriate and should be dropped? Notice that you do not ask the faculty to reword or reorganize the general categories. During this stage of the process, it is more useful to have them focus on the specific statements, rather than trying to reconceptualize the general categories.

Also, at this stage of refining the goal statement, it is not necessary to get parent and student input, although you may certainly do so if you wish. However, since their contributions are more important during the next stage of setting priorities, you may wish to restrict your surveying of those groups to that stage and not involve them in the refining process.

Use the results of the small group discussions to develop the final version of the goal statement. Rewrite any statements that the faculty felt were unclear. Add any goal statement suggested by one or more of the groups; eliminate those items that all the groups felt were inappropriate. This process will result in a clearer and more comprehensive version that can then be used in the process of setting priorities.

ASSESSING GOAL PRIORITIES

This clearer and more comprehensive goal statement can then be used to assess priorities. The process used here will depend, of course, on such factors as the nature of the school (whether public, church-related, or independent), the size of the faculty and the student body, and the general plans of the school district of which that school is a part. The process will also be affected by the availability of data processing resources. Since the process requires the reduction and analysis of a large data base, you should explore the feasibility of handling the data analysis by a computer. The process described in the following paragraphs is one that has been found to be generally successful in a variety of settings.

Goal Priorities Survey for Teachers

First, assess faculty priorities by distributing in a faculty meeting the survey shown in Figure 4-1 (or your own modification of it). Clarify the instructions, explain any items that might be confusing, and stress the importance of the process. Give the faculty ample time to complete the form during the meeting. Since you are assessing individual faculty perceptions, the form should be completed without discussion of its content.

Goal Priorities Survey for Students

Next, assess student priorities by having teachers distribute the same form during one of the "homebase" periods. Since some of the educational jargon may be confusing to students, the teachers should take the time to explain what each item means. Again, however, the student responses should be made without discussion of the substance, since you wish to get individual responses that have not been influenced by peer opinion.

Goal Priorities Survey for Parents

Finally, survey all parents by mail. In order to get a high rate of return and ensure that the results are representative, you may wish to take certain precautionary steps. Ask the parents' organization to devote some time during one of its meetings to the process of setting goals and its importance. Publicize the process through parent newsletters, flyers delivered by the students, and news releases in the local paper. And when mailing out the survey, enclose a self-addressed stamped envelope to ensure a higher rate of return.

Then, when all the returns are in, compute for each group the percentage distribution for each response to each item; the percentage figure will be the easiest to use in the next stage of the process.

IDENTIFYING PRIORITY GOALS

The next stage in the process is to use the data gathered to identify the priority goals. There are several processes that might be used here; the procedure outlined here has worked well in several middle schools.

First, summarize the results of the surveys, showing the percentage distributions for each response on each item, for all groups surveyed. Distribute that summary to all the faculty, asking them to review the results carefully and to discuss them informally with colleagues. Then again provide time in faculty team meetings for a more structured discussion, asking the faculty to pay special attention to the following items:

- Those items about which there seemed to be major faculty disagreement. If the majority of the faculty did not agree on a particular priority rating for a given item, then there is probably need for full discussion of that item.
- Those items to which two-thirds of the faculty gave a "high" priority rating but that did not elicit a similar level of parent support. This discrepancy also signals the need for discussion.

After that discussion, ask the faculty once again to respond to the survey. Indicate that any item which two-thirds of the faculty indicate is a "high" priority will be then presented to students and parents as a school priority, pending further review. Collate and analyze the results from this second faculty survey, noting all those items to which two-thirds or more of the faculty have a "high" priority rating.

The process suggested here is obviously a variation of the Delphi technique, which has been used successfully with groups as a means of assessing expert opinion about an open-ended issue.

DEVELOPING A CONSENSUS OF GOALS

By using the procedures described here, you have been able to identify those goals that at least two-thirds of the faculty believe should have a high priority. You should therefore be able to use those data in developing a next-to-final draft of the school's goal statement. You may wish to use a form like the one shown in Figure 4-2. Observe several features of this form. First, it retains the general categories used in the survey, to emphasize the importance of the conceptualization. Second, it uses the pronoun *we* to stress a shared responsibility. Finally, it makes a clear distinction between the priority goals and all the rest, using somewhat neutral language to introduce goals that did not receive a high rating.

That form should then be used in several different ways. First, faculty should discuss it again to be sure that they are ready to support it as a definite statement of school priorities. Second, the statement should be discussed in home-base meetings with students. In such discussions, the faculty should discuss openly both the process used and the results obtained. The teachers should make clear to the students the rationale for soliciting student input, without letting student preferences determine school priorities. It might be useful here to make an analogy with the way Congress makes laws for the country: Elected representatives are sensitive to the wishes of constituents, but they do not let constituent opinion determine the nature of legislation. The teachers should also take time to discuss specific issues on which students and teachers disagreed, noting that such disagreements are bound to occur among groups with different roles, perspectives, and objectives.

The next step in the consensus-building process is to work with parents. Here the objective is to resolve any major differences between faculty and parent perception, not simply to inform parents of a faculty decision. One useful way of achieving this outcome is to invite all parents and teachers to an open discussion of the topic. At such a session, the principal reviews the process used and summarizes the results, noting any items where there were major differences between the responses of the two groups. Then a faculty member speaks briefly about the teachers' perceptions, and a representative of the parents' association clarifies parent feelings. Those presentations are followed by small group discussions, with each group including both teachers and parents.

After the meeting, a steering group composed of administrators, teachers, and parents meets to review the results of that meeting. The group might decide to hold additional discussions or to amend the goal statement so that it is more inclusive and less divisive. Any amended version, of course, is submitted to the faculty for additional discussion.

STRESSING PRIORITY GOALS

The final step in the whole process is to publicize the priority goals and to continue to express them clearly to all involved. First, they should be emphasized with the faculty, since the faculty are primarily responsible for their accomplishment. They should become part of the faculty handbook and should be discussed from time to time in faculty and team meetings as a means of reminding faculty of their importance. And, as will be noted in subsequent chapters, they should play an important role in program planning and development.

The goals must also be stressed with the students. Some schools have found it effective to print large posters with the priority goals clearly displayed; those posters are then hung in every classroom as well as on corridor and cafeteria bulletin boards. Some principals report that they begin morning announcements with a statement of one of the goals. Teachers should be encouraged to show students how both the curricular and the extracurricular program contribute to the priority goals.

Finally, of course, the priority goals need to be communicated clearly to parents and to the community. Newsletters to the parents can stress the goals and the contributions that parents can make to their accomplishment. Some of the parent meetings can be devoted to the goals and the means by which the school is attempting to accomplish them. And news releases about the process and its outcome can be used to inform the general community.

This process obviously is a time-consuming one. However, its importance is clear. If the school has clear priorities and those priorities are understood and supported by all, it is more likely to be an excellent middle school.

Note

1. The College Board, *Academic Preparation for College: What Students Need to Know and Be Able to Do* (New York: The College Board, 1983).

FIGURE 4-1. Goal priorities survey

Directions: Several goals suggested for middle-school education are listed here. Read each goal statement and indicate what priority you think that goal should have for all the students in our middle school. Report your rating by circling the letter H if you think that goal should have a high priority; the letter M if you think that goal should have a middle priority; and the letter L if a low priority.

GOAL	YOUR RATING

LEARNING SKILLS The middle-school student will learn to:

1. Read with understanding and with critical judgment.	H	M	L
2. Write clearly and effectively.	H	M	L
3. Speak and listen well.	H	M	L
4. Use mathematical problem-solving processes.	H	M	L
5. Reason logically and think critically.	H	M	L
6. Study effectively.	H	M	L
7. Use the computer to solve problems and to compose.	H	M	L

BASIC ACADEMIC SUBJECTS The middle-school student will learn the important concepts and skills of:

8. English.	H	M	L
9. Mathematics.	H	M	L
10. Science.	H	M	L
11. Social studies.	H	M	L
12. A foreign language.	H	M	L
13. The arts.	H	M	L

HEALTH AND PHYSICAL EDUCATION The middle-school student will:

14. Understand the nature and importance of physical and mental health.	H	M	L
15. Develop physical fitness and recreation skills.	H	M	L

continued

FIGURE 4-1. (cont.)

GOAL	YOUR RATING

CREATIVE THINKING AND CREATIVE EXPRESSION
The middle-school student will:

16. Learn how to express ideas and images creatively in words, sounds, fabric, color, wood, and other media.　　　　　H　M　L

17. Learn how to think creatively and solve problems creatively.　　　　　H　M　L

PERSONAL SKILLS AND ATTITUDES The middle-school student will:

18. Develop a positive self-image.　　　H　M　L

19. Make sound moral decisions.　　　H　M　L

20. Develop special interests and leisure activities.　　　H　M　L

21. Learn how to cope with changes in family, community, and society.　　　H　M　L

22. Learn how to make sound decisions about careers, about spending and saving, about the use of television, and about other important personal issues.　　　H　M　L

23. Develop desirable attitudes toward work and study.　　　H　M　L

INTERPERSONAL SKILLS AND ATTITUDES The middle-school student will:

24. Learn how to work cooperatively with others.　　　H　M　L

25. Value his or her own ethnic identity and respect the contributions of other ethnic groups.　　　H　M　L

26. Treat others with respect, regardless of race, sex, or ethnic identity.　　　H　M　L

27. Learn how to be a contributing member of the family.　　　H　M　L

28. Develop the attitudes of responsible citizenship.　　　H　M　L

29. Develop a concern for humanity and an appreciation of global interdependence.　　　H　M　L

FIGURE 4-2. The goals of Washington Middle School

These are the goals that have a high priority for us:

LEARNING SKILLS Our students will be able to:

1. Read with understanding and with critical judgment.
2. Write clearly and effectively.
3. Speak and listen well.
4. Use mathematical problem-solving processes.
5. Reason logically and think creatively.
6. Study effectively.

We also will work toward accomplishing this goal:

LEARNING SKILLS Our students will be able to:

Use the computer to solve problems and to compose.

5

Aligning Goals and the Educational Program

Aligning School Goals and Programs

1. Appoint a coordinating task force and working committees on curriculum, teaching and learning, activity program, and guidance program.

2. Each committee identifies the goals its program should be primarily responsible for and those it should reinforce.

3. The task force then synthesizes the four reports, resolving issues of overlap and omission.

4. The results are then shared with faculty and parents.

By using the processes explained in Chapter 4, you should now have a clear set of goals for the middle school. It is of course desirable to have a set of goals that everyone understands and accepts, but it is even more important to institute those goals through the educational program. (We use the term *educational program* to refer to the four components that directly affect the growth and development of the students: the curriculum, the teaching and learning processes, the activity program, and the guidance program.) Our experience suggests that in too many middle schools the goals and the educational program are only loosely related. Too often, goals are promulgated—and then programs are developed without reference to those goals. The research clearly indicates that middle schools will be more effective if goals and programs are closely linked.

This linkage can be most effectively accomplished through a process we call "program alignment." It is a process for allocating a shared responsibility for achieving goals to the several educational programs. This chapter will offer a rationale for aligning goals and programs and then explain in greater detail a process for effecting goal and program alignment.

THE RATIONALE FOR PROGRAM ALIGNMENT

There are three reasons for aligning goals with educational programs.

Rational Decisions Are Possible

The first reason is that the alignment process enables middle-school leaders to make more rational decisions about implementing and evaluating the school's educational program. Consider the activity program, for example. In the typical middle school, activities are implemented just because an administrator or teacher thinks that a particular activity is needed. Any evaluation that is carried out is often done without reference to the goals of the program and their relationship to school outcomes: "Let's drop the Community Service Club—attendance is declining and the sponsor has lost interest." Contrast that school with one where goals and programs have been aligned. The activity program has been allocated responsibility for achieving certain of the school's goals. New programs are initiated only when they can demonstrate that they are likely to make a contribution to those goals. And evaluation is carried out with reference to the goals of the program: "Let's continue the Community Service Club; even though enrollments are down, it seems to be enhancing the self-image of participants."

Reasonable Expectations Are Established

The second reason is that the process of allocating shared responsibility to the various programs is likely to result in establishing reasonable expectations for those components, for the process results in a rational delineation of responsibilities. Such a delineation seems especially important in relation to the curriculum. Some educators erroneously assume that all of the school's goals should be accomplished through the curriculum; the result of such an error is an overloaded curriculum that accomplishes little because it attempts too much. Even if the faculty believe in a school where the curriculum is central, that curriculum will probably be more effective if it is structured to accomplish a specifically delineated set of outcomes, rather than being burdened with all the goals of the school.

A More Effective School Is Created

The most important reason, of course, is that the goal (program alignment process) is likely to result in a more effective school. The research on effective schools suggests clearly that the more effective schools are goal oriented: All aspects of the educational program have clearly set purposes that are related to the goals of the school. The clarity of purpose and the sharing of responsibility both result in greater efficiency and increased effectiveness.

THE PROGRAM ALIGNMENT PROCESS

The process of aligning the goals of the school with the educational program is a major undertaking that at its best involves the entire faculty, since such decisions in essence speak as the philosophy of the school. Some faculties will want a school that places the activity program at the center; others will value a school where guidance plays a major role. Some will want to maximize the contributions made by the teaching and learning processes; others will place most emphasis upon the curriculum. There is no best pattern here; it is clarity of purpose and function that is important.

Using the Task Force

Although total faculty involvement is highly desirable, the complexity of the process suggests that it can best be directed by a task force representing the instructional leadership of the school. The composition of this task force will vary with the size and organizational structure of the school, but it typically includes the following members:

- a representative of the district's curriculum office
- the middle-school principal
- team leaders or department heads
- one or more classroom teachers
- a representative of the parents' group

A working group of this sort should probably not include more than eight individuals; larger groups become unwieldy, even though they may be more representative.

Committee Structure

We have found in the schools we have worked with that the best process for getting faculty input is to devote an inservice day to the task of aligning goals and programs. The entire faculty is divided into four working committees, each one devoted to one of the program areas. The inservice session begins with the principal's making a brief general presentation, stressing the importance of the process and explaining the day's schedule and activities. Each committee then meets together, under the leadership of one of the task-force members, and holds an open discussion of its program area. For example, the guidance committee might examine such issues as these:

- What resources (people, money, space) are available for our guidance program?
- How important is the guidance program in our school?
- What is the general faculty attitude toward guidance?

The results of such a discussion are then used by the committee in answering the two basic questions for that session:

1. Which goals should the guidance program be *primarily* responsible for?
2. Which program goals can the guidance department *reinforce*?

Each committee prepares a written summary of its answers to those two questions and makes a brief oral presentation to the entire faculty at the end of the inservice session.

Synthesizing the Reports

It is then the job of the task force to synthesize and harmonize the four committee reports. The task force can simplify their work here by developing a matrix like the one shown in Figure 5-1. Across the top are listed the four components of the educational program: curriculum, teaching and learning processes, activity program, and guidance program. Down the left-hand side are listed first the priority goals and then all the other goals of the school. Listing the priority goals first is a good way to remind the faculty of the central importance of those goals.

The recommendations made by each of the four committees are then entered into the matrix. Through analyzing the data displayed on the matrix, the task force first resolves the issue of overlap and duplication. Do two or more of the programs claim primary responsibility for a particular goal? If so, should we give primary responsibility to only one of the programs? Our recommendation here is that only one program should have primary responsibility for each goal, but this is a decision that individual schools should make. The task force then examines the problem of omission. Are any of the goals not claimed as a primary responsibility by any of the programs? If so, which program can most readily make that goal its primary responsibility?

The task force then examines critically its own decisions from three different perspectives:

1. Does the general distribution of goals to programs seem to reflect the type of middle school we desire?
2. Does the distribution of responsibility for a particular goal seem likely to ensure its attainment? Are the goals adequately provided for?
3. Does the distribution of responsibilities to a given program seem to be a balanced one, so that the purposes of that program are likely to be achieved?

The answers to those questions should enable the task force to make any changes it deems necessary to achieve the desired coverage and balance. That tentative consensus is then shared with the faculty, preferably presented and reviewed in team meetings, with ample time for open discussion. The results of those discussions are then reported back to the task-force members, who can then revise the matrix to reflect general faculty perceptions.

The intent here is not to deliberate at length in order to achieve complete agreement; the purpose instead is to make a systematic allocation that reflects general faculty and leadership values, while permitting and even encouraging some open disagreement.

Informing Parents

The results of all these deliberations are shared with parents. The purpose of such sharing is to *inform* the parents, not to involve them directly in the decision-making process. They should be actively involved in identifying the goals of the school, but the decisions about alignment and allocation should be left primarily to the faculty. Those decisions are matters of implementation, not policy formulation. This process of informing the parents should be an ongoing one. The parent representative on the task force should be sure to keep the parents' organization fully informed as the task force conducts the process explained here. Then the middle-school principal can use one of the regular parent meetings to explain the process, present the results, and encourage parents to raise questions. From time to time, newsletters to the parents might focus on a particular program component and explain how it is attempting to discharge its goal-oriented responsibilities.

FIGURE 5-1. Relating goals to program components

Code: *p* = *goal will be* primarily *accomplished through this component*
     r = *goal will be* reinforced *through this component*

GOALS: THE MIDDLE-SCHOOL STUDENT SHOULD BE ABLE TO:	*CURRIC*	*TCH/LRN*	*ACTIV*	*GUID*
1. Read with understanding and with critical judgment.	p			
2. Write clearly and effectively.	p			
3. Speak and listen well.		p		
4. Use mathematical problem-solving processes.	p	r		
5. Reason logically and think critically.	p	r		
6. Study effectively.	p	r		r
7. Use the computer to solve problems and to compose.	r	p		
8. Learn important concepts and skills of English.	p	r		
9. Learn important concepts and skills of mathematics.	p	r		
10. Learn important concepts and skills of science.	p	r		
11. Learn important concepts and skills of social studies.	p	r		
12. Learn important concepts and skills of a foreign language.	p	r		
13. Learn important concepts and skills of the arts.	p	r		
14. Understand the nature and importance of physical and mental health.	p	r	r	r
15. Develop physical fitness and recreation skills.	p	r	r	

continued

FIGURE 5-1. (cont.)

GOALS: THE MIDDLE-SCHOOL STUDENT SHOULD BE ABLE TO:	CURRIC	TCH/LRN	ACTIV	GUID
16. Learn how to express ideas and images creatively in words, sounds, fabric, color, wood, and other media.	p	r	r	
17. Learn how to think creatively and solve problems.	r	p	r	r
18. Develop a positive self-image.	r	p	r	r
19. Make sound moral decisions.	p	r	r	r
20. Develop special interests.			p	r
21. Cope with changes.	p			r
22. Make sound personal decisions.	r		r	p
23. Develop positive work and study attitudes.		p		r
24. Learn how to work cooperatively with others.		r	p	
25. Value his or her own ethnic identity and respect the contributions of other ethnic groups.	p	r	r	r
26. Treat others with respect, regardless of race, sex, or ethnic identity.	r	p	r	r
27. Learn how to be a contributing member of the family.	p			r
28. Develop the attitudes of responsible citizenship.	p	r	r	r
29. Develop a concern for humanity and an appreciation of global interdependence.	p	r		

PART THREE

PROGRAMS
FOR EFFECTIVE
MIDDLE SCHOOLS

6

Aligning the Curriculum

The Curriculum of an Effective Middle School

1. The curriculum reflects and is developed from the goals of the school.

2. The curriculum facilitates the mastery of essential learning and inquiry skills.

3. The curriculum facilitates the learning of the important skills and concepts of the basic academic subjects.

4. The curriculum fosters the physical and emotional development of the students through a sound program in health and physical education.

5. The curriculum enhances the ability of the students to think creatively and to express themselves in creative forms.

6. The curriculum contributes to the development of personal and interpersonal skills and attitudes, giving specific attention to those skills and attitudes especially important for young adolescents in our society.

7. The curriculum is seen as relevant by the students and responds to their diverse needs.

By applying the processes described in Chapter 5, you now have identified those goals that will be both primarily accomplished and those that will be reinforced through the curriculum. The next major step in improving middle schools is to align the curriculum goals with the specific subjects offered in the school. As noted in the chapter-opening summary, in effective middle schools the curriculum is closely related to—or aligned with—the goals of the school. This chapter will present a rationale and explain a process for goal-curriculum alignment.

A RATIONALE FOR ALIGNING GOALS AND THE CURRICULUM

Although it is possible to develop effective curricula without reference to the goals of the school, it is argued here that aligning goals and curricula is an important step in developing excellent middle schools.

Bring Together All Departments

The first argument for goal and curriculum alignment is that the process is likely to have a unifying effect. The typical secondary school is "loosely coupled"; each department goes its own separate way, acting as an autonomous unit independent of all other departments.[1] Aligning goals and curricula is one way of tightening the coupling: The process reminds departments that they are joined in common pursuits. If, for example, all departments decide to work together toward the goal of "writing clearly and effectively," the resulting cooperative efforts are likely to bring the departments closer together.

Facilitate Curriculum Development

The second argument is that with the clarification of and emphasis on the outcomes desired in each curriculum, the alignment process tends to facilitate curriculum development. Supervisors and teachers tend to have an implicit understanding of what they are trying to achieve, but they typically develop curricula without reference to school goals. The result often is a curriculum without purpose. Units are added just because someone decides that they might be interesting to the students, and important outcomes are often neglected because everyone else believes that they are "someone else's job." Thus, most teachers feel that it is important to teach logical reasoning and critical thinking, but those thinking skills are usually ignored because they were not stated as specific goals for one or more of the school's subjects. If, however, the goal of facilitating critical thinking is stated as a desired outcome for both the English and the social studies curriculum, for example, then it is more likely that in each of those disciplines, units will be planned to achieve such a goal.

Monitor Curriculum Evaluation

Finally, the alignment process facilitates curriculum evaluation. As we note in the following section, it is basic to what we term "curriculum diagnosis"—assessing the fit between goals and courses. And it is useful in monitoring the curriculum and making summative evaluations of the curriculum—both of which are discussed more fully in Chapter 14. It would be extremely difficult to evaluate any curriculum if the evaluators could not identify its goals.

THE PROCESS FOR ALIGNING
GOALS AND CURRICULA

The process for aligning goals and curricula is similar to that used for aligning goals and programs: There is general faculty involvement, with leadership provided by a task force, perhaps the same one used in aligning goals and programs. Again, our experience suggests that an inservice day is the best time for accomplishing this important task. The principal should begin the session by presenting to the faculty all those school goals for which the curriculum has primary responsibility; those goals that the curriculum also reinforces can be dealt with at a later stage of the process. The concern here is to focus on what might be termed the "curriculum-based goals," those goals accomplished primarily through the curriculum.

Use of Subject Committees

Now the faculty meets in subject-matter committees. Each committee reviews the curriculum-based goals one at a time—and for each goal, reaches one of the following conclusions: Our subject will *emphasize* this goal; our subject will *contribute* to this goal; our subject will *ignore* this goal. Again, the inservice day should end with a brief summary by each committee and reminder by the principal of the next steps to be taken in the process.

The task force then collates the reports of the subject-matter committees, using a matrix like the one shown in Figure 6-1. Listed across the top of the matrix are the subjects, with the required subjects first. Down the left-hand side are listed the curriculum-based goals. Note that in this figure we have used the "learning skills" goals as an example, to illustrate how they might be treated differently across the curriculum.

Now the task force again evaluates the responses of the subject-matter committees, asking these questions:

- For each curriculum-based goal, is there at least one required subject that will emphasize this goal?
- For each complex curriculum goal, like critical thinking, is there one or more required subjects that will contribute to that goal? Are complex goals appropriately reinforced through the contributions of several different curricula?
- Do the subject-matter committees seem to have made appropriate choices? Is there a good fit between the goals emphasized and the nature of that discipline or area of study?
- Is there good balance across the subjects? Given the time provided in the curriculum, have some subjects attempted too much—or others too little?
- Are the indicators of curricular excellence present in our curriculum, as manifested in this process?

The task-force members revise the matrix to reflect their proposed recommendations. The revised matrix is then discussed once more by subject-matter teams to be sure that each subject-matter group approves the recommendations affecting their subject. Any concerns are resolved through an open discussion by the task force and the subject-matter team involved.

Sharing the Results

The results of this process of aligning goals and curricula are shared with faculty, parents, and students—through quite different processes. First, the task force produces for the faculty a publication that provides a complete summary of the results of the procedures just described. We have found that the clearest way of organizing this publication for the faculty is as follows:

1. Begin with a brief description of the process.
2. List all the curriculum-based goals—those that will be primarily accomplished through the curriculum.
3. Devote one section to each subject-matter area, showing first the goals that that subject will emphasize and then the goals to which it will contribute.
4. Conclude the publication with a reminder of those school goals that are only reinforced through the curriculum—those that are primarily accomplished through other components of the educational program.

The summary publication can be discussed at a faculty meeting, primarily to remind the faculty of the importance of the alignment process.

Because parents are less likely to be interested in the detailed explanation included in this publication, they probably can best be informed through an evening parents' meeting. The principal should present a rationale for the process, provide an overview of the procedures used, and summarize the results. The parents can then divide into subject-matter groups led by a teacher who teaches that subject. In those group discussions they can raise questions about the goals for that subject and the methods by which those goals will be attained.

Students should be reminded of the goals in every classroom, as appropriate. Each teacher should post in the classroom a list of the goals that relate to the subject being taught and from time to time point out to students how a given lesson relates to the instructional goals.

As the next chapter will indicate, the curriculum-based goals can provide an excellent foundation for developing a sharply focused course structure.

USING CURRICULAR GOALS TO DIAGNOSE THE CURRICULUM

Once this process of curriculum alignment has been initially accomplished, it is undertaken periodically as the key component of curriculum diagnosis. *Curriculum diagnosis*, as the term is used here, is a process of assessing whether there is a good fit between curricular goals and curricular offerings. The diagnosis is performed perhaps once every four years, using a process similar to the following: First, the faculty involved in teaching each required and elective course are asked to submit a current list of the goals for that course, indicating again those that they emphasize and those to which they contribute. Note that this diagnostic process begins with specific subject reports, not school-wide lists of goals. It is a "bottom-up" process. Those reports are collated in a matrix similar to that shown in Figure 6-1. Now the leadership team critically reviews the data displayed in the matrix, asking these questions:

1. Is every curriculum-based goal emphasized in at least one required subject? If not, should that goal be assigned to an existing course—or should a new course be added?

2. Is every more complex curriculum-based goal reinforced across the curriculum, with two or more required or elective subjects contributing to it? If not, which courses should be contributing to that goal?

3. Are there any goals that are emphasized in too many required subjects? Should a particular goal receive less emphasis?

4. If we need to economize by reducing the number of elective courses, which electives seem to be making the least contribution to school curricular goals?

5. Does the school's curriculum in general adequately reflect the indicators of curriculum excellence?

Curriculum diagnosis is thus the first important step in a rational process of curriculum improvement—and it is based upon and derives from curriculum alignment.

Note

1. Karl E. Weick, "Educational Organizations as Loosely Coupled Systems," *Administrative Science Quarterly,* 21 (1976), 1–19.

FIGURE 6-1. Aligning curriculum-based goals and subjects

GOALS: The middle-school student should be able to:	ENGLISH	SOCIAL STUDIES	MATH	SCIENCE	ART	MUSIC	HOME EC	INDUSTRIAL ARTS
1. Read with understanding and critical judgment.	e	c	c	c				
2. Write clearly.	e	c	c	c				
3. Speak and listen well.	e	c	c	c	c	c	c	c
4. Use problem solving.			e	c			c	c
5. Reason logically and think critically.	e	e	e	e	c			
6. Study effectively.	e	c	c	c	c	c	e	e
7. Use a computer to compose and solve problems.	e	c	e	c				

Code: e = emphasize this goal
         c = contribute to this goal

7

Developing
the Mastery Curriculum

Key Steps in Developing the Mastery Curriculum

1. Orient the faculty on the three basic types of curricular outcomes: mastery (basic and needing structure); organic (basic, but not structured); and enrichment (not basic for all students).

2. Departmental teams identify each curricular goal as mastery, organic, or enrichment.

3. Departmental teams identify for each mastery goal the key concepts, skills, and units required, entering their decisions in a mastery scope-and-sequence chart.

4. Grade-level teams use charts to generate mastery objectives.

5. Mastery objectives are then collated and critiqued.

6. Final version of mastery objectives are provided to teams to assist them in unit and lesson planning.

By using the processes explained in the previous chapters, the middle-school faculty is now able to identify for each subject its curriculum-based goals. The next important step is to use those goals in developing what we call the "mastery curriculum," that focused aspect of the curriculum which will chiefly reflect the indicators of effectiveness noted in Chapter 6. This chapter clarifies the nature of the mastery curriculum and then explains how it can be developed.

THE NATURE OF THE MASTERY CURRICULUM

The concept of the mastery curriculum has been developed by Glatthorn from his experience in working with several school districts in curriculum improvement projects. After examining numerous curriculum guides and working with frustrated administrators and teachers, he concluded that most district curriculum guides were not used by teachers because they were not sufficiently focused. They included two types of learnings that, according to his perceptions, did not belong in district curriculum guides: enrichment learnings that were really not essential for all students; and organic learnings that did not require curricular structuring. His work has led him to conclude that a curriculum which focuses on the mastery skills and concepts will be much more effective.

The Enrichment Curriculum

To understand better these three types of curricula—enrichment, organic, and mastery—think of any school subject you know well. First, divide that discipline into those learnings that are basic or essential for all students and those learnings that are useful for enrichment only. The enrichment skills and concepts are those that experienced teachers would consider interesting, but not really essential. In working with teachers, Glatthorn helps them identify the enrichment content by raising the issue this way:

> You are presently teaching a concept or skill that students have great difficulty learning. It is interesting, but not really essential for all students. If you dropped it from the curriculum, there would not be any real harm. Such a concept or skill should be part of the enrichment curriculum.

By identifying the enrichment content, you are left with what is basic—that which is essential for all students. Now divide that basic content into two types: the structured and the nonstructured. Structured learnings, as the term is used here, are those concepts and skills that require careful planning, organizing, and sequencing. Nonstructured learnings are those that can be developed without such careful planning. That division of the basic content yields the mastery curriculum (that which is basic and structured) and the organic (that which is basic and nonstructured). Figure 7-1 presents a schematic illustrating the distinctions explained here.

The Mastery Curriculum

The distinction between the mastery curriculum and the organic curriculum is perhaps the more important one. The mastery curriculum meets two criteria: It is considered essential for all students, and it needs careful structuring. It is characterized by these features:

- It should be systematically planned.
- It should be carefully sequenced and articulated from grade to grade.
- It should be specified as a set of learning objectives.
- It should be carefully assessed and measured.
- It should be represented in a K–12 scope-and-sequence chart and delineated in district curriculum guides.
- Its achievement can be facilitated through the use of good textbooks.
- All teachers should agree to emphasize it in their lesson planning and teaching.
- It should be mastered by all students—except those who are emotionally or mentally handicapped.

The Organic Curriculum

The organic curriculum is just as essential for students—but it does not require careful structuring. Organic learnings are developed informally and incidentally, day by day. Here are some organic outcomes: enjoy poetry, listen courteously, speak clearly, have an inquiring mind, have a good self-image, develop an interest in the political process. All those outcomes are certainly essential—but they do not need careful planning. Contrast these features of the organic curriculum with those listed previously for the mastery curriculum:

- It does not need careful planning.
- It does not have to be sequenced and articulated from grade to grade.
- It does not have to be specified as a set of behavioral objectives.
- It does not have to be assessed and measured.
- It does not have to be mapped in a scope-and-sequence chart or delineated in a curriculum guide.
- Its development does not require a textbook.
- It should be emphasized day by day, by all teachers.
- It should be gradually developed, not mastered, by all students.

The folly of including organic outcomes in district curriculum guides is illustrated by these examples of objectives taken from some middle-school guides we have examined:

- 8th grade mathematics: enjoy problem solving
- 7th grade sciences: develop scientific curiosity
- 6th grade language arts: listen courteously

Those outcomes are all important, but they should not be tied to a particular grade level or taught as parts of structured units.

Helping teachers identify the mastery curriculum in their subjects has several advantages. It results in a simpler curriculum guide that is free of the clutter of organic and enrichment outcomes. It focuses their attention on what is essential. And it helps them plan what is best planned, leaving organic outcomes to be nurtured in the daily interactions of the classroom.

DEVELOPING THE MASTERY CURRICULUM

The process of developing the mastery curriculum for a middle school is a complex and time-consuming one—but the evidence suggests that it is worth the effort and time. We describe in the following section a systematic process that Glatthorn has used effectively with several middle schools, but feel free to modify it to suit local conditions.

Faculty Orientation

The principal should meet with the faculty to present the basic concepts of the mastery, organic, and enrichment curricula. Because these concepts are essential in using the process, there should be ample time for questions and discussion to ensure that the basic ideas are fully understood by all. Teachers should then meet in subject-matter committees to consider each of the curriculum-based goals for a particular subject and determine whether that goal should be part of the mastery curriculum, the organic curriculum, the enrichment curriculum—or any combination of those. Figure 7-2 shows how one group of English teachers decided that issue. Notice that the goal of "understanding the important concepts and skills of English" has been subdivided into the two areas of literature and grammar. Similar divisions would be made in the other major disciplines: The subject-matter committee for each of those disciplines would decide on the major subdivisions that best reflect the nature of that discipline.

Grade-Level Analysis

Through that process the subject-matter committees have identified those curriculum-based goals that they think should be accomplished through the mastery curriculum: They are essential for all students and they need careful structuring. The next step is for the subject-matter committees to take each of those mastery goals and determine for each grade level the general concepts, skills, and units that will enable students to accomplish those goals. We stress here that the planning at this stage should focus on general learnings, not specific outcomes. The determination of specific learning objectives will come at a later point in the process.

The committees' tentative decisions should be reflected in a mastery scope-and-sequence chart. The chart should be constructed by listing at the left-hand side the mastery goals and across the top the grade levels. In each appropriate cell the general concepts, skills, and units are listed. Figure 7-3 shows a mastery scope-and-sequence chart developed by one group of English teachers.

That mastery scope-and-sequence chart in Figure 7-3 illustrates some important matters relating to this process. First, observe that the entries are rather general; there is no attempt to write specific learning objectives, only to show the placement of general skills, concepts, and units. The mastery scope and sequence is a general map, not a detailed set of directions. Next, there is some repetition from grade to grade: Expository writing, for example, is taught in each of the grades. The sequential development of expository writing skills will be reflected at the next level of curriculum development, not here. Note also that there may be some gaps in the scope and sequence; in this case, no decision-making skills or concepts are planned for grade 7.

Generating Mastery Objectives

The next stage in the process is to use the mastery scope-and-sequence chart as a guide for generating mastery objectives, grade by grade. This should be done by grade-level teams of teachers, who understand best the special nature of the students at that grade level. Those grade-level teams should take each of the entries on the scope-and-sequence chart and write more specific learning objectives. Figure 7-4 shows the objectives developed by sixth-grade language arts teachers for the "critical reading" goal. Notice that those objectives are specific without being couched in the overly technical language of behavioral objectives. All that matters is clarity and specificity, not precision.

Review of Objectives

These grade-level mastery objectives are then collated subject by subject and then critically reviewed. This review process attempts to assess the extent to which the curriculum objectives meet certain standards of excellence. Specifically, the curriculum review should focus on the following issues:

1. Does the placement of objectives reflect our best knowledge of adolescent development?
2. Do the objectives reflect our best current knowledge of that subject area or discipline?
3. Do the objectives show a desirable progression and development from grade to grade?
4. Is there sufficient reinforcement, without excessive repetition?
5. Do the objectives sufficiently provide for the learnings necessary for achieving that master goal?
6. Does the number of objectives for a given grade seem appropriate, so that the curriculum for that grade level is neither too light nor too heavy?
7. Do the objectives adequately articulate with the curriculum of sending and receiving schools? Do they build on and lead to the curricular objectives of those schools?
8. Do the objectives taken together sufficiently reflect the indicators of excellence as they relate to this particular subject?

That review should probably be conducted by a special task force, with representatives from the leadership team, the faculty, and the school district curriculum office, assisted if necessary by curriculum consultants. And any revisions suggested as an outcome of this process should be carefully reviewed by the teachers, who should have the authority to make a final decision. Because the classroom teachers will ultimately decide what they wish to teach, the mastery curriculum should reflect their informed decisions, even when those decisions seem in conflict with the recommendations of experts.

Unit and Lesson Planning

The final version of the mastery objectives should then be made available to grade-level teams for their unit and lesson planning. We have found that the best format is a loose-leaf notebook for each grade that contains the following:

- A review of the research on the cognitive development of adolescents.
- The scope-and-sequence chart for each subject, showing all grade levels in that school.
- The mastery objectives for each subject, for that grade level only.
- Suggestions for enriching the curriculum for that grade.
- Suggestions for achieving organic outcomes for that grade.

Notice that the mastery curriculum notebook neither specifies units of study nor recommends particular teaching methods. The intent here is to give teachers much freedom about planning units and choosing methods, just as long as they accomplish the objective specified. These matters of planning units and choosing methods may be left to individual teachers or teams. In fact, teachers are encouraged to make the notebook their own curriculum guide by adding articles from journals, inserting units and lessons they have developed, and including teaching materials produced by their colleagues.

These mastery curriculum notebooks have several advantages over the traditional curriculum guide. They focus only on the mastery curriculum, rather than attempt to be too comprehensive. Specifying only the mastery objectives gives teaching teams great flexibility in organizing units of study. The mastery objectives also provide a sound basis for monitoring the curriculum and assessing student progress. The loose-leaf format simplifies the task of revising and updating the guide and enables teachers to add their own instructional materials.

Observe also that the mastery curriculum notebook provides a useful resolution of the controversy over interdisciplinary units. Most experts on the middle school recommend interdisciplinary units that combine learnings from two or more disciplines, but most teachers are reluctant initially to embrace this approach. They worry about essential skills and concepts' being slighted in interdisciplinary units, are uncertain about their ability to plan complex units that integrate content from several disciplines, and are reluctant to give up the time needed to plan interdisciplinary units.

The mastery notebooks give teaching teams some options here. They may decide to organize subject-matter units until they have acquired more experience in working together; they can then use the same objectives as the basis of inter-disciplinary units. They may decide to plan only a few interdisciplinary units, perhaps one each marking period, using subject-matter units for the rest of the school year; thus, teachers and students experience the benefits of both approaches to curriculum planning. They are not locked into one particular approach.

Several examples of schools that have improved their curriculum with these approaches can be found in Appendix A.

FIGURE 7-1.   The three curricula

	BASIC	ENRICHMENT
STRUCTURED	mastery	enrichment
NONSTRUCTURED	organic	

FIGURE 7-2. The goals of English language arts

GOAL: THE MIDDLE-SCHOOL STUDENT SHOULD BE ABLE TO:	MASTERY	ORGANIC	ENRICHMENT
1. Read with understanding and critical judgment.	X	X	
2. Write clearly.	X	X	X
3. Speak and listen well.	X	X	
4. Reason logically and think critically.	X	X	X
5. Study effectively.	X	X	
6. Use computer to compose and to solve problems.	X		X
7. Understand essential concepts of English			
a. Concepts of grammar	X		X
b. Concepts of literature	X		X
8. Think creatively and solve problems creatively.	X	X	
9. Learn how to make decisions about careers, spending and saving, and use of television.	X		
10. Develop desirable attitudes toward work and study.		X	
11. Value his or her own ethnic identity and respect the contributions of other ethnic groups.	X	X	

FIGURE 7-3. Mastery scope and sequence for English

MASTERY GOAL	GRADE 6	GRADE 7	GRADE 8
critical reading	critical reading stories	critical reading articles	critical reading advertisements persuasion
writing	exposition persuasion narratives	exposition persuasion narratives	exposition persuasion narratives
speaking, listening	interviews	meetings	class discussions
critical thinking	inferring predicting	generalizing evaluating	detecting bias identifying fallacies
studying	library skills	test taking	reference skills
grammar	parts of speech	parts of sentences	combining and expanding sentences
literature	short stories and novels	plays	poems
creative thinking	brainstorming	synectics	creative problem solving
decision making	television	—	careers
ethnicity	black writers	eastern European writers	Hispanic writers

FIGURE 7-4. Mastery objectives for English language arts

Grade: *6*   Team: *Walker, Danforth, Parpart*

Mastery goal: *Critical reading of stories*
Mastery objectives:

1. Infer setting from clues in story.
2. Predict endings of stories.
3. Infer motivation from actions.

8

Supervising to Improve Middle-School Instruction

Teaching and Learning in an Effective Middle School

1. Give special attention to assessing cognitive readiness.
2. Use the computer and television to improve instructional efficiency.
3. Alternate modes and methods of learning.
4. Emphasize concept development by full explication, detailed exemplification, and guided discussion.
5. Strengthen achievement motivation of young adolescents by helping them set reasonable goals, acquire needed skills, and implement plans for achieving those goals.
6. Attempt to develop learner autonomy by making appropriate provisions for independent learning.
7. Make appropriate provisions for cooperative group learning.

If you have decided to focus on the improvement of middle-school teaching by emphasizing the indicators just listed, how do you accomplish that goal? One answer, of course, is through a comprehensive staff development program as described in Chapter 15. A more direct approach is through teacher supervision. However, several studies indicate that the standard approaches to supervision are not very productive.[1] We therefore present in this chapter what we have found to be a more effective model: differentiated supervision for middle schools.

DIFFERENTIATED SUPERVISION: AN OVERVIEW AND A RATIONALE

The differentiated model, found to be effective in several field tests, is a supervision model that is based upon several studies of effective middle-school teaching, incorporates the best available research on supervision, and provides options for the teachers who are to be supervised.[2] In explaining how to apply the model, it might be useful at this juncture to describe it briefly and present a rationale for its use.

The Basic Elements of Differentiated Supervision

The basic elements in the model are these:

Develop a description of effective teaching. Administrators and teachers begin by developing their own description of effective middle-school teaching. This description comes from two main sources: a review of the indicators of excellence listed at the beginning of this chapter; and a review of the more specific research on effective middle-school teaching. This description of effective middle-school teaching is used as the basis of all supervision and teacher evaluation that goes on in the school.

Supervise several teachers. A small number of carefully selected teachers are given clinical supervision. This is a systematic process of diagnosing teacher performance, identifying one skill for focused improvement, coaching the teacher in acquiring that skill, and repeating the cycle until significant improvement has been achieved.

Guide remaining teachers. The rest of the teachers are guided in selecting one of the other supervisory options. With appropriate guidance, they may select cooperative professional development (a peer process of observing and debriefing), self-directed improvement (an individualized and goal-oriented process of professional growth), or instructional monitoring (an organized system of brief "drop-in" visits by an administrator).

Each of these elements will be described more fully in the following sections.

The Rationale for Using Differentiated Supervision

The rationale for the differentiated model is based upon several well-tested assumptions. First, there is now a developing body of knowledge about effective middle-school teaching that can provide useful guidelines for supervision. (See the references cited in Figure 8-1.) That research is neither definitive nor conclusive, but it does point the way to good middle-school instruction. It can provide a sound basis for all supervision as long as it is supplemented with the experiential knowledge of informed practitioners.

The Diagnostic/Coaching Process

The next assumption relates specifically to clinical supervision: Clinical supervision will be most effective if it begins with a research-based diagnosis of performance, uses that diagnosis to identify one critical skill needed for improvement, and employs coaching techniques to assist in the development of that skill. Note that the diagnostic-coaching approach focuses on one major skill at a time, rather than trying to effect several changes at once. This diagnostic/coaching process marks a major departure from the standard "observe/confer" approach to clinical supervision, which often seems unsystematic and unfocused.

Options for Teachers and Administrators

The third assumption is that there should be supervisory options available for both administrators and teachers. This commitment to options challenges the conventional wisdom that all teachers should be given clinical supervision. There are two major problems with this conventional wisdom. The first is that school administrators simply do not have the time to provide clinical supervision to all teachers. The second is that not all teachers need clinical supervision; it is most effective for and most needed by beginning teachers who are learning their craft and experienced teachers who are having serious problems.

DEVELOPING A SCHOOL-BASED DESCRIPTION OF EFFECTIVE TEACHING

The first step in improving teaching through the differentiated model is to develop a school-based description of effective middle-school teaching. Begin by discussing with the staff the general indicators of excellence and the specific research on effective middle-school teaching. If you wish, you may simplify this step by reproducing and distributing copies of Figure 8-1, which presents a synthesis of the indicators and the research, developed from a careful analysis of all the major studies on effective teaching at the middle-school level and the studies previously cited in this work. Teachers then have an opportunity to discuss that list in team meetings, in an atmosphere of intellectual openness. The stance here is neither to ask teachers to accept that research unquestioningly nor to encourage them to challenge it unthinkingly. Instead, a message of this sort is conveyed:

> Here is a synthesis of several studies of middle-school teaching. Since it has been developed from several reliable studies, it provides some tentative guidelines for us. Reflect about your own experience in light of that research and discuss with your colleagues how your experience with our students either confirms or raises some questions about that research.

As a result of that general faculty discussion, the faculty may decide that they wish to modify that statement so that it reflects their experience with their students. They should be invited to add clarifying statements, change the wording of items, or include additional skills that they believe are generally effective with pupils in that school. The goal here is to achieve a faculty consensus about effective teaching that represents a synthesis of empirical research and the experience of successful teachers. That faculty statement of effective middle-school teaching should also be reviewed to be sure that it encompasses and reflects the school's instructional goals.

Adding Specific Skills by Organizing Teachers into Subject-Matter Groups

The next step in the process is to enable teachers to supplement that general list by adding subject-specific skills—teaching skills that are effective with a particular subject-matter area. Obviously the best basis for accomplishing this step is to organize the teachers into subject-matter groups. Each such group should have an opportunity to review the research relating to the subject its members teach and then discuss that research in light of their experience. Here the goal is to develop a brief list of subject-specific skills that can supplement the general list. Figure 8-2 shows one such list developed by a middle-school mathematics team. The teachers reviewed several studies of effective mathematics teaching and reflected about their own teaching; as a result, they decided that those three specific skills for mathematics teachers should be added to the general school list.

The process described in the foregoing paragraph accomplishes several important objectives. It acquaints teachers with the research on middle-school teaching, it provides an opportunity for them to reflect about their own teaching, and it results in a school-based list of general and specific teaching skills that can be used in the remaining phases of the differentiated model.

OFFERING TEACHERS THE SUPERVISORY OPTIONS

With that list of skills developed, teachers are offered the four supervisory options, with guidance. The principal meets with the faculty and provides a brief overview of each option. In this briefing process, the principal may find it useful to distribute a written summary so that teachers can have a clearer understanding of the basic principles. The principal should also make it clear at this time that although teacher preferences will be given serious consideration, the final choices will be determined by the principal in conference with the teacher.

The teachers are then surveyed about their preferences. In general, the principal should let each teacher use the type of supervision preferred, with some exceptions. Any teacher new to the building, any beginning teacher, and any teacher having serious problems should be counseled into selecting clinical supervision. The evidence suggests that beginning teachers and teachers with problems need the intensive support of the clinical process; teachers new to the building should start with the clinical mode until the principal has had a chance to assess their competence.

So that clinical supervision is not viewed as a remedial process for the incompetent, the principal should also encourage one or two highly effective teachers to choose it for at least a period of time. Every teacher, regardless of experience and competence, can derive some benefit from effective clinical supervision.

MAKING CLINICAL SUPERVISION MORE EFFECTIVE

How can clinical supervision be made more effective for those needing it or choosing it? Several excellent textbooks deal with clinical supervision, so there is no need here to offer a detailed explanation of the standard approach. Rather it seems more useful to focus on those aspects that make our approach different from most of those offered.

The Pre-Observation Conference: Discussing Behaviors and Lessons

The process begins with a pre-observation conference. The supervisor (and we use the term here to refer to any administrator or staff member trained in clinical supervision and given supervisory responsibility) and the teacher discuss together the combined, revised list of effective teaching behaviors to be sure that they both understand and agree on the behaviors desired. They then discuss unit and lesson planning: The teacher explains his or her preferred planning style, gives an overview of the year's work, presents an overview of the units being taught, and clarifies the plans for the week ahead; the supervisor plays an active role in the discussion, raising questions about time allocations, asking questions about goals and objectives, and speaking generally about learning strategies effective with middle-school learners. The conference concludes with the supervisor's explaining the nature of the diagnostic observation that will next be made.

The Diagnostic Observation: Collecting Data

Diagnostic observation plays a crucial part in the entire process. The purpose of the diagnostic observation is to collect full data about all teaching/learning transactions in order to identify one critical area for improvement. To do so, the supervisor should make an unannounced visit to a class that he or she believes is typical; the unannounced visit ensures that the supervisor will observe an unrehearsed performance.

There are several ways to collect the diagnostic data. One method that seems to work well is to use a form like the one shown in Figure 8-3. Notice the diagnostic code at the top of the form; it identifies the five general aspects of effective middle-school teaching and also includes a code number for any special skills relevant to that subject. In order to make the coding process simple and to focus attention on the general areas of strength and weakness, only the general aspects of effective teaching are listed here, not the specific behaviors. The specific behaviors will be examined in the next phase.

During the observation, the observer keeps a running record of the time in the left-hand column and, in a condensed narrative form, notes in the main section all the significant teacher and pupil behaviors. This condensed narrative should be comprehensive, specific, and objective. The supervisor should attempt to record all the important transactions so that a full record is available for post-observation analysis. The data should be as specific as possible: number of pupils engaging in a particular behavior, verbatim notes of important questions and answers, identification of pupils when important. And, the supervisor should make the record as objective as possible, avoiding judgmental language and clearly distinguishing between inferences and observable behaviors.

Analyze the information gathered. After the observation has been completed, the supervisor spends some time alone analyzing the observational data in order to prepare for the diagnostic conference. The objective here is to review the notes carefully to identify general areas of strength and weakness. Note again that the diagnosis begins with the examination of general aspects, not specific behaviors. In identifying these general areas, the diagnostic code can be very useful. As the supervisor reviews the observational record, he or she should use the code numbers to enter in the "plus" column any occasions when a particular aspect of effective teaching was significantly present—and enter in the "minus" column those occasions when a particular aspect was noticeably absent. The code numbers placed appropriately should simplify the supervisor's job of noting patterns of successful and less successful behavior.

Prioritize the teacher's needs. If the observational analysis suggests that there is more than one area in which improvement is needed, the supervisor attempts to put the teacher's needs in priority order by weighing two important factors:

- *Significance:* Which aspect of teaching seems to interfere most with the learning of these pupils?
- *Readiness:* Which aspect of teaching does the teacher seem most ready to deal with?

The analysis phase ends with the supervisor's preparing a tentative agenda for the diagnostic conference that simply notes all the areas of strength and the one priority area for improvement.

The Diagnostic Conference: Solving Problems

With the tentative agenda prepared, the supervisor then meets with the teacher in a diagnostic conference. To the extent possible, the conference should have a collaborative, problem-solving focus, with the supervisor and the teacher both playing active roles in reviewing the class and identifying an area for improvement. If the teacher seems very perceptive and autonomous, the supervisor may play a less active role, essentially letting the teacher identify both the strengths and the one area for improvement. If the teacher seems uncertain and dependent, the supervisor should perhaps be more direct in calling to the teacher's attention the priority area for improvement. Regardless of the style used, the diagnostic conference should end with teacher and supervisor agreeing on the priority need.

A Training Session: Getting the Required Help

So a need has been identified. Now the supervisor must be sure that the teacher gets the required help. The supervisor might decide to provide the assistance directly or to call upon some other resource person, such as a department head, an expert consultant, or a skilled colleague. One or more training sessions should be held in order to assist the teacher in bringing about the improvement needed.

These training sessions will be more effective if the resource person has done some preliminary work. For each of the general aspects of teacher effectiveness, the resource person should prepare a more detailed analysis that provides specific research-based information on the skills involved. See, for example, the analysis of "conditions for productive learning" summarized in Figure 8-4. It identifies the three major skill areas involved (structure, clarity, and accountability) and specifies for each the desired behaviors.

The more detailed analysis will be useful in two important ways. First, it provides a focus for the training. The trainer and the teacher know exactly what they are trying to accomplish. Instead of talking vaguely about "structure," they can discuss the usefulness of lesson overviews, analyze their limitations, and develop together some overviews that the teacher can try with forthcoming lessons.

The Focused Observation: Determining If Improvement Has Been Achieved

The second use of the detailed analysis is that it provides a structure for the next observation, which in this case is a focused observation. Unlike the diagnostic observation, which attempted to note all the major teaching/learning transactions, the focused observation limits its attention to the area for which training has just been provided. In the example previously discussed, the supervisor would observe only to determine to what extent the teacher has been able to establish the conditions for effective learning. Obviously, the detailed analysis used in the training will be helpful in guiding the focused observation.

In making this focused observation, the supervisor can use a form similar to the one shown in Figure 8-5. Although it is similar in general format to the one used in the diagnostic observation, it is specifically designed to help the supervisor collect data relating solely to the area of concern. It lists and provides a numerical code for the desired behaviors, reminding the supervisor what to observe for and enabling the supervisor to analyze the observational data rather quickly.

The Follow-up Conference: Making Final Recommendations or Comments

Following the focused observation and analysis, the supervisor and teacher confer again. Was the skill area sufficiently mastered? If so, would another diagnostic observation be useful to establish the next area for development? If not, is additional training needed? Or should the supervisor do one more focused observation on the same skill area, as a way of giving the teacher another chance to demonstrate success?

The clinical supervision process, then, is rational and systematic, employing sound learning principles in a logical sequence:

- Diagnose present performance.
- Analyze performance data to identify priority areas.
- Provide training where it is specifically needed.
- Assess mastery of specific skills.

USING COOPERATIVE PROFESSIONAL DEVELOPMENT WITH EXPERIENCED TEACHERS

Cooperative professional development is essentially a process in which two to four teachers work together as a team for their common growth. Because it is much less intensive and systematic than clinical supervision, it should probably be provided only to experienced and competent teachers. Although it usually will not bring about significant improvement in teaching, several pilot tests indicate that it can have several positive effects.[3] It increases the professional dialogue among teachers. It emphasizes the central importance of teaching in the business of the school. And it seems to give teachers an increased sense of power.

Orienting Teachers

The principal should orient interested teachers to cooperative professional development so that they understand what is involved. It should be stressed first that in no way will information from cooperative observations be used in the teacher evaluation system. The principal should also make clear to the teachers how they will be given time to observe one another's classes and to confer after the observation. In some schools, teachers are expected to use their preparation periods; in others, teachers are asked to "cover" one another's classes so that the cooperative process can work; in still others, substitutes are used.

Arranging Teams

After this orientation, teachers who decide to participate are asked to express a preference for the colleagues with whom they would like to work. Usually it is desirable to have the teachers indicate first, second, and third choices, so that you have more flexibility in arranging teams. In middle schools with team teaching, it would obviously be desirable for the members of a teaching team to work together in the cooperative mode, unless they prefer to collaborate with members of other teams. Also keep in mind that the system is easier to implement if cooperative teams are kept small; teams of two involve the fewest complications.

Once the teams are established, the principal should only occasionally monitor the progress of the cooperative program, encouraging the teachers involved to assume responsibility for this part of the program. If the principal plays too active a role in the cooperative mode, the teachers may begin to suspect the principal of trying to use the cooperative mode as a means of obtaining evaluative data in a covert manner.

Developing Informal Contracts

The cooperative teams meet together to establish informally the contract governing their relationship. They should resolve these issues:

1. How many times should we observe one another's classes? They should agree to make at least two observations during the year—more if possible.
2. Do we expect a debriefing session after each observation? Some type of interaction after each observation is desirable, but the participants may decide to speak only briefly and informally, rather than holding a formal debriefing conference.
3. Do we plan to use the list of effective teaching skills as the basis for our observations? This list can provide a useful basis for the cooperative mode, as well as the clinical, but experienced and competent teachers may prefer not to be restricted to this list.
4. Do we expect to collaborate in ways other than observing and debriefing? Some teachers involved in the cooperative mode may decide to work together on curriculum materials or to exchange classes from time to time.

With this basic contract established, the participants proceed. They talk informally about their classes and their teaching, observe one another's classes, and give one another nonjudgmental feedback about the observation. It is a low-key, simple process in which colleagues give one another feedback and support. It will not bring about major improvements, but it will enhance the professional climate of the school.

SELF-DIRECTED IMPROVEMENT FOR AUTONOMOUS TEACHERS

Self-directed improvement is a process in which experienced and competent teachers work alone to effect professional improvement. It is designed for autonomous individuals who either do not have the time for cooperative professional development or who simply prefer to work on their own. Again, the process begins with an orientation for interested teachers. The principal explains how the process is designed to function, indicates what resources are available to support the system, and again stresses that its intent is supervisory, not evaluative.

Goal Setting by Individual Teachers

Teachers who choose self-directed professional development should be asked to complete a form similar to that shown in Figure 8-6. The form enables participants to be clear about their goals, methods, resources, and assessment measures. The teacher first specifies only one or two professional goals for the year; the system seems to work better when the teacher focuses on a limited number of goals, rather than a long list. And the goals need not be stated in quantifiable terms; such quantification is unnecessary and tends to make teachers feel negative about goal specification.

Achieving the Goals

The teacher then indicates what methods will probably be used to accomplish the goal; the objective here is to help the teacher think through issues of method, not to make an unalterable commitment. Next, the teacher indicates what resources—time, money, materials, programs, and people—would be helpful in achieving the goal. Finally, the teacher indicates what methods will be used to assess progress.

The completed form is submitted to the principal, who should then meet with the teacher to clarify any ambiguities and to suggest any needed modifications. The administrator may suggest some rewording of the goal statement, offer some suggestions about methods to be used, review the resources requested, and discuss the assessment processes. The tone of this conference should be constructive and supportive; the administrator's goal is to help the teacher develop a feasible plan, not to impose administrative requirements.

Conducting Informal Conferences

The self-directed mode seems to work best when the principal acts as a key resource throughout the process. In addition to holding the initial conference, the principal should also try to provide within reason all the resources requested, confer with the teacher from time to time to check informally on progress, and hold an informal end-of-year conference to help the teacher make a final assessment of achievement.

INSTRUCTIONAL MONITORING AS A SUPERVISORY OPTION

"Instructional monitoring" is a system in which the principal or some other administrator from time to time throughout the year makes brief and unannounced drop-in visits to the classroom. It is offered as an option to experienced and competent teachers who do not need clinical supervision and do not want to participate in either the cooperative or self-directed mode.

A Brief Orientation Session

In this case only a brief orientation session is needed, as instructional monitoring in many ways only systematizes what good principals have always done. One important matter to emphasize is that, unlike the other modes, instructional monitoring does have an evaluative element: The administrator monitoring teaching will be picking up information that will inevitably be used in the evaluation process, and it is important to be honest about this issue. It is also important to clarify how the teachers will receive feedback about the visits. An explanation of this sort is usually helpful:

> "I'll be making several monitoring visits each day, so it will not always be possible to give you personal feedback after each visit. I will be making brief notes on cards, and you may see those cards if you wish. If I see evidence of what might be a serious problem, I will talk with you briefly soon after the visit."

A Regular Schedule of Brief Visits

To make the monitoring more useful, the administrator develops a regular monitoring schedule. Most principals who monitor regularly find it useful to reserve one period early in the day and one toward the end of the day—crucial times for assessing the general tone of the school. Some principals like to monitor by grade—making a sweep of first the sixth grade, followed by the seventh and then the eighth. Others prefer to monitor by subject, monitoring English language arts one day, math the next. The important point is to be systematic, so that the visits provide useful information about what is going on in the school.

The visits should be brief, lasting perhaps only ten minutes. That is time enough to get a general sense of what is happening instructionally. The administrator should take a seat where he or she can observe the teacher and most of the class. The observations should focus on the key elements of what is occurring: what methods the teacher is using, what learning processes the students are employing, how many students are actively involved, how many are not. Brief notes on the highlights of the observation can be made on a 3" × 5" card like the one shown in Figure 8-7. Notice that it records information in brief form about the essentials.

After about ten minutes, the administrator should leave, making a nonverbal signal of acknowledgment to the teacher. If there is time, the administrator should speak briefly some time that day with every teacher observed; even a few comments of praise often make a difference. At the least, as indicated previously, the administrator should be sure to confer briefly with any teacher with whom problems were perceived, just to give that teacher an opportunity to clarify the situation or present additional information.

The Value of Monitoring

Although most supervision textbooks deprecate such "drop-in" supervision, some recent research on effective schools indicates that effective principals play an active monitoring role.[4] Such monitoring has some very helpful effects. It gets the principal out of the office into the mainstream of school activity. It conveys a sense of concern. It results in a visible administrative presence that discourages nonconforming behavior. And it gives the principal some very useful information about the general climate of the school.

Specific programs to improve teaching and supervision can be found in Appendix B.

Notes

1. Arthur A. Blumberg, *Supervisors and Teachers: A Cold War,* 2nd ed. (Berkeley, CA: McCutchan, 1980).

2. Allan A. Glatthorn, *Differentiated Supervision* (Alexandria, VA: Association for Supervision and Curriculum Development, 1984).

3. *Ibid.*

4. David C. Dwyer, Ginny V. Lee, Brian Rowan, and Steven T. Bossert, *Five Principals in Action: Perspectives on Instructional Management* (San Francisco, CA: Far West Laboratory for Educational Research and Development, 1983).

**FIGURE 8-1. Effective middle-school teaching:
a synthesis of the research**

The effective middle school teacher:

1. Establishes a desired classroom environment by

   a. Using class time efficiently.
   b. Maintaining and communicating a task orientation.
   c. Managing pupil movement and pupil talking in a manner consonant with learning objectives.

2. Maintains desirable relationships with pupils by

   a. Holding and communicating high expectations for them.
   b. Showing warmth and positive feelings toward them.
   c. Communicating enthusiasm about them and about teaching.

3. Establishes conditions for productive learning by

   a. Providing clear and organized structure for lessons and units.
   b. Clarifying learning objectives and tasks.
   c. Holding pupils accountable for in-class tasks and homework.

4. Uses effective teaching and learning techniques by

   a. Engaging pupils in learning tasks related to objectives.
   b. Providing activities appropriate to pupils' developmental levels.
   c. Making appropriate use of active learning strategies, including appropriate use of computers, television, and cooperative learning.
   d. Alternating modes and methods of learning.
   e. Emphasizing concept development by full explication, detailed exemplification, and guided discussion.
   f. Strengthening achievement motivation and developing learner autonomy.

5. Effectively monitors pupil learning by

   a. Diagnosing the pupil's cognitive readiness.
   b. Monitoring the pupil's progress closely.
   c. Giving pupils appropriate feedback.

SOURCES: Carolyn M. Evertson, Linda M. Anderson, and Jere E. Brophy, Texas Junior High School Study: Process and Outcome Relationships *(Austin, TX: Research and Development Center for Teacher Education, 1976); J. Howard Johnston, "Middle School Research: What We Know and What We Need to Find Out," in* Perspectives on Middle Schools Research, *Christina K. McCann (Cincinnati: University of Cincinnati, 1980); David B. Strahan,* Competencies for Middle School Teachers: A Review of Empirical Studies of Teacher Effects *(Laramie, WY: University of Wyoming, 1979).*

FIGURE 8-2.   Teaching skills effective in middle-school mathematics

The effective middle-school mathematics teacher:

1. Emphasizes whole-class instruction.

2. Stresses problem-solving skills.

3. Provides for guided and independent practice of skills and concepts.

FIGURE 8-3.   Diagnostic observation

Diagnostic Code:

1	classroom environment	4	effective techniques
2	pupil relationships	5	monitoring learning
3	productive conditions	6	special for *social studies*

Teacher's Name: *Williamson*   Date: *October 6*   Period: *3*

TIME	OBSERVATIONS	+	−
10:00	Arrive rm 103. JW not present. 2 students arguing with each other; much loud talking. Take seat in back of room. Students aware of my presence, begin to settle down.		1
10:05	JW arrives, sees me, seems embarrassed. "OK, let's settle down. Get out your homework." Begins by asking students to read answers to questions at end of chapter. Calls on volunteers—mostly those sitting in front of him. Several students seem not to have done homework—but pretend they have.		3

FIGURE 8-4 Conditions for productive learning

STRUCTURE

1. Reviews previous learning
2. Gives overview of lesson
3. Makes connections between parts of lesson

CLARITY

4. States learning objectives clearly
5. Gives clear directions for tasks
6. Shows relationship of tasks to objectives

ACCOUNTABILITY

7. Checks class work efficiently
8. Checks homework efficiently

FIGURE 8-5. Focused observation

Focus: Establishes conditions for productive learning

Focused code:

1 Reviews previous learning	5 Gives clear directions for tasks
2 Gives overview of lesson	
3 Makes connections between parts of lesson	6 Shows relationships of tasks to objectives
4 States learning objectives clearly	7 Checks class work efficiently
	8 Checks homework efficiently

Teacher's Name: *Williamson*   Date: *October 20*   Period: *3*

TIME	OBSERVATIONS	+	−
10:00	Arrived 103. JW writing questions on board; pupils settling down for class. JW checks two absence notes, seems to make visual check of attendance.		
10:05	"Let's review where we are. Write your answers to the three questions on the board."	1	

FIGURE 8-6. Goal setting for self-improvement

Teacher's name: *Barbara Parpart*   Date: *October 1*

Teacher's goal(s) for the year:

1. Learn how to use the word processor to facilitate the composing process.

Methods that will probably be used to achieve goal:

1. Read current articles on word processors and composing
2. Attend workshop being offered at state college
3. Observe in Central High where word processors are being used

Resources needed:

1. Suggestions for readings
2. Workshop fee—$25.00
3. Two professional days—one for workshop, one for observing

How will accomplishment of goal be assessed:

1. Will confer with principal in January and in May
2. Will submit final report in May

FIGURE 8-7.   Instructional monitoring notes

10/6   Period 4 (11:45–11:55), H. Walker   7th gr. lang. arts

Walker at desk checking papers when I arrive. Students at first noisy, then get quiet when they see me. Walker explains that students are in small groups discussing short story they have read. I listen in on some of the discussions. Two of the groups seem confused as to what they are supposed to be doing.

Reminder: Confer with Walker on need to monitor small group work.

9

Improving the Activity Program

The Activity Program of an Effective Middle School

1. The activity program includes diverse activities that develop and reward multiple talents.

2. The activity program includes activities that will encourage healthy heterosexual interactions, without compulsory dating and dancing.

3. The activity program includes activities that enable young adolescents to develop social and interpersonal skills.

The best middle schools must have strong activity programs that reflect the indicators listed here. That is a belief that middle-school leaders have always advocated, even before the recent research substantiating its validity. But that conclusion needs special emphasis now, when too much of the discussion of "school effectiveness" focuses only on academic achievement. That concern for academic rigor, while indeed a legitimate one, should not mislead us into equating excellence with academic quality. At the middle-school level especially, excellence in education must include the special contributions that a strong activity program can make. This chapter will present a rationale for such a program and then discuss in detail how middle schools can strengthen this important component.

RATIONALE FOR A STRONG ACTIVITY PROGRAM FOR YOUNG ADOLESCENTS

The basic argument for a strong activity program is that young adolescents have needs that cannot be met solely through the academic component of the school day. Consider these needs of the young:

- They need to develop leadership and decision-making skills. Such skills cannot be acquired through reading, listening, and discussion, the standard learning activities of the classroom. They can best be acquired by struggling with real problems in a low-risk environment, under the guidance of a sensitive adult. That's the kind of environment a good activity program provides.

- They need healthy interactions with members of the same sex and the opposite sex. As we have seen in Chapter 3, early adolescence is a time when both types of interactions are needed. Young men and young women especially need to learn new ways of being with each other, in an informal environment that has less control than the classroom but more structure than the unchaperoned party. A strong activity program will provide natural opportunities for both same-sex and opposite-sex interactions.

- They need to develop multiple talents. There are many kinds of "intelligence," but the standard academic program develops only two, verbal and mathematical reasoning.[1] Young adolescents need challenging activities that call upon and nurture diverse skills. And they also need opportunities to earn legitimate rewards through the use of such skills.

- They need to develop interpersonal skills. As they struggle to understand themselves and to get beyond an immobilizing self-consciousness, they need a supportive environment in which they can learn how to relate to both adults and peers. In the typical classroom they are frozen into the student role: The student speaks only when called on, answers teacher questions, and speaks to peers only when the teacher isn't watching. While such "on-task" behavior probably leads to better understanding of cognitive concepts, it does not help the young adolescent acquire such important interpersonal skills as getting acquainted, sharing feelings, and expressing differences. Such skills can best be developed through the less formal environment provided by a good activity program.

- They need to develop new relationships. Too many schools are composed of only classes and cliques. The classes are the academic groups, often stratified by ability; students spend most of the day with peers of similar academic talent. The cliques are the peer groups, usually stratified by ethnicity and social class; they dominate the lives of the young adolescent outside of school and even have a strong influence on classroom interactions. A good activity program enables the young to break out of the class and clique structure—to form new friendships and create new alliances. One middle-school principal spoke of his school band in this manner: "It's an awful musical group—but it's the only place where poor whites and blacks mix." And such activities as sports, glee club, band, and musical comedy productions may be the only real places where young people of different social classes and ethnic groups mix on an equal basis.

- They need to develop new interests. They are too old for dolls and too young for cars. They need a chance to work with an adult who can stimulate new interests and make new hobbies seem exciting. Early adolescence should be a time for exploring and experimenting—and you can't do that in a highly structured classroom, where dabbling is considered frivolous.

- They need a change of pace. They need to be highly active, and they need time to relax. The academic classroom places them in a passive role, where sitting quietly is prized. And the structured learning environment demands focused attention—daydreaming is frowned upon. A good activity program provides this needed change of pace: They can move around, release their energy, and escape the pressures of answering questions and paying attention.

- They need opportunities to celebrate and perform. The basic human needs for ritual, for ceremony, and for celebration are especially strong in the early adolescent. And the chief justification for assemblies, dances, parties, concerts, and plays is that those activities meet those basic adolescent needs.

- They need opportunities to serve. An important part of the young adolescent's growth toward maturity is fostered by opportunities for service—helping others through personal efforts, not material gifts. Too many adults who complain about the selfishness of the young fail to realize how few opportunities they provide the young for unselfish service. The usual academic classroom discourages service and cooperation. A strong activities program would meet this need.

HOW A STRONG ACTIVITY PROGRAM MEETS INDIVIDUAL NEEDS

As indicated in the foregoing list, these needs are not met in the standard classroom. And a good activity program is justified because it meets those needs through several kinds of differences that distinguish it from the classroom.

A different environment. The standard classroom is a useful environment for learning academic concepts; it is not conducive to fostering interpersonal relationships and stimulating creativity. A good activity program will provide a changed environment in which such skills can be developed. It will be an environment in which people can interact more freely and less formally, where risks can be taken with less fear of failure, where rules can be developed as the need arises, and where real problems can be solved.

Different roles and relationships. In the classroom the young adolescent plays only one role—that of student—and engages in rule-governed relationships with teachers and fellow students. The developmental needs of young adolescents require different roles and relationships. They need to serve, not to be catered to. They need to teach, not just learn. They need to identify problems, not simply solve those that are posed for them.

A different spirit and mood. The mood of the task-oriented classroom is serious and businesslike, with the participants concerned with efficiency and productivity. Such a mood is appropriate for learning mathematics, but it does not meet the basic human need for playfulness. The young adolescent needs a time to laugh, to fantasize, to celebrate—to escape the solemn business of being a good student. The right kind of activity program provides for those changes.

A different view of learning. In the standard academic classroom, most learning is viewed as the acquisition of concepts through verbal means—listening, discussing, reading, and writing. A good activity program offers a different view. Learning is the growth that comes from solving real problems. In the mathematics classroom the student solves problems about the speed of trains and the height of buildings. In the activity program the student develops a club's budget and determines the best way of raising funds to meet expenses.

A different view of ability. In the classroom, academic ability is emphasized and rewarded: IQ and achievement scores are the measures of success. In a good activity program, other talents are demanded and prized: the ability to plan, to sing, to resolve disputes, to use the body gracefully. And success is measured in terms of real accomplishments, not performance on examinations.

These differences can best be provided through a comprehensive activity program.

THE COMPONENTS OF A COMPREHENSIVE ACTIVITY PROGRAM

A comprehensive activity program includes three basic components: athletics, celebrations, and interest groups.

The Athletic Program

The ideal athletic program includes the optimal mix of interscholastic and intramural sports. The interscholastic program can provide an opportunity for the highly talented to compete and can energize the competitive spirit of the rest of the student body. What kinds of interscholastic sports should be offered? The principals of effective middle schools who were surveyed about this issue believed that only interscholastic track, basketball, gymnastics, swimming, and soccer should be offered at grades 5 and 6. In grade 7 they would add volleyball, tennis, and girls' softball. Boys' football should not be offered until grade 8, in the view of these leaders.[2]

The intramural program, with less pressure and reduced competition, is perhaps even more important for developing adolescents. About half of these same principals of effective middle schools reported that they would emphasize intramurals, rather than interscholastic sports, at grade 8 and below. And about half of the parents surveyed in the same study supported this view.

Celebrations

We use the term *celebrations* here to include assemblies and social activities. A strong assembly program serves several functions. It strengthens the bonds of community by bringing everyone together for a shared experience. It provides valuable opportunities for the young to perform for their peers, their parents, and their teachers. And it marks off seasons and holidays, dividing the long school year into shorter segments that the young adolescent can manage. And there is always a need for appropriate social activities: class parties and mixers quietly chaperoned by sensitive adults who know what to look for and what to ignore. As noted previously, most experts recommend that such social activities for young adolescents provide an atmosphere that enables the awkward and the shy to make contact at their own pace, in their own style—that does not push immature adolescents into intense heterosexual relationships.

Interest Groups

"Interest groups" is a broad term that includes several types of activities: clubs, publications, dramatics, and musical groups. These special interest groups play a vital role in diversifying the activity program. The athletic program gives the physically talented a chance to excel; the assembly program provides opportunities for gifted performers. A strong club program meets the needs of all the rest. Interestingly enough, schools that include grades 7 to 9 are more likely to have club programs than schools that include grades 6 to 8 or 5 to 8, according to a recent survey.[3]

Optional Components

In addition to these three basic components, some middle-school programs also include student government and honor society. We consider these optional components, because both seem less essential in excellent middle schools. First, student government, as it operates in many schools, does not reach enough students and seems not to accomplish its goals. In too many schools, it is not a representative body that makes meaningful decisions; it is, instead, an elite group that spends its time debating trivial issues. It makes more sense to provide meaningful opportunities for all students to participate in real decision making. The leadership team should assess student perceptions of such important issues as school climate and curriculum. Classroom teachers should get appropriate student input into the content of learning. And activity sponsors, working with smaller groups of students in a more open environment, can help students make all the important decisions about the conduct of their program.

Honor societies were developed as a means of giving recognition to the academically talented and seem to flourish in academically oriented high schools. But they are not much in evidence in schools for younger adolescents; less than one-third of the grades 6 to 8 schools surveyed indicated that they sponsored an honor society. Such reluctance is understandable. In the view of many middle-school administrators and teachers, honor societies often produce unhealthy academic competition and foster a sense of academic elitism. And they reward only the academically talented—the ones who are usually rewarded in the classroom. It makes more sense to provide a diversified and extensive reward system so that those who excel in any activity can be recognized.

DIAGNOSING THE ACTIVITY PROGRAM

Strengthening all the components of the activity program begins with a careful diagnosis of its strengths and weaknesses. Such a diagnosis can be based upon the criteria listed in Figure 9-1. These criteria have been developed by analyzing the needs served by activity programs and by reviewing the literature on effective activity programs and the indicators of excellence noted previously. Four of the criteria relate to the administrative structure of the program—support, time, program diversity, and the reward system—and fall within the purview of the school administrators. Three criteria relate to the learning structure of the program—the environment, the leadership, and the nature of learning—and fall within the purview of the activity sponsors.

These criteria should be useful in diagnosing the activity program. Three diagnostic procedures are recommended: faculty survey, student survey, and administrative analysis. The faculty and student surveys, using forms similar to those shown in Figures 9-2 and 9-3, can be useful in identifying how those groups perceive the strengths and weaknesses of the program; specific uses of the data are noted in the following section of this chapter.

The administrative analysis is a complex process that is concerned essentially with determining if there is sufficient diversity in both the content that is offered and the talents that are nurtured. Activity programs can have one of five different content emphases:

1. Service to others: activities that enable students to serve others. Examples: audio-visual aides; teacher aides; tutors; water safety monitors; community volunteers.

2. Hobbies and special interests: activities that broaden and develop the special interests of students. Examples: current events; local history; stamp collecting; photography; sports.

3. Skill acquisition and personal improvement: activities that help students acquire special skills. Examples: word processing; cooking; small engine repair; home repair; computer programming; grooming.

4. Performance and communication: activities that enable students to perform publicly and communicate through the mass media. Examples: dramatics; chorus; band; newspaper; radio and television.

5. Future: activities that help the students think systematically about the future. Examples: careers; Future Teachers of America; families of the future.

Obviously, these categories are not mutually exclusive; however, they can be useful in determining if the content of the activity program is sufficiently diversified. A good activity program for middle-school students includes offerings from these five content areas.

The second dimension of diversity is the talents nurtured. Although there are several ways of conceptualizing human talent, there are eight that seem important in the development of the young: artistic; interpersonal; leadership and managerial; mechanical; musical; physical; scientific–mathematical; verbal. All eight should be represented in a strong activity program.

A useful way to make these two analyses is to construct analytical grids for content and talent. Down the left-hand side list all the activities. Across the top on one grid list the content foci. Then consider each activity and determine its content emphasis. Make the same kind of analysis of the talent emphasis. Figures 9-4 and 9-5 illustrate how these grids can provide a visual representation of diversity in both dimensions.

IMPROVING THE ADMINISTRATIVE
STRUCTURE FOR THE PROGRAM

Using the diagnostic data derived from the surveys and the analysis just described, the principal and the administrative staff assume primary responsibility for building support, finding time, diversifying the program, and rewarding achievement.

Building Support for Your Activities

A strong program is possible only if it has the support of all involved. The leadership team will first of all need to enlist the support of the superintendent, so that adequate fiscal resources are provided and the necessary logistical supports are made available. The best source of pressure here is a successful program that brings positive publicity to the school and builds a climate of parent support.

Faculty support. Faculty support might be more difficult to achieve, since many middle-school teachers have a strong academic orientation that causes them to be biased against activities they consider frivolous. First, in selecting faculty, administrators should choose teachers who understand the importance of a diversified program. Second, in developing the specific components of the program, administrators should encourage teachers to sponsor activities that relate either to the subject they teach or the hobbies they pursue. A third way to ensure teacher support is to reward activity sponsorship—by factoring it into the performance appraisal system and by giving public recognition to successful sponsors. Finally, the principal can develop faculty support through both the formal and informal staff development processes. Timely reminders at faculty meetings, items in the faculty bulletin, and words of commendation on the public address system are all useful ways of reminding teachers that a successful activity program is important.

Student support. Students will support any activity program that is responsive to their needs. They need no special inducement; a successful program builds its own constituency. In fact, effective middle-school principals note that no amount of scolding about "school spirit" can force students to support a program that is controlled by adults to satisfy adult needs.

Parent support. Special efforts are needed, however, to enlist the support of parents. Here again the best way of building parent support is to offer a program that provides opportunities for all students to succeed. If students come home from school enthusiastic about a club project or excited about a talent show, most parents will quickly get the point. Some middle schools increase parent support by enlisting parents as volunteers to assist in the activity program. Others devote time in parent meetings to discussions of the value of the activity program.

Finding Time to Fit It All In

If the activity program is important for all students, then it must be scheduled in a manner than enables all to participate. Thus, after-school programs in schools to which most students are bused are unsatisfactory because they attract only a small percentage of the students whose parents can provide transportation or who are willing to wait for a special late bus. On the other hand, the activity program should not intrude excessively into instructional time. The research is conclusive about the relationship of instructional time to achievement—and effective principals' protecting instructional time.[4]

The best solution seems to be one widely used in middle schools: building an activity period into the master schedule. The time for such a period can be gained in several ways: reducing the time allocated to one of the nonacademic areas; lengthening the school day; or reducing on a particular day the length of each instructional period.

Faculty views about the issue of time, as reflected in the faculty survey, should be given greatest weight, since the matter of instructional time is a major concern of most teachers. Student responses to item #3 in the student survey form will also provide information about their perceptions.

Diversifying the Program

The results of the administrative analysis explained in the foregoing section should be the major factor in assessing the diversity of the program and in determining if any modifications are needed. The analysis should indicate which type of activities are needed and which might be overemphasized. A more balanced program can then be developed by enlisting the aid of those teachers who are willing to drop an activity in an area where several others are offered and to add an activity in an area of need. Some middle schools also report success in using carefully selected parents and community volunteers to sponsor activities. Retired people can be an excellent resource for such programs.

Rewarding Outstanding Achievement

The final aspect of the administrative structure is the reward system. In the typical school, only academic and athletic talents are rewarded; most youngsters thus have little opportunity for public recognition. In an excellent middle school, every student has a chance to earn *legitimate* rewards. Notice the emphasis on legitimate awards. Students must believe that they have earned a real award through significant accomplishment. They do not value awards bestowed too liberally on the undeserving. The data gathered in both the faculty and the student survey can be helpful in understanding their perceptions of this issue.

A productive reward can be established in the following manner:

● The leadership team develops an awards policy, specifying the number of rewards, the type of recognition given for special accomplishment, and the general criteria for selection.

- The members of each activity group establish the specific criteria for its club or organization. The members then use those criteria in identifying the members to be honored, with the activity sponsor providing the guidance necessary to avoid flagrant favoritism.

- The recipients are then honored at a suitable ceremony—an awards banquet or an awards assembly.

- The awards are publicized in the school and community newspaper.

Such a system provides reasonable guidelines within which students can learn how to make their own choices about achievement and recognition.

IMPROVING THE LEARNING STRUCTURE OF THE ACTIVITY PROGRAM

A sound administrative structure can provide the necessary support for the activity program—but an effective learning structure is also required if the activity program is to meet the needs of the students. In too many schools the club meeting looks like another class—the teacher is talking and students are listening. This problem seems to stem from two causes: The teachers don't take the program seriously, as they believe that it is not valued by administrators; and the teachers lack the skills required for conducting an effective program. The first problem can be dealt with by supporting the program in meaningful ways: providing time for it; securing the needed resources; rewarding successful teacher performance; and making activity sponsorship a part of the performance appraisal system.

The second problem of skill deficiency is more complex. The difficulty is, of course, that teachers are trained to teach in standard classroom setting; they are usually not trained in the special skills needed for effective activity sponsorship. The solution here is a program that develops these skills. Begin by assessing teachers' interest in the following staff development topics:

1. Working with students to develop rules and guidelines.
2. Handling behavior problems in the activity setting.
3. Dealing with cliques and gangs in activities.
4. Developing student leadership.
5. Planning and implementing short-term activities.
6. Planning and managing long-term projects.
7. Coping with student boredom and flagging interest.
8. Communicating with parents about the activity program.
9. Implementing a fair reward system.

Then plan programs that deal with those topics teachers consider important. The best programs will give teachers an opportunity to share successful techniques with one another and learn about effective programs in other middle schools.

An example of an excellent activity program can be found in Appendix C.

Notes

1. Howard Gardner, *Frames of Mind: The Theory of Multiple Intelligences* (New York: Basic Books, 1983).

2. James W. Keefe and others, *The Middle Level Principalship, Volume 2: The Effective Middle Level Principal* (Reston, VA: National Association of Secondary School Principals, 1983).

3. *Ibid.*

4. P. Berman and M. McLaughlin, *Federal Programs Supporting Educational Change, Vol. 8: Implementing and Sustaining Innovation* (Santa Monica, CA: Rand Corp., 1978).

FIGURE 9-1. Criteria for a strong activity program

THE ADMINISTRATIVE STRUCTURE FOR THE PROGRAM

1. **Support:** The activity program is supported by administrators, teachers, students, and parents—all of whom are committed to it because they understand its importance.

2. **Time:** The activity program is scheduled in a manner that enables all students to participate without losing excessive amounts of instructional time.

3. **Program Diversity:** The activity program appeals to diverse interests, encourages healthy heterosexual interactions, nurtures multiple talents, and develops interpersonal skills.

4. **Reward System:** The activity program provides opportunities for all students to earn legitimate awards. Diverse accomplishments are publicly recognized.

THE LEARNING STRUCTURE FOR THE PROGRAM

5. **Environment:** The activity program takes place in a less structured environment, providing for freedom within broader limits than those provided in the classroom.

6. **Leadership:** The activity program provides meaningful opportunities for students to lead, to decide, and to solve problems.

7. **Nature of Learning:** The activity program enables students to learn by creating, playing, and doing, rather than simply through passive listening.

FIGURE 9-2. **Survey of faculty attitudes about activity program**

Directions: Listed below are several statements describing our school's activity program. Indicate to what extent you agree or disagree with that statement, circling one of these symbols:

SA—strongly agree	*D—disagree*
A—agree	*SD—strongly disagree*
?—uncertain	

STATEMENT: OUR ACTIVITY PROGRAM: *YOUR RESPONSE*

1. Is strongly supported by administrators.	SA	A	?	D	SD
2. Is strongly supported by the teachers.	SA	A	?	D	SD
3. Is strongly supported by the students.	SA	A	?	D	SD
4. Is strongly supported by the parents.	SA	A	?	D	SD
5. Is given adequate time.	SA	A	?	D	SD
6. Does not intrude excessively into academic time.	SA	A	?	D	SD
7. Responds to diverse student needs, interests, and talents.	SA	A	?	D	SD
8. Provides opportunities for all students to earn legitimate rewards.	SA	A	?	D	SD
9. Provides students with sufficient freedom.	SA	A	?	D	SD
10. Provides meaningful opportunities for student leadership.	SA	A	?	D	SD
11. Enables students to learn in a variety of active learning modes.	SA	A	?	D	SD

FIGURE 9-3. Survey of student attitudes about activity program

Directions: We would like to know what you think about our activity program. The activity program includes our assemblies, our sports teams, our clubs, and our student groups. Below are listed several statements about the program. Read each one. Decide what you think about that statement and circle one of the following answers:

SA—strongly agree	D—disagree
A—agree	SD—strongly disagree
?—uncertain	

STATEMENT	YOUR OPINION
1. Our teachers take an active interest in our activity program.	SA A ? D SD
2. My parents think that our activity program is a good idea.	SA A ? D SD
3. We have enough time for our activities.	SA A ? D SD
4. The activity program has clubs and programs that interest me.	SA A ? D SD
5. In our school, activity awards are given to students who deserve them.	SA A ? D SD
6. We can relax and have some fun in our activity program.	SA A ? D SD
7. In our activity program, students have a chance to make decisions.	SA A ? D SD
8. We do things in our activity program; we just don't sit around.	SA A ? D SD

9. What do you like best about our activity program. _____
_____
_____

10. How do you think our activity program could be improved? _____
_____
_____

FIGURE 9-4. Analyzing the activity program: content focus

ACTIVITY	SERVICE	HOBBIES	SKILLS	PERFORMANCE	FUTURE
1. A-V aides	X				
2. Careers					X
3. Chorus				X	
4. Ceramics		X			
5. Etiquette			X		

FIGURE 9-5. Analyzing the activity program: talent focus

ACTIVITY	ARTISTIC	INTER-PERSONAL	LEADER-SHIP	MECHANICAL	MUSICAL	PHYSICAL	SCIEN-TIFIC– MATHE-MATICAL	VERBAL
1. A-V aides		X						
2. Career	X	X	X	X	X		X	X
3. Chorus					X			
4. Ceramics	X							
5. Etiquette		X						

10

Improving the Guidance Program

Guidance in an Effective Middle School

1. The school provides continued guidance for students trying to make wise choices from many options.

2. The guidance program provides all young adolescents with the help they need to achieve developmental tasks: cope with feelings, develop perspective about problems, and find needed resources.

3. The school provides special support and services to those encountering serious problems.

As noted in Chapter 3, the period of early adolescence seems to be a time of great change and stress. At this time young adolescents need the advice and support of caring adults at school who can help them cope with and learn from the special problems of growing up. This chapter explains how that crucial function can be provided through a strong and diversified guidance program that reflects both the indicators of excellence noted above and the experience of effective middle schools.

CRITERIA FOR EFFECTIVE
GUIDANCE PROGRAMS

What constitutes an effective guidance program for early adolescents? The answer is not in counselor–pupil ratios or in numbers of specialized personnel with impressive-sounding titles. Instead, the criteria focus on the services provided, so that middle-school leaders have some flexibility in determining who can best offer those services. The criteria listed in Figure 10-1, therefore, emphasize functions, not personnel; they present a synthesis of the indicators of excellence and the research on effective middle-school guidance programs.

All Adolescents Need Contact with a Staff Member

The first criterion is probably the most important: Every middle-school youngster should be known well by at least one staff member—whether that individual is an adviser, a classroom teacher, a counselor, or an administrator. The importance of this criterion can best be appreciated by understanding the transitional role of the middle school in relation to teacher contact. In most elementary schools, the pupil has only one teacher, who is assisted by some specialists in art and music. In high school the student has contact with perhaps seven different teachers. Thus, one of the functions of the middle school is to help the student make the transition from one teacher concerned with the child to several teachers interested primarily in their disciplines. The evidence suggests that the middle school can best perform this function if it ensures that every student is known well by one staff member, while that student at the same time is taking courses with several teachers.

That staff member performs several important roles for that student. The staff member acts as an advocate and "ombudsperson" for the student when advocacy is needed. Other teachers have a fragmentary view of the student, but that one member of the staff tries to get a total perspective: test performance, achievement in all subjects, physical and emotional health, peer relationships, activity involvement, discipline record. And that staff member who knows the student best helps the rest of the faculty see the student whole.

Most Adolescents Need Academic Guidance

The second criterion relates to the academic advising function. The middle-school student will need help with choosing electives, improving study skills, coping with academic difficulties, making better use of school time, thinking about careers, and making tentative long-term educational plans. These issues become more important at the high school level, but they cannot be safely ignored in the middle school. Almost every major study of young adolescents indicates that academic performance is one of their main worries.

Adolescents Need Help Growing Up

The next criterion deals with the help the student receives in handling all the normal personal problems of growing up. As noted earlier, the early adolescent years seem to be a period when such problems become most acute. These young people are beset with a host of worries: Am I popular? Am I normal? Why are these changes in my body taking place? Why don't people like me better? Should I use drugs? Is it all right to have intercourse? Why do I seem to get into so much trouble? Am I as smart as I should be? They don't need a psychiatrist, necessarily; but they do need a sensitive and caring adult who can listen to them, act as a sounding board, and even give advice when needed.

But many young adolescents will at some point need professional help in dealing with crises of a physical, social, or emotional nature. Coping with serious family problems, getting help with drug and alcohol abuse, dealing with severe emotional problems—all these are crises that require professional intervention. The school may not have such personnel on its staff, but it should be able to provide those services on a referral basis.

All Adolescents Need Administrative Services

The last criterion deals with the routine administrative services that every student needs. The homeroom or the adviser room should be effectively performing a range of such functions: maintaining up-to-date records, communicating with parents, orienting the students to school facilities and services, and serving as the main channel of communication between the school and the student. It is the one place where all students can be reached.

ORGANIZING THE SCHOOL FOR A STRONG GUIDANCE PROGRAM

How should personnel be used in a strong program that meets those criteria? Middle schools have tried a variety of patterns, including the use of peer counseling, contracted professional services, guidance aides, teacher–counselors, and even computers. However, two patterns of personnel use seem to predominate: the counselor-centered program and the adviser-centered program. Either approach can be made to work effectively if both counselors and teachers are committed to the importance of the guidance function and if they are prepared to diagnose the existing program and remedy its deficiencies.

The Counselor-Centered Program

The counselor-centered program, perhaps the more conventional approach and more frequently used in schools organized as junior highs, relies primarily upon a certified guidance counselor to provide for academic advising, personal guidance, and crisis intervention. The guidance counselor's services are supplemented by the efforts of the homeroom teacher or adviser, who assists with the academic advising, provides administrative services through the homeroom, and supposedly is the staff member who best knows the student. The advantages of the counselor-centered approach are obvious: The individual primarily responsible for providing the academic advising and personal counseling is a trained professional concerned solely with the guidance function and not distracted by other responsibilities. The main drawback to this approach is that it requires one counselor to provide critically needed guidance services to large numbers of students; counselor-student ratios of 1:400 are not uncommon in large middle schools. The results of such overburdened staff are predictable: Only those students with serious problems get attention.

The Adviser-Centered Program

The adviser-centered program, perhaps more common in middle schools, relies primarily upon a teacher–adviser (sometimes called the homeroom teacher, the counselor–teacher, or the homebase teacher). The adviser is responsible for twenty-five to thirty-five students, is expected to know those students well, and provides the academic and personal guidance in the homeroom setting, which also serves as the administrative unit. The guidance counselor provides the crisis intervention services and works closely with and assists the advisers. The adviser program has much to recommend it. Its chief strength is that it decentralizes the guidance functions and in the process reduces loads. Instead of one guidance counselor trying to counsel 300 students, there are ten teacher–advisers, and each counsels thirty. And in such a program, the adviser is more likely to know the student well, since that expectation has been built into the role. There are, however, two problems with the adviser system. First, the advisers are expected to perform several functions for which they have not been trained; counseling is a professional skill not easily acquired. Second, the adviser is primarily a teacher, busy with lesson planning, teaching, and grading papers; the counseling function often takes a lower priority since it is more easily deferred.

DIAGNOSING YOUR EXISTING GUIDANCE PROGRAM

In diagnosing most of the programmatic components in the middle school, multiple data sources are necessary. In diagnosing the guidance program you can rely primarily upon student input, supplemented with faculty discussion and analysis.

The primary objective in diagnosing the guidance program from the student's point of view is to understand how effectively services are being delivered to the client—as the client perceives the matter. At the same time that counselors and teachers believe that an existing program is highly effective, students may feel that they are not receiving the help they need. One useful way of obtaining student perception is to use a questionnaire similar to the one shown in Figure 10-2. Using language that young adolescents can understand, it asks students for three essential pieces of information: which adults are most of all providing specific guidance functions; which adult knows the student best of all; and how well the student feels known.

Best results will be obtained if any survey of this sort is administered in a class setting where the teacher can explain its purpose, clarify the directions, and assure the students of anonymity. Students will probably want to discuss the survey, as it raises issues important to them; however, such discussion should come after the students have completed and turned in the survey form, so that their answers are not influenced by the perceptions of assertive peers.

The survey form has been designed so that it can yield several types of information; note that it requests identifying data about section membership and sex, since those would seem to be the most important analytical dimensions. However, these are the key questions that the leadership team should seek to have answered in the data analysis:

1. By analyzing the percentage of "nobody" responses for each item, which specific services are being delivered least effectively? This information indicates in what particular areas students feel they are not being helped; it might suggest to the faculty, for example, that students believe that they are getting the academic advising they need but are not getting help with personal problems.

2. By analyzing the total responses for each source of help (counselor, adviser, etc.), which sources seem most effective in delivering those services? The data here, obviously, will help the leadership team and the faculty compare the way they intend to have guidance services delivered with the way students perceive they are in fact being delivered.

The survey returns should be discussed with the faculty in a special meeting. The principal should summarize and explain the results and then ask the faculty to meet in small groups to discuss their implications and offer suggestions as to how the guidance program might be improved. The specific improvements explained in the following section could well provide a basis for such faculty recommendations.

IMPROVING YOUR GUIDANCE PROGRAM

The standard method for improving guidance services is to hire additional personnel—counselors, psychologists, and secretaries. Although such solutions can obviously play a part, most school districts are unwilling or unable to spend additional money on guidance services during years of declining enrollments and shrinking resources. The following methods, which are not quite so costly, have been used successfully by several middle schools.

Allow Teachers to Supplement Your Services

Even if a school is relying upon a counselor-centered guidance program, it can strengthen its program by providing more time for the homeroom or adviser-room teacher to supplement those services. In too many schools the homeroom period lasts only ten or fifteen minutes each day—just not enough time to do the job. As one middle-school teacher wryly remarked, "I have ten minutes each morning—to check attendance, collect absence notes, read the morning announcements, distribute messages to individual students—and give thirty students the personal guidance they need."

Middle schools report several different approaches to providing additional time for the advising function. In many schools, one period each week is set aside for this purpose and is built into the school's master schedule; for example, on Thursday, period 3 might be the advising period. Other schools use a rotating period. In one week the guidance period would come on a Monday, with every period that day shortened by five to eight minutes; the following week, it would come on a Tuesday, and so on throughout the year. Schools allocating a block of time to teaching teams would have greater flexibility, of course; the team would simply be instructed to devote forty to fifty minutes each week to advising and would adjust its own schedule accordingly. And some schools individualize the advising schedule by giving the teacher one period each week for advising; the adviser meets with students individually, requesting that classroom teachers excuse them for as much time as is needed.

Regardless of the scheduling solution chosen, adequate time must be found. If advising young adolescents is a responsibility of teachers, they need the time to do it.

Diversify Guidance Department Resources

A few venturesome middle schools have attempted to diversify their guidance resources. The counselor and the teacher are expected to be responsible for the sensitive issues involved in personal guidance, but the more routine aspects of academic advising can be handled by parent volunteers and carefully selected guidance aides. More mature students can also be used if they are given proper training and supervision. All such efforts need to be well coordinated, of course. The middle-school youngster will be confused if he or she hears quite different messages from counselor, teacher, aide, and peer.

Provide Additional Training for Your Staff

Even if the school relies primarily upon its counselors for guidance services, the program can be strengthened by providing effective staff development for the advisers. Teachers acting as advisers need to develop the necessary skills, even if they are not perceived as the primary source of guidance services.

The staff development program should begin with a needs assessment, surveying the faculty with a form similar to the one shown in Figure 10-3; additional needs-assessment approaches are suggested in Chapter 14. The guidance counselors should play a key role in such staff development, assisted by experienced teachers who are known to be effective advisers.

Develop Group Guidance Materials

Another effective improvement strategy is the development of group guidance materials; such materials can be developed as a part of the staff development program or as a separate aspect of the improvement effort. These group guidance materials should be simple and easy to use; in fact, they can be developed in both format and content so that students can use them in leading group guidance sessions. Figure 10-4 shows a discussion guide that could be used in this manner. Note that it summarizes the important facts, suggests some questions to raise, and offers some simple advice about leading discussions.

These student-led guidance discussions can be useful both to learn some important facts and concepts and also to develop discussion skills.

All these approaches can strengthen a guidance progam without adding excessive costs.

Three examples of excellent guidance programs can be found in Appendix D.

FIGURE 10-1.   Criteria for guidance program

Each student in the school is known well by at least one member of the staff, who has a total perspective of the student and keeps the rest of the faculty informed about the student's program, progress, and problems.

Each student in the school receives adequate academic advising about such matters as course selection, study skills, career exploration, academic improvement, and long-term planning.

Each student in the school receives appropriate help and effective guidance in such areas of personal growth as developing new interests, making sound moral choices, developing a realistic self-image, making friends, coping with stress, discerning feelings, solving personal problems, understanding physical and sexual development, and developing social skills.

Each student in the school has available, when needed, competent professional help and special support in handling serious problems of a physical, social, and emotional nature.

Each student in the school has a primary administrative "home" that successfully performs several administrative functions: record keeping; reporting; communicating with parents; communicating with students about school affairs; and orienting the student to school facilities, services, and regulations.

FIGURE 10-2. Getting the help you need

Directions: You can help us help you by filling out this form. Listed below you will find some questions that most students want answers to and need help with. Who helps you with these questions? Listed across the top are people in the school who might help you most. For each question listed, put an "X" in the column showing who gives you the most help with this question. Notice that one of the columns is headed "Nobody." Put an "X" in this column if you feel that you are not getting the help you need in answering this question.

WHO HELPS YOU MOST OF ALL?

QUESTIONS STUDENTS ASK	Counselor	Adviser	Classroom Teacher	Principal or Asst. Principal	Other Student	Nobody
1. What courses should I take next year?						
2. What careers should I be thinking about?						
3. How can I improve my grades?						
4. How can I use my time in school better?						
5. How can I improve my study habits?						
6. What clubs and activities should I join?						
7. What are the important rules and regulations in this school?						
8. Am I making good progress in my school subjects?						

continued

FIGURE 10-2. (cont.)

QUESTIONS STUDENTS ASK	WHO HELPS YOU MOST OF ALL?					
	Counselor	Adviser	Classroom Teacher	Principal or Asst. Principal	Other Student	Nobody
9. How can I find my way around this school?						
10. How can I develop new interests and hobbies?						
11. How can I make more friends?						
12. How can I get along better with other students?						
13. How can I stay out of trouble in school?						
14. How can I handle my feelings in a grown-up way?						
15. How can I know what is the right and moral thing to do?						
16. How can I get along better with my teachers?						
17. What abilities and skills do I have?						

continued

FIGURE 10-2. (cont.)

QUESTIONS STUDENTS ASK	WHO HELPS YOU MOST OF ALL?					
	Counselor	Adviser	Classroom Teacher	Principal or Asst. Principal	Other Student	Nobody
18. What are my weak areas in school?						
19. How can I get help when I'm in trouble?						
20. How can I feel better about myself?						

Other information: To help us use your answers, please give us the following information:

1. What section/grade are you in? _____

2. Are you a boy _____ or a girl _____?

3. Which adult in the school do you think knows you best of all? _____

_____

4. How well do you think that person knows you? Check one:

_____ very well _____ about average _____ not well at all

FIGURE 10-3. Staff development needs assessment of guidance services

Directions: The following topics are being considered as possible foci for our staff development efforts to improve guidance services. Please indicate the extent of your interest in those topics by circling one of the following: VI, very interested; MI, moderately interested; NI, not interested.

TOPIC	EXTENT OF YOUR INTEREST		
1. Using small groups for guidance purposes	VI	MI	NI
2. Facilitating moral development	VI	MI	NI
3. Providing career guidance	VI	MI	NI
4. Discussing issues of human sexuality	VI	MI	NI
5. Dealing with alcohol and drug abuse	VI	MI	NI
6. Improving students' self-image	VI	MI	NI
7. Working with parents of children in trouble	VI	MI	NI
8. Knowing about and using community resources	VI	MI	NI
9. Improving intergroup relations	VI	MI	NI
10. Helping students improve academic performance	VI	MI	NI

Please list any other topic not mentioned above in which you would be very interested:

**FIGURE 10-4. Thinking about careers: a discussion
guide for student group leaders**

THE FACTS THAT STUDENTS NEED TO KNOW

1. Most young people change their minds several times about the careers they plan to follow.

2. Most people change careers two or more times during their lives.

3. Many people do not make good career plans; they think about only a few career possibilities and choose careers for which they are not suited.

4. Many careers that will be most needed by the year 2000 are not even in existence now.

5. By the year 2000 there will probably be less need for people to do the following jobs: work on assembly lines, teach school, work in banks, farm, work in mines, and build houses.

6. By the year 2000 there will probably be more need for people to do the following jobs: provide health care, repair computers, take care of older people, send and receive information, provide security, take care of pre-schoolers.

QUESTIONS TO DISCUSS

1. What career do you think you might follow when you are an adult?

2. Why does that career interest you?

3. If we cannot be sure what careers will be needed, how can we best prepare ourselves?

4. Can you imagine a new career that will be important in the year 2000, one that does not exist now?

5. Can you think of a career now in existence that might disappear by the year 2000?

continued

FIGURE 10-4. (cont.)

TIPS FOR DISCUSSION LEADERS

1. Remind students that only one person should speak at a time.

2. Be sure that everyone has a chance to speak. Call on any student who has not had a chance.

3. If a student tries to talk too much, say something like this: "Your ideas are good, but let's give everyone else a chance to talk."

4. Students will have different opinions about the questions listed. Ask students to explain their opinions. Make sure the group understands that there are no right or wrong answers.

5. At the end of the discussion, ask one of the students to summarize what has been learned.

PART FOUR

THE PROPER
ENVIRONMENT
FOR EFFECTIVE
MIDDLE SCHOOLS

11

Improving School Climate

The School Climate in an Effective Middle School

1. The school is characterized by an academic ambience; there is a shared concern for achievement.

2. Administrators and teachers have high expectations for students.

3. There is a clear sense of order about the school; there are a few rules, which are clear, reasonable, and enforced.

4. Administrators and teachers stress the importance of school discipline as a means of maintaining the school as a social order and developing a respect for authority and an appreciation of the need for rules.

5. The school provides a stable and predictable environment for adolescents experiencing instability and uncertainty.

One important aspect of middle-school excellence is the climate of the school. Even if the curriculum is sound and the teaching is effective, the school will not achieve excellence unless the climate is supportive in the ways suggested by the indicators listed above. The research is generally conclusive about the relationship of several climate factors to student achievement.[1] And several leading educators have pointed out that climate is intrinsically important: Even if it could not be linked to achievement, it would still deserve attention.[2] This chapter will explain the concept more fully, review the research on climate factors, describe a process for assessing school climate, and present a strategy for improving climate. Since school climate is such a complex factor and is so much dependent upon local conditions, the emphasis in this chapter is on a process to be used, rather than upon specific programmatic changes.

THE NATURE OF SCHOOL CLIMATE

Most experts who examine and discuss school climate define it generally as the total environmental quality of the school. That environmental quality is made up of four components: *ecology, milieu, social system,* and *culture.*[3] The ecology is the physical and material aspects of the school environment—the size of the school, the condition of the building, the appearance of the facilities. The milieu is the characteristics of persons and groups within the school—teacher characteristics, student abilities, teacher morale, student morale. The social system is the pattern of personal and organizational relationships—how leadership is provided, how decisions are made, how groups relate to one another, how people communicate. The culture is the values and belief systems—the norms, expectations, and goals of the organization and its members. All four aspects interact in a rather complex way, even though they may be isolated for analysis.

The findings summarized in Figure 11-1 about the elements of the school as a social system yield this general portrait of the effective school:

> There is a principal who plays an active and involved role in both instruction and in school activities—and who defends classroom time against unnecessary intrusions. All relationships—between administrators and teachers, among the teachers, between teachers and students, and between school and community—are in general positive. Teachers and students are appropriately involved in making the important decisions. There is a sense of trust and honesty, with much open communication. And students have ample opportunities to participate and get involved.

It is more than a place of learning; it is in addition a caring community.

And, as Figure 11-1 indicates, the culture is important. There is a consensus about goals and norms. All participants—administrators, teachers, and students—place high value on academics. People expect much of one another. Teachers are strongly committed to improving pupil performance. There are appropriate opportunities for students to cooperate in both informal and formal groups. And administrators and teachers are consistent and fair in enforcing the school's rules. That excellent school is a community with a shared belief system.

THE RESEARCH ON SCHOOL CLIMATE

Which climate factors seem to be related most directly to student achievement? The answer is a complex one. *Climate* is an elusive and ambiguous concept that is difficult to research; and several studies have resulted in somewhat conflicting results. However, a comprehensive review of more than 200 studies enables the careful reader to identify those factors that seem to be consistently supported.[4] Figure 11-1 synthesizes the findings from that review, using the terms previously identified and including the indicators noted at the opening of this chapter.

Note that there are no ecological factors listed, since the research here is inconclusive. Although two studies found that the decoration and care of the school were associated with higher student achievement, several other studies reported no significant relationships between most ecological factors and student achievement.[5]

As indicated in Figure 11-1, both teacher and student morale are important elements in the milieu. If teachers are in general satisfied with their school and have a positive attitude toward their work, their schools tend to have higher achievement. Similar relationships exist between student morale and achievement: Students seem to do better academically when they feel good about their school and have a high academic self-concept.

DIAGNOSING THE CLIMATE OF THE SCHOOL

Because climate is to a great extent a matter of perception, the best way to diagnose climate factors is to survey the perceptions of those involved. In making such a survey, you can use one of the published instruments described in Figure 11-2; all of these instruments meet the basic tests for reliability and validity. Or you can make an informal assessment by using the two instruments shown in Figures 11-3 and 11-4; they are useful for making general assessments for local school use, even though they have not been fully validated for research purposes.

The Faculty's Assessment

The first, "Our School—How It Looks to the Faculty," is designed to be used with the faculty; it includes twenty-two items in a Likert-type scale that assess teacher perceptions about the factors identified in the research as important aspects of climate. They have been reorganized in a way that will simplify the analysis and use of the results: items 1–8 are concerned with general aspects; items

9–11, with those related primarily to administrators; items 12–16, with those related to teachers; items 17–21, with those related to students; and item 22, with the aspect related to the parents.

The faculty assessment can be administered at any faculty meeting, with the principal explaining the nature of the instrument and the use of the results.

The Student and Parental Assessment

The second instrument, "Our School—How It Looks to Students and Parents," assesses the same twenty-two factors but uses language that students and parents are more likely to understand. The items are listed in the same order as on the faculty instrument, making it easy to compare results.

Students can be surveyed in their homebase room; each teacher who administers the instruments to students should, of course, explain what the instrument attempts to measure and stress the importance of responding seriously and conscientiously. How parents can best be surveyed is a more complex matter. Parent input is important here. Previous experience with surveying parents suggests that the best results will be obtained by mailing the survey form to the home, with a self-addressed stamped envelope enclosed.

The instruments have been designed so that they can be easily scored—by hand, if the numbers are small, or by computer, if they are large. Each of the five responses is given a numerical equivalent (strongly agree, 5; agree, 4; uncertain, 3; disagree, 2; strongly disagree, 1) so that the average or mean response for each item can be computed by simple arithmetical computations.

Analysis of the Assessments' Results

The results should be analyzed from two perspectives. First, identify those aspects about which there is substantial disagreement in the perceptions of the three groups surveyed. Minor variations between perceptions of faculty, students, and parents are both predictable and unavoidable, as the three groups have different biases and perspectives. However, major discrepancies about any item probably indicate the need for further analysis and exploration. The best way to explore differences in perception is through an open discussion in which each person is encouraged to discuss freely his or her beliefs about the matter in question, while the group listens to understand. The goal in such discussions is not to establish who is right—only to share one's own beliefs and to understand the perceptions of others.

Let's take an example. Suppose teachers report agreement with the statement that "teachers and students get along well" (item 16)—but most students report disagreement. The issue should then be explored in classroom discussions. The teacher should report the results of the survey, express his or her beliefs about the issue, and cite evidence to support those beliefs. Then the students should have an opportunity to express and defend their views, with the teacher listening to understand, not to challenge. From such discussions few minds are changed, but some beliefs are better understood: "We teachers think that teacher–student relationships are good because there are no major conflicts—but students believe relationships are not good because teachers seem too distant and remote."

Next, identify those items where the perceptions of respondents suggest that a major problem exists. In general the perceptions of faculty should be given greatest weight in analyzing items 1–15; the perceptions of students are probably most valid in assessing the aspects covered by items 16–21; and parent perceptions are most informative about item 22. However, an average score below 3.0 for any item from any of the three groups indicates an aspect of climate that perhaps warrants the special attention suggested in the following section.

A STRATEGY FOR IMPROVING SCHOOL CLIMATE

By using the processes explained previously, the faculty should be able to better understand the major areas of disagreement and to identify those aspects of climate that seem less than satisfactory. They should then be ready to implement a specific strategy for climate improvement.

Set Priorities and Make a Strategic Plan

Our experience suggests that the best strategy is one that involves thoughtful prioritizing and strategic planning. The prioritizing is necessary for three reasons: Climate factors are complex variables that are not easily remedied; teachers usually feel overwhelmed by complicated improvement plans that have too many objectives; and success is more likely to be achieved by action that focuses on just a few factors about which there is a shared concern.

One useful way to prioritize is to use a form similar to that shown in Figure 11-5. Note that in this example six aspects are identified as possibly needing attention. However, the faculty are given three choices as to what they wish to do about each. A faculty might decide that its best choice is simply to accept the situation as it is: The members may not value the type of change suggested by a particular aspect—or may feel that a given aspect would be too difficult to alter. For example, many faculties with whom we have worked were not strongly committed to giving students more opportunity to share in decision making; they preferred to accept the situation, without trying to study it or change it.

Second, a faculty might decide that a given aspect needs further study, either because there were marked differences in perceptions or because the complexity of the problem suggests the need for additional information. Suppose, for example, that students and parents disagree with the statement "You can believe what the principal and teachers tell you." Further study would be needed here to pinpoint the sources of distrust. Is the problem with teacher–parent conferences, with the school's public relations program, or with the way the school handles conflicts and crises? Useful data about such questions could be gathered through interviews, focused surveys, and group discussions.

How to Find the Best Solutions

Finally, the faculty might decide that a given aspect should be changed. They do not want to accept the situation as it is, and they want to do more than just study the problem. They believe that action is called for. If action is called for, how can the best improvement plan be developed? We would like to describe here a general process that seems to have worked well in several schools. It involves four phases: Analyzing, brainstorming, evaluating, and strategizing. In explaining how the process works in these four phases, we will use this aspect of school climate as an example: "Students help one another in class and in activities." We will assume that the faculty, student, and parent surveys have indicated that this aspect needs attention—and that the faculty members have decided that they would like to effect some change here.

Analyzing. In the analyzing stage, you should accomplish four related tasks to help the faculty members understand the nature and importance of each specific aspect of climate they wish to change. First, identify the climate aspect that will be the focus of change efforts. Then review and summarize the related literature about that aspect of climate, to establish a rationale for its importance. Next, summarize the ratings given by the three groups surveyed. Finally, re-state the climate aspect as a problem to be solved. The results of the analysis should be shared with the faculty, perhaps by using a form similar to that shown in Figure 11-6. Observe that the form also includes space for solutions, the focus of the next stage.

Brainstorming. When you brainstorm, you produce creative solutions to the problem. Although some prefer to carry out this stage through brainstorming in groups, we have secured better results in what are called "nominal groups."[6] The nominal group process, which combines the advantages of both individual and group thinking, follows several closely related steps:

1. Brief the faculty about the problem, using a form similar to that shown in Figure 11-6.
2. Divide the faculty into groups of five or six, with a leader for each group. Ask each group to sit together at a table.
3. Ask each member in a group to work individually, without consulting other members, for about fifteen minutes. Each participant should list on the

form five or more solutions that might solve the problem. They can be either previously tried solutions or completely new ideas.

4. At the end of fifteen minutes, provide time for the group leader to collate and record all the solutions developed by the individual members. The leader calls on each person, one at a time, to read one idea; the leader records each idea on newsprint, without noting the name of the contributor. This continues in round-robin fashion, until every idea has been recorded.

5. When all ideas have been recorded, the group leader should lead a discussion of any of the ideas about which members have questions or that members wish to advocate strongly.

6. When the discussion period has concluded, the group leader should then ask participants to rank the solutions. Each participant identifies and ranks five ideas that he or she considers best, giving a score of 5 to the best idea and 1 to the fifth-best idea.

7. Ask each group to present its five best ideas to the entire faculty. A recorder can then develop a combined list, eliminating any duplicate suggestions.

8. The faculty should then discuss the combined list and use the same ranking process to identify those five ideas that have the greatest promise and strongest support.

What kinds of ideas might be produced through this nominal group process? Let's go back to the aspect previously identified—"Students help one another in class and in activities." Here are some examples that illustrate the range of suggestions possible:

- Use cooperative learning groups in each class.
- Establish a cross-age tutoring project.
- Award a "distinguished service prize" to students who cooperate effectively.
- Teach a unit on cooperative societies in social studies class.
- Appoint "editors" in each English language arts class who can help classmates with writing problems.
- Select "problem solvers" in math class—students who can help classmates with problem-solving strategies.
- Include cooperative games in the activities program.
- Hold discussions in homeroom on the differences between cheating and helping one another.
- Encourage team projects in creative arts.
- Change the grading system so that it motivates cooperation, not competition.
- Hold staff development programs to teach teachers how to help students build upon one another's ideas.

● Work with parents to help them develop cooperative home environments.

Evaluating. Such a list of solutions obviously needs careful evaluation—and that's the goal of the evaluating stage. Whereas the brainstorming stage requires openness and creativity, the evaluating stage places a premium on critical judgment. Assemble a small group of administrators and teachers who seem to have the best understanding of the school and its students—and who know how to ask the hard questions. Ask them to evaluate each of the ideas on the basis of the following criteria:

● Is the solution likely to be effective in improving climate?
● Is it likely that the solution will have strong support from all constituencies—faculty, students, parents, the school board?
● Is the solution economically feasible?
● Is it likely that the solution can be implemented successfully without overtaxing resources?

This evaluation process should enable the leadership group to identify one or two solutions that can improve the school climate without overtaxing resources. If you wish, you can use a form like that shown in Figure 11-7 to simplify the prioritizing process.

Strategizing. Now you need to strategize. At the strategizing stage, assemble a group of administrators and teachers who have effective planning skills. Their task is to develop an action plan for implementing the solutions—identifying the steps that must be taken, assigning responsibilities for each task, and specifying deadlines.

Most strategies for planning climate improvement will deal with one or more of five factors: administration, staff development, curriculum, student/parent orientation, and evaluation. Administrative planning involves such steps as securing superintendent and board approval, preparing budget requests, and producing reports. Almost any climate change will require some staff development, to ensure that teachers have the skills needed to implement the change effectively. Many climate changes will also affect the curriculum; therefore, curricular modifications may need to be considered. All changes that directly affect students should be communicated clearly to them and to their parents. And for all climate improvements, a systematic evaluation plan should be developed, specifying both the formative assessments to be made while the project is underway and the summative assessment to be conducted at the end of the first year of implementation.

These decisions can be recorded on a strategic planning schedule, with the time periods listed across the top and the five planning factors down the left-hand side. The entries in the cell should specify the steps to be taken and the individual responsible. A portion of such a chart is shown in Figure 11-8.

Improving school climate is a complicated business. "Quick fixes" are not likely to work. It requires the careful analysis, ideation, evaluation, and planning described in this chapter.

Middle schools that have been especially effective in improving school climate are listed in Appendix E.

Notes

1. Carolyn S. Anderson, "The Search for School Climate: A Review of the Research," *Review of Educational Research*, 92 (1982), 368–420.

2. John I. Goodlad, "Schools Can Make a Difference," *Educational Leadership*, 33 (1975), 108–17.

3. R. Tagiuri, "The Concept of Organizational Climate," in *Organizational Climate: Exploration of a Concept* (Boston: Harvard University, 1968).

4. Carolyn S. Anderson, "The Search for School Climate: A Review of the Research," *Review of Educational Research*, 92, (1982), 368–420.

5. Michael Rutter and others, *Fifteen Thousand Hours: Secondary Schools and Their Effects on Children* (Cambridge, MA: Harvard University Press, 1979); Phi Delta Kappa, *Why Do Some Schools Succeed? The Phi Delta Kappa Study of Exceptional Elementary Schools* (Bloomington, IN, 1980).

6. A. L. Delbecq and A. H. Van de Ven, "A Group Process Model for Problem Identification and Program Planning," *Journal of Applied Behavioral Science*, 7 (1971), 466–92.

FIGURE 11-1. School climate factors associated with student achievement

---

MILIEU FACTORS

● Teacher morale: good general morale; positive attitude toward work; general satisfaction with school.

● Student morale: good general morale; high academic self-concept.

SOCIAL SYSTEM FACTORS

● Instructional program: high proportion of time spent on instruction.

● Administrator–teacher rapport: much administrator support, collegiality.

● Teacher-shared decision making: teachers involved in decisions.

● Communication: good communication; much trust, respect, caring.

● Teacher–student relationships: shared activities.

● Student-shared decision making: students involved in decisions.

● Opportunity for student participation: much freedom to use building, to participate in activities, to associate with one another.

● Teacher–teacher relationships: much teacher cooperation and concern.

● Community–school relationships: positive parent–administrator and parent–teacher relationships.

● Involvement in instruction: strong administrative leadership; active involvement of administrators in instruction and activities.

continued

FIGURE 11-1. (cont.)

CULTURE FACTORS

- Teacher commitment: strong commitment to improve pupil performance.

- Peer norms: academics valued by student body.

- Cooperative emphasis: emphasis on cooperation; existence of student groups.

- Expectations of teachers: high expectations of administrators for staff.

- Expectations of students: high expectations of administrators and teachers for pupils.

- Emphasis on academics: strong emphasis on academics, orderly atmosphere.

- Consistency in administering rewards and punishments: consistently applied disciplinary rules.

- Consensus on curriculum: agreement by all participants on school curricula.

- Consensus on discipline: agreement by all on school norms and rules; emphasis on social order and stable environment of school.

- Goals: clear goals; clearly defined limits for behavior.

FIGURE 11-2. A selection of published instruments for assessing school climate

ORGANIZATIONAL CLIMATE DESCRIPTION QUESTIONNAIRE (OCDQ)

One of the earliest instruments; used in more than one hundred studies of elementary and secondary schools. Some researchers question its usefulness in predicting student achievement. A. W. Halpin and D. B. Croft, *The Organizational Climate of Schools* (Chicago: University of Chicago Press, 1963).

MY SCHOOL INVENTORY (MSI)

Developed initially for use in elementary schools; has been used in many studies of school climate. G. I. Anderson, *The Assessment of Learning Environments: A Manual for the Learning Environment Inventory and My Class Inventory* (Halifax, Nova Scotia: Atlantic Institute of Education, 1973).

ELEMENTARY SCHOOL ENVIRONMENT SURVEY (ESES)

Uses student perceptions of teacher and pupil values to develop school profiles. R. L. Sinclair, "Elementary School Educational Environments: Towards Schools That Are Responsive to Students," *National Elementary Principal,* 49 (1970), 53–58.

THE SCHOOL SURVEY (SS)

Measures teacher satisfaction with the work environment; has been widely used in climate research. R. J. Coughlan, "Dimensions of School Morale," *American Educational Research Journal,* 7 (1970), 221–35.

QUALITY OF SCHOOL LIFE SCALE (QSL)

Assesses student perceptions of school climate; has been used in several studies of elementary and middle-school students. (J. L. Epstein and J. M. McPartland, The Concept and Measurement of the Quality of School Life," *American Educational Research Journal,* 13 (1976), 15–30.

FIGURE 11-3. Our school: how it looks to the faculty

Directions: Below you will find several statements about our school. Read each statement. Then decide how much you agree or disagree with that statement. Circle one of the following as your answer:

SA—strongly agree	*D—disagree*
A—agree	*SD—strongly disagree*
?—uncertain	

IN OUR SCHOOL...		RESPONSE			

1. There is a clear set of goals. SA   A   ?   D   SD

2. Administrators and faculty emphasize and reward academic achievement. SA   A   ?   D   SD

3. There is open and honest communication. SA   A   ?   D   SD

4. Instructional time is valued and used well. SA   A   ?   D   SD

5. There is consistency in administering rewards and punishment. SA   A   ?   D   SD

6. There is strong administrative leadership. SA   A   ?   D   SD

7. There is general agreement about the curriculum. SA   A   ?   D   SD

8. There is general agreement about disciplinary policies. SA   A   ?   D   SD

9. Administrators have high expectations for the faculty. SA   A   ?   D   SD

10. Administrators and teachers get along well. SA   A   ?   D   SD

11. Administrators and teachers have high expectations for the students. SA   A   ?   D   SD

12. Teacher morale is generally high. SA   A   ?   D   SD

13. Teachers have an opportunity to share in decision making. SA   A   ?   D   SD

continued

FIGURE 11-3. (cont.)

IN OUR SCHOOL…	RESPONSE				
14. The teachers get along well with one another.	SA	A	?	D	SD
15. Teachers work hard to improve students' academic performance.	SA	A	?	D	SD
16. Teachers and students get along well.	SA	A	?	D	SD
17. Student morale is generally good.	SA	A	?	D	SD
18. Students have an opportunity to share in decision making.	SA	A	?	D	SD
19. Students have many opportunities to participate in school activities.	SA	A	?	D	SD
20. The students value academic achievement.	SA	A	?	D	SD
21. Students help one another in class and in activities.	SA	A	?	D	SD
22. There are good relationships with the parents.	SA	A	?	D	SD

FIGURE 11-4. Our school: how it looks to students and parents

Directions: Below are several opinions about our school. Read each one. Then decide how much you agree or disagree with each one. Circle one of the following to show how much you agree or disagree:

SA—strongly agree	*D—disagree*
A—agree	*SD—strongly disagree*
?—uncertain	

Your answers will help us make the school better.

OPINIONS: IN OUR SCHOOL...		YOUR ANSWER			

1. Everyone understands what this school is trying to achieve.   SA   A   ?   D   SD

2. The principal and the teachers stress the importance of studying and doing well in class.   SA   A   ?   D   SD

3. You can believe what the principal and the teachers tell you.   SA   A   ?   D   SD

4. Teachers don't waste time in class.   SA   A   ?   D   SD

5. The principal and teachers are fair in the way they discipline.   SA   A   ?   D   SD

6. The principal really seems to care about making the school a good one.   SA   A   ?   D   SD

7. The principal and the teachers seem to agree about what should be learned.   SA   A   ?   D   SD

8. The principal and the teachers seem to agree about the rules of the school.   SA   A   ?   D   SD

9. The principal seems to expect teachers to do a good job.   SA   A   ?   D   SD

10. The principal and the teachers seem to get along well with one another.   SA   A   ?   D   SD

continued

FIGURE 11-4. (cont.)

OPINIONS: IN OUR SCHOOL...	YOUR ANSWER				
11. The principal and the teachers expect all students to do well in their classwork.	SA	A	?	D	SD
12. The teachers seem to enjoy teaching in the school.	SA	A	?	D	SD
13. The teachers have a chance to make decisions about the school.	SA	A	?	D	SD
14. The teachers seem to get along well with one another.	SA	A	?	D	SD
15. The teachers try hard to help all students learn.	SA	A	?	D	SD
16. Teachers and students get along well with each other.	SA	A	?	D	SD
17. Students feel good about themselves and the school.	SA	A	?	D	SD
18. Students have a chance to decide important things.	SA	A	?	D	SD
19. Students have many opportunities to participate in activities.	SA	A	?	D	SD
20. Students care about getting good grades.	SA	A	?	D	SD
21. Students help one another in class and activities.	SA	A	?	D	SD
22. Most parents think that the school is a good one.	SA	A	?	D	SD

FIGURE 11-5.   Prioritizing the climate factors

To the faculty: The results of our recent survey on school climate suggest that the following aspects might need attention. Consider each aspect. Then indicate your opinion as to what we should do about that aspect, circling one of these words:

ACCEPT: *you think we should accept this situation the way it is, without trying to study it or change it.*

STUDY: *you think we should study this aspect of climate further, in order to understand the situation better.*

CHANGE: *you think we should work together to attempt to change this aspect of our school climate.*

ASPECT NEEDING ATTENTION	YOUR RESPONSE		
3. There is open and honest communication.	Accept	Study	Change
4. Instructional time is valued and used well.	Accept	Study	Change
7. There is general agreement about the curriculum.	Accept	Study	Change
8. There is general agreement about disciplinary policies.	Accept	Study	Change
18. Students have an opportunity to share in decision making.	Accept	Study	Change
21. Students help one another in class and in activities.	Accept	Study	Change

FIGURE 11-6. Issue analysis

THE CLIMATE ASPECT

Students help one another in class and in activities.

WHY IT IS IMPORTANT

1. This aspect seems related to student achievement: Students seem to achieve better when they have many opportunities for cooperation.

2. Our society needs people who know how to work together; students can learn those useful skills in a supportive environment with the right kind of teaching.

3. The research suggests that cooperative learning approaches improve students' relationships with one another and their attitudes toward school.

OUR SCORES

Average teachers' ratings: 2.9

Average students' ratings: 1.8

Average parents' ratings: 3.1

THE PROBLEM STATEMENT

How might we give students more opportunities to help one another in class and in activities—and to learn the skills they need for successful cooperation?

YOUR IDEAS

1. _____

2. _____

3. _____

4. _____

5. _____

FIGURE 11-7. Evaluating solutions

SOLUTION	EFFECTIVENESS	SUPPORT	ECONOMIC FEASIBILITY	IMPLEMENTATION	TOTAL
Cooperative learning groups	5	4	5	4	18
Cross-age tutor	4	3	4	4	15
Cooperative games	5	3	3	5	16
Team projects	3	4	4	4	15
Grading system	5	3	4	2	14

FIGURE 11-8. Strategic planning chart for cooperative learning

FACTOR	MARCH	APRIL	MAY	JUNE
Administration	Proposal to superintendent (Walker)	Submit budget request (Jones)		
Staff development		Draft staff development plan (Walker)	Review by faculty (Jones)	Submit to superintendent (Walker)
Curriculum		Develop plan for summary review (Albert)		Choose staff for summary review (Albert)
Student/parent orientation		Develop orientation plan (James)		Prepare student-parent flyer (White)
Evaluation		Develop detailed evaluation plan (Walker)		

12

Improving the Organizational Structure

The Framework of an Effective Middle School

1. The organizational structure of the school is an organic one, evolving in response to teacher perceptions of student needs.

2. The school creates a sense of smallness by using a "house" system staffed with teams of teachers.

3. Teaching teams have a great deal of influence over school-wide matters and classroom issues.

4. The school schedule allows for periods of both activity and relaxation.

5. The school makes provisions for flexible grouping, so that students can for at least part of the time be with peers at similar stages of development.

Over the course of the past few decades, educational reformers have advocated several organizational models, such as the Trump plan, open education, and Individually Guided Education. Each of these organizational models has often been adopted enthusiastically by middle schools—and then discarded when some newer fad appeared. Rather than repeating this cycle of adoption and rejection, middle-school leaders working closely with the teachers should determine for their schools which particular aspects of organizational structure are most strongly supported by the research and are most likely to be useful for their schools. That essentially is the approach advocated in this chapter.

THE ORGANIZATIONAL STRUCTURE'S NATURE AND IMPACT

"Organizational structure," as the term is used here, is the set of processes for organizing the time, space, and personnel in a school for instructional purposes. It includes first of all the basic structure of the school. Is the organizational structure adopted as a "package" of educational innovations—or is it developed organically by the staff and modified to meet the changing needs of teachers and students? Also, is the school divided into smaller self-contained "houses"—or is it one large entity organized by grade levels? Organizational structure next includes two related aspects of teacher assignment. Do teachers work alone in self-contained classrooms—or as cooperative members of teams? If teams are used, are those teams organized on an interdisciplinary basis or by subject matter?

Third, it includes the means by which students are assigned to learning groups. Are they grouped heterogeneously or homogeneously? Is grade level, developmental level, or ability level the basis for sorting students into groups? Do they work individually, in small groups, as a whole class, or in large groups? Finally, it involves the way time is divided and allocated—the nature of the school's master schedule.

The research on the organizational structure of schools seems less conclusive in its general findings than the research on other aspects of middle schools. For most of the components of structure, there are fewer definitive studies, and in many cases the results are conflicting. Consequently, the research summary in Figure 12-1 should be interpreted as a set of tentative guidelines, not as a series of prescriptions: It represents a synthesis of the effectiveness guidelines research on organizational structures.

Those guidelines taken together suggest that the more effective middle school might be described in this fashion:

> It is organized into several houses or mini-schools. Teachers work in interdisciplinary teams, with a semi-departmentalized structure. For the most part, students are grouped heterogeneously and spend most of their learning time working as a class or in small groups. The schedule is flexible and academically oriented, but there is sufficient time for activities and relaxation.

But note again that these organizational matters are best determined by the faculty and are frequently reassessed: The structure is an organic one, a home-grown solution to a set of local conditions.

IMPROVING THE BASIC ORGANIZATIONAL STRUCTURE

The basic structure of the organization involves both the process by which the structural aspects are determined and the type of units into which the school is divided. Each of these will be examined here.

An Organic Process

First, the staff should use an organic process for determining the structure, since such an approach seems more effective than simply adopting and retaining some package of innovations. After examining four exemplary middle schools, one researcher reached this conclusion about organizational structure: "The schools have in common an organic structure evolving in response to the staff's evaluation of students' needs. Each school has made decisions that the other schools have rejected...."[1]

Decentralized approach. Although the specific nature of that "organic structure" will, of course, vary with each school, there are two general approaches that might be used. The first is a "bottom-up" or decentralized approach that relies on the insightfulness and creativity of the teaching staff. In this decentralized approach, the leaders establish the basic organizing framework for the entire school and then give to each teaching team the greatest autonomy in determining the specific structures it needs and in making modifications as the need develops. As Figure 12-2 indicates, in each dimension of organizational structure, the school leaders determine the broad guidelines; the teaching teams make the specific day-to-day decisions and are encouraged to make changes as they perceive the need for modifications.

This decentralized approach has certain obvious advantages and disadvantages. First, it provides for maximum flexibility; teaching teams can decide from week to week how to modify the organizational structure, subject to appropriate administrative review. Also, it gives teachers a greater sense of autonomy; they are making the key decisions that affect their professional roles. Finally, it could be argued that the decentralized approach is more likely to provide the optimal set of structures for a particular group of students, as those structures are determined by those closest to the students.

However, the decentralized approach also has certain drawbacks. First, its administrative looseness may result in problems of coordination: Schedules don't match, shared facilities are overtaxed, corridor traffic is unpredictable. Second, it can result in an undesirable lack of uniformity in such key areas as curricular content and student discipline. Finally, it increases the administrative responsibility of teachers and can thus result in diminished instructional effectiveness.

Centralized approach. The other "top-down" or centralized approach begins with the leadership team, in consultation with the teachers, determining at the outset the set of structures that will be used to organize the school and then using a problem-solving process in making organic modifications as needed. The initial determination is made on the basis of the administrators' assessments of such factors as facilities, teacher maturity and competence, and student needs.

After that set of structures is in effect for two or three years, the leaders then conduct a systematic diagnosis of the effectiveness of those structures. In making this diagnosis, they consider such indicators as student achievement, discipline referrals, and activity-participation records. They also make an assessment of teachers' perceptions of the effectiveness of those structures by using a survey form like the one shown in Figure 12-3. It summarizes the research on each programmatic component, provides space to describe the school's present approach, and assesses the faculty's readiness to change.

All these diagnostic data enable the leadership team to determine which structures to change, which to leave as they are, and which to study with greater care. The process can still be considered an organic one, as it uses a data-based problem-solving process to make continuing changes; however, the impetus and direction come from the top.

The Nature of Units

The second aspect of the basic structure involves the nature of the units into which the school is divided. Most effective middle schools are larger schools that have been subdivided into smaller units called mini-schools or houses. Such an arrangement gives teachers and students the advantages of both bigness and smallness. The larger school can offer more activities and curricular options; the smaller units give teachers a chance to know and work closely with a particular group of students—and give students better opportunities to form meaningful relationships with peers.

In creating these houses, several choices are available, with definite advantages and disadvantages accruing to each.

- *Houses organized by grade level, with a grade-level team assigned to each.* Thus, there would be a sixth-grade house, a seventh-grade house, and an eighth-grade house; each team would develop its own grade-level program, within general school guidelines. The grade-level house is probably the simplest to administer and schedule, as each grade can be treated as a self-contained entity. The main drawback is that it tends to overemphasize grade level as a determiner of student placement and curriculum content.

- *Houses organized as multi-grade units with generally similar programs.* Thus, a grades 6–8 school of 900 students might be organized into six houses, with each house including students from all three grades. The multi-grade house encourages teachers to minimize grade-level distinctions and to place students more appropriately for instruction. Such multi-grade units, however, seem more complex to administer, as they usually require the part-time services of specialized personnel.

- *Multi-grade mini-schools, with each mini-school designed as an alternative school with its own curriculum and learning environment.* Thus, one large middle school might be divided into three alternative schools: an intellectually rigorous "academy" with a strong emphasis on the academic disciplines and much use of independent study; a "service corps" with a curriculum emphasizing community problems and experiential learning; and a "basics" school offering a curriculum stressing reading, writing, and mathematics in a highly structured environment.

Such alternative schools seem no longer to be in vogue, especially at the middle-school level, but the research indicates that in general they have been effective in providing a more productive environment for many students.[2] Alternative schools have been successful when they operated with clear decision-making and disciplinary structures, when they were directed by leaders who knew how to design learning environments, and when they were staffed by teachers who had special skills in relating to students. They have been less successful when they were unstructured "free schools" that permitted students to learn only what they wanted to study in an environment without limits.

These decisions about the number and type of mini-schools will, of course, be influenced by such factors as the size of the school, the facilities available, and the nature of the student body. The experts seem to recommend the multi-grade house system, but the decision is best left to the leadership team and the teachers.

Monitoring the structure. Once the houses have been established, the leadership team should closely monitor their operations. A review of the literature and an analysis of our own experience suggest that certain predictable problems will develop, each of which will need special attention. The first is a leadership problem. House leaders will become overwhelmed with their multiple responsibilities and will not be sure how to provide the leadership the teachers need. Those leaders will need both time to do the job and training to develop their skills. The second is a curriculum problem. Some teaching teams will make unwise use of their curricular autonomy and choose content solely on the basis of teachers' interest. The implementation of the mastery curriculum approach described in Chapter 7 should remedy this situation. The final problem involves the teachers' perceptions of their role. Left to their own devices, some teachers will focus solely on their instructional role, forgetting that the house structure was intended to facilitate their guidance function. Here, some intensive staff development will be needed both to alter their perceptions and to teach them the skills.

IMPROVING TEACHER ASSIGNMENT PRACTICES

Teacher assignment involves two related matters—whether teachers will work alone or as a team and whether they will teach one or several subjects. Several different patterns are presently in use in middle schools.

- Teachers work alone in self-contained classrooms, with each teacher responsible for all academic areas of the curriculum. This essentially is the elementary model: A sixth-grade teacher teaches English language arts, mathematics, science, and social studies to a class of thirty pupils who remain with that teacher most of the day.

- Teachers work alone, but each teacher teaches one subject. This is the typical secondary model: The sixth-grade class goes to an English teacher, then to a math teacher, and so on.

- Teachers work as members of departmentalized teams; there is an English team, a math team, a science team, and a social studies team. The departmentalized teams usually plan together and teach together, often combining large-group, whole-class, and small-group instruction. For example, one of the three English language arts teachers assigned to sixth grade would present a twenty-minute lecture to ninety students on the propaganda techniques used in the mass media; the students would then meet for twenty minutes in small groups, with each group chaired by a student leader and the three teachers moving from group to group.

- Teachers work as members of interdisciplinary teams, so that each team includes a teacher with competence in one of the academic disciplines. Thus a sixth-grade team might include one language arts teacher, one social studies teacher, one math teacher, and one science teacher, supplemented by the part-time assignment of specialists in art, music, and other nonacademic areas. These interdisciplinary teams might plan and teach interdisciplinary units in what are usually called "humanities" programs—or they might plan as a team but teach their disciplines independently.

Advantages of Interdisciplinary Teams

A recent survey of middle-school principals indicated that both the more effective principals and the general group surveyed preferred a combination of the secondary "subject specialist" model and the interdisciplinary team model.[3] In general, the interdisciplinary team model is both recommended by the experts and tentatively supported by the research. The teaming enables teachers to share information about and perceptions of their students; it also facilitates their collaborative planning. As Goodlad notes, teaming is thus one of the most effective means of reducing the fragmentation of the program and the isolation of the teachers.[4] And interdisciplinary teams reportedly are more child-centered; subject-matter teams seem to reinforce the primacy of the discipline.

Such interdisciplinary teams should also enable the principal to assign teachers so that they are teaching in one or two areas of special competence. After grade 5, some form of specialization seems desirable; the research suggests that at that point teachers with depth in particular subject-matter areas like science and mathematics get better results in student achievement than do teachers responsible for several areas of the curriculum.

It should be stressed again, however, that any teacher-assignment model that both administrators and teachers support can be made to work; all that matters is effective learning and positive attitudes, not a particular organizational scheme. And these matters of how teachers work together and what they teach affect the teachers' daily lives so directly that faculty preferences should be given primary consideration in establishing the teaching teams.

Making Team Teaching Work

In establishing and maintaining the effectiveness of those teams, school administrators can be guided by the research on team teaching.[5] First, in constituting the membership of teams, they should attempt to place together teachers who have generally similar values about student discipline. Although a certain amount of professional conflict is productive, the research suggests that where there are serious differences about behavioral norms, the conflict becomes divisive and counterproductive.

Second, each team needs a leader who understands and knows how to apply the special skills of colleagial leadership. Typically such leaders do not have access to three important sources of power: They cannot reward; they cannot punish; and they have little formal authority. In such a situation, the research suggests that they need to rely on other power sources: their expert knowledge; their control of information; and their attractiveness as individuals.[6] They will need to be trained in the sensitive use of such power.

Next, team and individual responsibilities should be clearly delineated. With guidance from the principal, the teams should decide how extensively they will work together: Will they work as individuals or as a team in developing curricula, making instructional plans, asssessing student performance, and instructing classes? They also should understand their individual responsibilities in checking attendance, monitoring behavior, grading papers, and guiding learning.

Also, the teams should be given time within the school day to share information about students and to make instructional plans. Such discussions and planning require time, and busy teachers are reluctant to commit after-school time even when they acknowledge the importance of those functions.

With appropriate membership, effective leadership, clear responsibilities, and adequate time, teaching teams can make a major contribution to excellent middle schools.

IMPROVING STUDENT ASSIGNMENT PRACTICES

Student assignment practices involve two central matters of student group membership—the bases for grouping students and the size of instructional groups. Both issues bear directly on teachers and students and have a major impact on the nature of learning.

The Bases for Grouping Students

In determining on which bases students should be grouped for instruction, middle schools have six different choices.

- *Tracking.* Tracking is the process by which students are sorted into ability-based tracks or streams; the tracking determines both group membership and curriculum in all their subjects. Thus, a student in the low-ability track is with other less-able students every period of the school day.
- *Ability grouping by subject.* Subject-based ability grouping is supposedly more flexible than tracking. In this mode, students are grouped for instruction in a particular subject on the basis of their ability in that subject. Thus, a student might be in a high-ability English class but an average-ability math class. Proponents of subject-based ability grouping claim that it is not as rigid as tracking, but the data suggest otherwise: For most students, subject-based ability grouping turns out to be tracking.
- *Heterogeneous grouping.* Schools that use heterogeneous grouping believe in the virtues of diversity. Classes are either composed at random or are carefully structured to achieve a mix of student abilities.
- *Self-determined grouping.* Many schools that offer an "electives" curriculum use a type of student-determined grouping. Courses are developed at three levels of challenge or difficulty; students are fully informed about these levels and, with parent guidance, are expected to make an informed choice. Although self-determined grouping in actuality has results similar to those of ability grouping, its advocates believe that involving the student in the decision mitigates its pernicious effects.
- *Grouping by developmental level or learning style.* Eichorn has for years advocated and practiced what he terms "developmental grouping," in which

students are placed in multi-age groups according to their combined index of social, physical, mental, and academic maturity.[7] His studies indicate that students in schools that use developmental grouping have better achievement than comparable students in other schools. Some attempt to assess the young adolescent's developmental level or cognitive level. And some experts recommend that learning style should be the primary determiner of group placement, although very few middle schools have attempted to implement the recommendation.

- *Individualized placement.* There are several forms of individual placement in use in middle schools. In the usual model, students are assigned heterogeneously to a team of teachers, who then attempt to teach each student at his or her specific achievement level. Most approaches to individualized instruction use a diagnostic/prescription process: the Teacher diagnoses the student's present level of achievement and prescribes an appropriate set of learning objectives. Proponents claim many advantages for individualized instruction, but the research is somewhat discouraging. Although individualized learning approaches have been generally successful at the college level, they have not resulted in improved achievement at the elementary or secondary level, according to several studies.[8]

Ability grouping. While all six options are available, most middle schools use some form of ability grouping; it might therefore be useful to examine this particular option in greater detail.

Should middle schools use ability grouping? The answer can be considered from three different perspectives—the research, the practice of effective schools, and the preferences of teachers. First, the research in general is not conclusive about its use. According to numerous studies conducted over the past several years, ability grouping has no clear effect on achievement and is associated with some significant drawbacks: It typically results in stratification by social class and race, it often perpetuates negative stereotypes of those with limited academic ability, and it seems to result in an inferior education for the less able. In his comprehensive study of schooling, Goodlad found the curriculum for the "lower track" to be boring, trivial, and unchallenging.[9] The only argument for ability grouping that is supported by the research is that it results in more manageable classes: Extremely heterogeneous classes are more difficult for teachers to discipline.[10]

As stated, the research does not strongly support ability grouping, but the practice of effective schools tends to support it. In the study of principals of effective middle schools, 92 percent of the principals surveyed indicated that their schools used ability grouping; most reported that it was used at all age levels in certain subject areas.[11] Most of the principals whose schools use ability grouping relied primarily on three criteria for the placement of students: judgments of school staff, standardized achievement tests, and report card grades. And, as the effectiveness guidelines note, excellent schools provide some opportunity for students to be together with peers at a similar developmental level.

The preferences of teachers are very clear: Most are strongly in favor of ability grouping, especially for the subject they teach. They tend not to be impressed with the research. They want manageable classes, and they know from experience that heterogeneous classes are more difficult to plan for, to teach, and to discipline.

Determining the optimal approach. Given such conflicting perspectives, there is obviously no easy solution to the problem of determining the optimal approach for a given school. The best answer seems to be one that both embodies the advantages of several approaches and also has the strong support of the staff. The teachers should first be informed about the grouping options available as well as the research on grouping. They should also have an opportunity in such discussions to share their own experiences with and reactions to the several approaches. With that background established, they should then be involved in an assessment of present practice. A form like the one shown in Figure 12-4 can be useful here. It lists the criteria for assessing grouping practices and asks the teachers to evaluate the school's success on each.

The results of the survey can assist the leadership team in deciding which of four basic strategies would be most effective. One strategy focuses on the grouping systems: The school modifies its basic approach to grouping, perhaps using heterogeneous classes on a trial basis in selected subject areas. The second focuses on the placement process: The school develops more refined processes for placing students, using multiple criteria and making a determined effort to achieve greater integration of the social classes and races represented in the school. The third approach emphasizes the curriculum: The grouping system and placement criteria are left intact, but teams are given the charge of strengthening the curriculum, especially for the gifted and the less able. The final approach emphasizes instructional treatment: All other aspects of the grouping system are left unchanged, but teachers are given intensive staff development to assist them in individualizing instruction within present grouping patterns.

The intent here is to use a diagnostic problem-solving process that deals with specific issues, rather than advocating some doctrinaire stance on a very complicated issue.

The Size of Instructional Groups

In theory, instructional groups can vary in size—from 1 to 1000 or more. In actuality, middle schools tend to use either whole-class or small-group instruction. According to the Keefe study, large-group and individualized instruction were used infrequently.

This is one case in which research and practice are in accord. According to the research on teacher effectiveness, most of the basic skills are best imparted through whole-class instruction.[12] With a group of twenty-five to thirty-five students, a good teacher can effectively accomplish the tasks of direct instruction without encountering serious disciplinary or instructional problems. Larger sized groups, especially at the middle-school level, are very difficult to discipline and keep on task.

The direct instruction of class-size groups, however, should be supplemented with sufficient small-group learning. The small group of four to eight is optimal for several key teaching/learning activities: discussion, cooperative problem solving, remediation, and project work. However, these small groups will need to be monitored closely; the research suggests that off-task behavior increases markedly in unsupervised group activity.

Because most teachers seem inclined to use a whole-class approach, they will need most help with small-group instruction—in both seeing the need for it and in implementing it effectively. Many teachers seem reluctant to use small-group learning because they believe it should be used only for student-led discussions in English or social studies classes. However, the small group can be used in any subject area—for a variety of activities. Teachers will also need help with using small-group learning in their classes, as it does require some special approaches. The following skills can become the basis for a series of staff development sessions: using small groups to accomplish instructional goals, determining size and membership of learning groups, developing student leadership in group settings, monitoring small group learning and keeping groups on task, assessing and grading group performance.

MAKING MORE EFFECTIVE USE OF TIME

The last aspect of organizational structure involves the way time is both divided and allocated—the essential decisions reflected in the school's master schedule. In dividing time, middle schools have three general choices: the period schedule, the modular schedule, or the block-of-time schedule. The period schedule divides the day into six to eight instructional periods of forty to fifty minutes, the schedule that secondary schools have traditionally used. It has persisted because it seems to work: It provides the teacher with enough time to teach a few concepts, check on student learning, and provide some directed practice. And it is not over-long for most secondary students; they can sit still for forty minutes without causing too much trouble or doing too much daydreaming.

Modular Schedules

Critics, however, have attacked the traditional period because of its inflexibility; they claim that it is too long for some kinds of learning (such as lectures) and too short for others (such as laboratory work). Consequently, some middle schools have adopted a modular schedule. The modular schedule uses shorter time increments—usually of fifteen or twenty minutes—as the basic building blocks of the school's schedules. Teaching teams can then specify how many modules they need for a particular subject each day of the week. Thus, an English class might meet for two "mods" on Monday, one on Tuesday, none on Wednesday, three on Thursday, and one on Friday. The advantage of the modular schedule, obviously, is that it provides somewhat greater flexibility; a twenty-minute module enables teachers to have instructional periods of twenty, forty, sixty, or eighty minutes.

However, the modular schedule has two drawbacks, both of which have limited the extent to which it has been used in middle schools. First, the modularized master schedule is somewhat more difficult to develop than the period schedule, especially when it is combined with flexible group size. Second, once established, it is as inflexible as the period schedule; a teacher scheduled for a sixty-minute class on a particular day might really need only twenty minutes—but has no choice, since the master schedule calls for a sixty-minute session.

Block-of-Time Schedules

Most middle schools have found the block-of-time schedule easier to develop and more flexible to implement. In the block-of-time schedule, a team of teachers is assigned a block of time (usually from 60 to 120 minutes) that they may then subdivide as they see fit. Most teams working in a block-of-time schedule agree on a standard allocation that they then vary for special needs, rather than decide each day's schedule on an *ad hoc* basis.

Because the type of master schedule does not seem as important as other aspects of organizational structure, teacher preference should play a determining role. Even though effective middle schools tend to use a block-of-time schedule, the research suggests that any type of master schedule that the teachers support can be made to work.

The allocation of time is a more critical matter. Here middle-school leaders need to balance their concern for students' academic achievement with their interest in students' emotional well-being. The direct relationship between time allocated to the basics and to achievement in those areas is clearly recognized by numerous research studies. One comprehensive review of the research noted that effective principals allocated school time on the basis of program priorities and also prevented intrusions into high-priority activities.[13] Yet, as we have noted elsewhere in this book, the middle school must be concerned with something more than academic achievement. The young adolescent needs time to relax—and time to pursue activities that will develop new interests and reward special talents.

Achieving this optimal balance requires both careful planning and close monitoring. First, leaders must plan the master schedule so that it provides for time allocations that reflect their program goals. One way of making these planning decisions is to determine at the outset how much time proportionately should be allocated to four types of school-day experiences: high-academic-pressure subjects (English, reading, mathematics, science, social studies, foreign language); moderate-academic-pressure subjects (health and physical education, art, music, industrial arts, home economics, typing); moderate-structure activities (clubs, homeroom, assemblies, study periods); and low-structure activities (lunch, "time off" periods, class parties).

There is no research on the issue, but the practice of effective middle schools suggests these ranges:

TYPE OF ACTIVITY	RANGE
High-academic-pressure subjects	50–60%
Moderate-academic-pressure subjects	15–25%
Moderate-structure activities	10–20%
Low-structure activities	15–20%

Once these decisions have been made by reflecting on program priorities, the leaders then must monitor intrusions. Such monitoring is essential simply because there are so many pressures to excuse students from planned programs: field trips, special committee meetings, medical and dental appointments, physical examinations, district and state testing programs, to name only a few. Each of these may be justified, but together they add up to a significant loss of instructional time, a loss that militates against middle-school effectiveness. Only clearly defined policies and consistent application of those policies can defend the school schedule against the criticisms of well-meaning individuals who are convinced that their causes are just.

> Several examples of effective middle-school structure are listed in Appendix F.

Notes

1. Joan Lipsitz, *Successful Schools for Young Adolescents* (New Brunswick, NJ: Transaction, 1984), pp. 193–94.

2. Mary A. Rawid, "Synthesis of Research on Schools of Choice," *Educational Leadership*, 41 (1984), 70–78.

3. James W. Keefe and others, *The Middle Level Principalship, Volume 2: The Effective Middle Level Principal* (Reston, VA: National Association of Secondary School Principals, 1983).

4. John I. Goodlad, *A Place Called School: Prospects for the Future* (New York: McGraw-Hill, 1984).

5. H. N. Sterns, "Team Teaching: Cooperative Organizational Concept," in *Handbook on Contemporary Education*, ed. S. E. Goodman (New York: Bowker, 1976).

6. Paul Hersey, Kenneth H. Blanchard, and Walter E. Natemeyer, *Situational Leadership, Perception, and the Impact of Power* (San Diego: Center for Leadership Studies, 1979).

7. Donald H. Eichorn, *The Middle School* (New York: Center for Applied Research in Education, 1966).

8. Robert L. Bangert, James A. Kulik, and Chenn-Lin C. Kulik, "Individual Systems of Instruction in Secondary Schools," *Review of Educational Research*, 53 (1983), 143–58.

9. John I. Goodlad, *A Place Called School: Prospects for the Future* (New York: McGraw-Hill, 1984).

10. Jane Stallings, "What Research Has to Say to Administrators of Secondary Schools about Effective Teaching and Staff Development," in *Creating Conditions for Effective Teaching*, ed. Kenneth Duckworth and others (Eugene, OR: Center for Educational Policy and Management, 1981), pp. 2–33.

11. James W. Keefe and others, *The Middle Level Principalship, Volume 2: The Effective Middle Level Principal* (Reston, VA: National Association of Secondary School Principals, 1983).

12. Donald M. Medley, "The Effectiveness of Teachers," in *Research on Teaching*, eds. P. L. Peterson and H. J. Walberg (Berkeley, CA: McCutchan, 1979), pp. 11–27.

13. K. A. Leithwood and D. J. Montgomery, "The Role of the Elementary School Principal in School Improvement," *Review of Educational Research*, 52 (1982), 309–39.

FIGURE 12-1. The research on middle-school organizational structure

The research on the organizational structure of middle schools suggests that the following characteristics are generally desirable.

THE BASIC STRUCTURE OF THE SCHOOL

● The organizational structure has been determined organically by the staff and is modified to meet the changing needs of teachers and students.

● The large school is divided into several smaller "houses" or mini-schools of 100 to 200 students; students spend most of their school day in such houses, where they become known by a small group of teachers.

TEACHER ASSIGNMENT

● Teachers work together in interdisciplinary teams and are given time to evaluate students and make appropriate instructional plans; those teams have a great deal of influence over school-wide and classroom issues.

● Teachers instruct in one or two areas of their instructional competence, rather than being responsible for the entire instructional program.

---

continued

FIGURE 12-1.   (cont.)

STUDENT ASSIGNMENT

● Students spend most of their learning time in heterogeneous groups; homogeneous grouping is used to provide for special needs and to enable students to spend part of their day with others at similar stages of development.

● Students work as a whole class and in small cooperative learning groups; individual work occurs less frequently.

USE OF TIME

● Blocks of time are allocated to teaching teams for them to use flexibly.

● The school schedule provides most time to academic learning, but appropriate amounts of time are allocated for activities and relaxation.

SOURCES: *Sandra B. Damico, Chad Green, and Afesa Bell-Nathaniel, "The Impact of School Organization on Interracial Contact Among Schools,"* Journal of Educational Equity and Leadership 2 (1982), 238–52; *Joan Lipsitz,* Successful Schools for Young Adolescents *(New Brunswick, NJ: Transaction, 1984); Mary H. Metz, "Sources of Constructive Social Relationships in an Urban Magnet School,"* American Journal of Education, *91 (1983), 202–44; Margaret C. Wang, "Adaptive Instruction: Building on Diversity,"* Theory Into Practice *19 (1980), 122–28.*

FIGURE 12-2. A model of decentralized decision making

ORGANIZATIONAL ASPECT	LEADERS DETERMINE	TEACHING TEAMS DECIDE
1. House patterns	Which students will be assigned to house	What types of programs the house will provide
2. Teacher assignment	General guidelines for effective use of staff	Whether teachers will teach as individuals or as teams
3. Teacher subject assignment	What mix of teachers will be assigned	What subjects teachers will teach
4. Student grouping	General guidelines for group membership	Which students will work together for various activities
5. Group size	General guidelines for determining group size	What size group will be used for specific activities
6. Time divisions	Basic divisions of school day; how much time will be allocated to team	How time will be segmented within blocks of time
7. Time emphasis	Minimum time to be allocated per week for each activity	Specific times for each activity

FIGURE 12-3. Assessment of the school's organizational structure

---

BASIC ORGANIZATION

The research suggests: Middle-school students should spend much of their time in smaller houses or mini-schools so that they can become known by a small group of teachers.

Our school _____

Your attitude: ___ Leave things the way they are

___ Take some action to change

___ Study the issue more

TEAM TEACHING

The research suggests: Teachers should work together in interdisciplinary teams, with adequate time to evaluate students and make instructional plans.

Our school _____

Your attitude: ___ Leave things the way they are

___ Take some action to change

___ Study the issue more

SUBJECT SPECIALIZATION

The research suggests: Teachers should instruct in one or two areas of their instructional competence, rather than being responsible for the entire instructional program.

Our school _____

Your attitude: ___ Leave things the way they are

___ Take some action to change

___ Study the issue more

ABILITY GROUPING

The research suggests: Students should spend most of their learning time in heterogeneous groups, with homogeneous grouping used selectively for special student needs.

Our school _____

Your attitude: ___ Leave things the way they are

___ Take some action to change

___ Study the issue more

continued

FIGURE 12-3. (cont.)

INSTRUCTIONAL GROUPING

The research suggests: Middle-school students should spend most of their time in whole-class and small-group learning, with less time in large-group instruction and individual study.

Our school _____

Your attitude: __ Leave things the way they are

__ Take some action to change

__ Study the issue more

SCHOOL SCHEDULE

The research suggests: Blocks of time should be allocated to teaching teams that can use that time flexibly to respond to student needs.

Our school _____

Your attitude: __ Leave things the way they are

__ Take some action to change

__ Study the issue more

USE OF TIME

The research suggests: The school schedule should provide most time to academic learning, but appropriate amounts of time should be made available for activities and relaxation.

Our school: _____

Your attitude: __ Leave things the way they are

__ Take some action to change

__ Study the issue more

FIGURE 12-4. Judging our grouping practices

THE CRITERIA	SCORE—GOOD, FAIR, POOR
1. Grouping practices should not stratify or segregate students by race or social class.	_____
2. Grouping practices should neither stigmatize students nor give them a false sense of superiority.	_____
3. Grouping practices should not unduly complicate the teacher's instructional or management responsibilities.	_____
4. Grouping decisions should employ multiple criteria and should be made with input from all those who know the student.	_____
5. Grouping decisions for all students should be reviewed periodically, with appropriate adjustments made.	_____
6. Grouping decisions should enable all students to make optimal academic progress.	_____
7. The curriculum for all groups should be challenging and interesting.	_____

13

Strengthening Parent and Community Relationships

The Community and an Effective Middle School

There are supportive community relationships, based upon the success of the school and frequent parent contact.

In too many middle schools, good community relationships are equated with effective publicity that creates an inflated image. Such a distorted view leads to misguided attempts to cover up problems and to sell the school like a commercial product. Excellent middle schools have good community relationships—but those healthy relationships come about from a sincere desire to work closely and communicate openly with parents and community. And the best school–community relationship, we will argue, will reflect the specialness of the school and the community it serves.

THE IMPORTANCE OF EFFECTIVE PARENT AND COMMUNITY RELATIONSHIPS

The argument for good school–community relationships can be made from both grounds of principle and practice. The basic principles are two-fold: In a democracy, the public schools belong to the people and are expected to serve the larger interests of that society. Both those principles of public ownership and societal responsibility require that schools be closely linked with and responsive to the communities they serve. The school board serves as the representative body that translates public sentiment into educational policy, but the individual school itself is obligated by principle to be closely related to its community. Even if effective community relationships had no practical consequences, they would be desirable simply because they are intrinsically worthwhile in a democratic school system.

Advantages for the School

Yet there are practical consequences, both for the school and the community. For the school, the results of good school–community relationships are obvious. Taxpayers are more disposed to support district budgets when school–community relationships are sound. Better teachers are attracted to schools that have strong community support, as long as that support does not become a demand for control. The school has better access to the rich resources of its community—its people, organizations, and natural resources. School leaders can more effectively focus on the essential tasks of educating children when their energies are not absorbed in dealing with community tension and conflict. And the students learn an important message about the nature of school and society.

Advantages for the Parents

Obviously, the parents and the community also gain when there are sound relationships with the schools. When parents and other citizens are fully informed about their schools, they can make better decisions about educational matters. When parents feel positive about their schools, they experience a sense of satisfaction about an important aspect of their and their children's lives. And when there is general community support for and pride in the schools, the community itself becomes a more attractive place to live.

THE COMPLEXITY OF GOOD SCHOOL–COMMUNITY RELATIONSHIPS

It is thus a relatively simple matter to argue for the desirability of "good school–community relationships." It is a much more complex undertaking to establish what those good relationships are and to realize them in practice. Several factors account for this complexity.

The Changing Sense of Community

The first factor is the changing sense of "community" in a time when middle schools often draw students from several distinct geographical areas. For example, Lipsitz in her study of exemplary middle schools makes the point that "...Noe [Middle School] has no neighborhood.... Students from the entire school system who are of middle-school age, scheduled to be bussed, and also academically gifted, are sent to Noe for one mandatory year of busing."[1] If "community" means "students' residential neighborhoods," then the Noe community is all of Jefferson County, Kentucky.

The Past Power Struggle and the Uneasy Truce

The second complicating factor is the struggle for power that during the 1960s and 1970s caused turmoil in the schools. In the 1950s it seemed clear that school administrators were in power, paternalistically deciding for students, teachers, and parents what the schools should be. Those administrators defined for everyone else what good school–community relationships should be: a complacent community kept at arms length, supporting with bountiful taxation a subservient faculty. In the '60s, students and parents used sit-ins and demonstrations to demand more power; in the '70s, teachers' unions used the strike to assert their own claims. There seems now to be an uneasy truce. Students worry about their future; parents are anxious about their jobs; teachers fear layoffs; and administrators compete for diminished resources. They all seem willing, therefore, to avoid confrontation over power issues and inclined to make compromises to maintain a fragile peace. But the truce has not resolved the basic question that provoked those previous struggles: Who owns the schools? With that question unanswered, the nature of good school–community relationships must remain somewhat ambiguous. Each of those constituencies has a different agenda and would define "good school–community relationships" in a very different manner.

The Changing Family Structure

The third complicating factor is the changing nature of the American family. It was relatively simple years ago for the schools to communicate with the family: There were two parents, with the mother usually working at home. Now communication is complicated: In many families, there is only one parent; and in two-parent families, both are likely to be working full time outside the home. It has thus become very difficult to call parents at home and to get parents to come to school during the day for conferences. It is even very difficult to get good attendance at evening meetings; working parents want to relax in the evening and spend time with their children, not attend PTA meetings. Thus, what some school administrators call "parental apathy" is simply a manifestation of a sensible desire to spend more time at home.

Different Expectations for the Schools

Another complicating factor is that the diversity of our society results in some very different expectations for the schools. Although there is a certain uniformity in the general vision of good schools and their community relationships (orderly schools that emphasize the basics and keep in close touch with parents), there are sharp differences about the details of that picture. Parents have very different priorities for their schools: The parents of middle-school youngsters in the South Bronx worry about the physical safety of their children; the parents in an affluent suburb of New York fret about how many foreign languages are taught. And they have different preferences about the nature and extent of their involvement in the schools: Working-class parents in a small rural town may want very active participation; affluent suburbanites may like it better if they just aren't bothered. "Good school–community relationships" are probably not the same thing in Keokuk, Iowa, and Scarsdale, New York.

The Nature of Middle Schools

A final complicating factor is the nature of middle schools themselves. To begin with, there is less consensus among professionals and citizens about the purposes of middle-school education. There is strong agreement about the purposes of early elementary education (teach the three R's) and of the high school years (stress the academics), but there is much confusion about middle-school priorities. Should affective goals come first—or should academics dominate? Should middle-school teachers reduce academic pressures or raise their standards? This absence of consensus complicates school–community relationships. And the special nature of early adolescents also muddies up the picture. Young adolescents struggling to achieve autonomy and independence are often embarrassed by parent involvement in school activities. For many twelve-year-olds, home and school are two separate worlds—and the less communication, the better.

All these factors mean that it is very difficult—if not foolhardy—to generalize about the nature of "good school–community relationships." Consider some evidence. One group of researchers discovered that in white middle-class schools, high parent involvement was positively associated with pupil achievement in the basics; in black schools serving working-class communities, parent involvement was negatively related with pupil achievement.[2] And in her study of effective middle schools, Lipsitz observes that the faculty of Noe are " ... grateful for the relatively high level of parental apathy in their district," whereas parental support has been crucial in the survival of the Region 7 (Detroit) Middle School.[3]

We are left then only with some very general guidelines—and an obvious need to develop a differentiated school-based approach to effective school–community relationships. We now turn to both of these matters.

GENERAL GUIDELINES FOR SCHOOL–COMMUNITY RELATIONSHIPS

A review of the literature on effective middle schools and an analysis of the special factors alluded to in the foregoing section have produced the guidelines listed in Figure 13-1. The first two guidelines—an emphasis on quality education and responsiveness to the milieu—are clearly the most important. They seem to be most basic in that they are most pervasive in their effects and they have the strongest support in the research.

Emphasize Quality Education

The first guideline states an obvious truth: There is no substitute for quality. Experienced middle-school principals know that their most effective public relations medium is a satisfied student. If a youngster goes home every day with glowing reports of her school and her teachers, the parents don't need any additional evidence. Good schools enjoy community support; poor schools do not. It's as simple as that.

Respond to the School Environment

The second important guideline is perhaps more complex. Effective middle schools are responsive to their milieu, their social and political environment.[4] Although they may from time to time test the limits of community tolerance, they stay within those limits, as to exceed them in any significant way will produce criticism and reduce support.

There are three specific types of responsiveness that seem crucial. First, the prevailing educational philosophy of the school should be consonant with that of the majority of its constituency. Radical educators do not last long in conservative communities. Second, the priority goals of the school should represent the general expectations of parents and community. If affective outcomes are given a low priority by parents, the school risks losing support if it explicitly gives those goals the greatest attention. Finally, the school's standards for student behavior should be those that parents and community members in general would support. Although parents seem willing to give teachers much latitude about instructional methods, they have very clear ideas about what constitutes desirable conduct, and they do not want those convictions challenged by adults whom they consider permissive or indulgent.

Inform Parents and the Community on all Fronts

The third guideline speaks of the responsibility to inform. To begin with, there should be full information about the students. Parents especially should be fully informed about students' academic progress, their problems, and their achievements. This last item needs emphasizing. Too often, parents hear from the school only when their child is in trouble; but many effective middle schools make a practice of sending home letters of praise for specific accomplishments. The community should also be kept informed about overall student achievement and about the accomplishments of groups and individuals.

Program information is also needed. The school should make every attempt to explain all major program components—curriculum, instruction, activities, and guidance—in language that the public will understand. Many middle schools have made two mistakes here. Some make excessive use of educational jargon: "Our interdisciplinary teams function in a multi-aged nongraded individualized program." Others err by overselling educational innovations: "This new independent study program will enable all students to become autonomous self-directing individuals."

Finally, the school should provide full information about its faculty. This is an area that most schools unwisely neglect: Too often, the public hears about teachers only when they are asking for more money. The school should provide for the community a general descriptive profile of its faculty and on a periodic basis feature individual teachers whose contributions are worthy of attention.

Provide for Parent and Community Input

The next guideline speaks to the other part of the communication cycle: The school provides channels for parent and community input and makes appropriate use of that input. As will be explained more fully in the next section of this chapter, this guideline needs to be sensitively applied so that the school achieves that delicate balance between community control and teacher autonomy. The effective principal plays a key role in achieving that balance by serving as a buffer between insistent parents and classroom teachers.

Use Outside Resources and Provide Services

The final two guidelines speak to the symbiotic nature of good school–community relationships: In the best relationships, schools use the community, and communities use the schools. The school uses the people, places, and institutions of the surrounding area as a vital means of enriching the educational program and extending the boundaries of education. And the school makes its own resources—its facilities, its staff, and its students—available to the community for appropriate educational purposes.

Taken together, these six guidelines provide a useful map for middle schools on the road to excellence. How to negotiate that journey is a more complex matter—one that individual schools must accomplish in their own way.

DEVELOPING A SCHOOL-BASED PARENT–COMMUNITY PROGRAM

The uniqueness of each school and its setting thus provides a rationale for each middle school to develop, within district guidelines, its own parent–community relations program. Developing a new program or improving an existing one can be accomplished by following the steps in the next section.

Improve Faculty Understanding of the Community

The first step is to understand the special nature of the community and to transmit that understanding to the faculty. In too many instances, the faculty's orientation to the community consists solely of a recital of its landmarks and some glib comments about its people. The goal, instead, is to be able to answer the following questions:

1. What smaller neighborhoods make up the larger community? How do those neighborhoods differ from one another?
2. What is the socio-economic and ethnic mix of the community? Note that in understanding a community's educational values, social class seems to be more important than race.
3. What religions and denominations are represented? Do the religious views of the people tend to be liberal or conservative? How important are church-related schools?
4. What are the general educational beliefs of the people in the community? What are their curricular priorities and their expectations about discipline?
5. To what extent do party politics affect school affairs? Which individuals control the political parties?
6. Who are the power brokers in the community? Which individuals exercise behind-the-scenes influence on key community issues?

Some of the answers to these questions can be secured, obviously, from such readily available sources as census information and registration and voting records. Some can be acquired by close attention to local news media. But the most important information—about attitudes and influence patterns—is not so easily obtained. Astute educational leaders cultivate their own informal sources: They listen to the breakfast talk at the local diner, eavesdrop on conversations at the country club, listen to the experts in the hair salon, learn from the custodians and the bus drivers, keep in touch with the local clergy. Even if they do not live in their school's community, they work hard at keeping informed by cultivating the grapevine.

More formal approaches can also be used. Some middle-school principals have found it effective to meet on a regular basis with community leaders—to exchange ideas, to elicit information, and to develop contacts. Others join service clubs for the same purposes—although it should be noted that the typical service club is not a representative group.

So those key questions can be answered through several sources—through public information, informal contacts, and more formal channels. They then must be shared with the faculty. Reports of successful practitioners suggest two complementary methods of educating the faculty about the community. The more factual and public information can be summarized in a publication—"A Profile of Our Community"—and discussed in general faculty meetings. More sensitive information—about the politics and power structure—is perhaps better shared in small group discussions. Even in small group discussions, discretion is advised. Statements about the power structure of the community can be misunderstood by the inattentive or distorted by mischief-makers.

Develop Policies and Guidelines

The second step in building a school-based community relations program is to develop policies and guidelines about parent and community relationships. In many school systems, the district office will have developed such statements; even in such a situation, middle-school leaders should request the opportunity to modify and amplify them to suit the special needs of their school. The need for such policy statements is supported by several research studies which indicate that most teachers prefer specific guidelines for dealing with parents and community representatives; in an ambiguous situation like a parent–teacher conference, they like the security provided by specific directions.

Policies and guidelines are probably needed for the following areas:

- Holding parent conferences.
- Handling confidential information about students.
- Dealing with controversial community issues.
- Handling citizen complaints about instructional materials.
- Using community resources—field trips, speakers, organizations.
- Making school resources (faculty and facilities) available to the community.

These policies and guidelines play such a crucial role in guiding teachers that they should be developed systematically and carefully. This process has worked well for many schools:

1. Appoint a small task force to do the substantive work. The task force should include representatives from the leadership team, faculty members, parent representatives, and whatever experts seem needed and available.

2. The task force should review existing documents that provide direction: state directives, statements from professional organizations, district policies, and guidelines from other middle schools.

3. The task force should develop a first draft of policies and guidelines that seem to reflect the special needs of that school.

4. That draft should be reviewed by the leadership team, by district officials, by the faculty, and by parent groups, where appropriate. Insofar as possible, the final document should represent a consensus of views, with parent and teacher opinions given major weight.

5. The final document should then be reviewed with the faculty and then made part of a permanent policy handbook. Figure 13-2 shows one useful format and suggests the kind of content that might be included. The final document should be clearly written and make use of captions, numbered lists, and underlining to simplify teacher use.

Assess Faculty and Parent Preferences for Parent Involvement

A key step in developing a school-based program is assessing faculty and parent preferences for parent involvement. The members of the leadership team can make better decisions about this matter if they understand the feelings of both faculty and parents.

In any discussion of this issue, the leaders should take pains to be sure that faculty and parents understand two key points. The first is that parent involvement is not an either/or proposition; rather there are degrees of involvement, as they relate differentially to aspects of the school program. Five levels of involvement might be specified:

- Parents determine alone: The parents make the decision.
- Parents determine with the faculty: The two groups share the decision-making function.
- Parents recommend: The faculty decides, but it gives parent recommendations careful consideration.
- Parents provide input: Parent views are solicited but are weighed as only one factor in making the decison.
- Parents are informed: The faculty decides without parent input—parents are informed about the decision.

The second key principle is that there is no right answer to these issues. Some educators and parents argue that the elected school board is the body that legally represents the views of all citizens, including parents—and that any parent involvement beyond participation in school board elections and meetings is unnecessary and unwise. At the other extreme there is a smaller number who believe in parent control, with the professional staff chosen only to carry out parent-determined decisions.

Since the issues are both complex and vital, they should be examined in a very systematic fashion. Some middle schools have successfully used a process like this one:

1. The general issue of parent involvement is raised in first a faculty meeting and then in a parent meeting, with a clear explanation of the two cardinal principles noted previously.

2. Faculty and parent views are surveyed, using a form like the one shown in Figure 13-3. Faculty views can be surveyed in a faculty meeting; the parent organization should be responsible for surveying parents. The parent survey should be accompanied by a letter explaining the issue and clarifying the degrees of involvement. In conducting both surveys, it should be made clear that the results will be used only for the guidance of administrators and teachers; respondents should not feel that they are voting on the issue.

3. The responses to the survey are collated and analyzed. The results are then reviewed with district administrators, who clarify the limits imposed by district policies and board actions.

4. The results are then discussed in a combined meeting of both faculty and parents. The meeting should start with a general presentation that highlights the findings, noting both agreement and disagreement in faculty and parent views. That general presentation should then be followed by discussion in small groups composed of both faculty and parents. The discusssion will be heated—but the airing of views is essential.

5. The leadership team then uses all the above information in setting and implementing policies governing parent involvement.

Is there some best set of policies governing these matters? Obviously there is not. In previous chapters we offered suggestions about where parent input is most desirable, but we believe that the degree and nature of parent involvement should be determined at the school level. In making these school-based decisions, the following guidelines, however, should prove to be useful:

● Any school-based policy should be consonant with district policies. School-based decisions should not contravene board policies.

● Parents should not be expected to make decisions about professional issues requiring a high degree of technical competence. Soliciting parent input does not mean ignoring professional expertise.

● No individual or small group of vocal parents should be able to dictate policy for all the rest. The leadership team should make systematic efforts to get the views of all parents, not simply those who attend PTA meetings.

• The more a policy directly affects the parents, the more they should be involved in the development of that policy. Most parents do not care very much about the school's curriculum; they see the curriculum as a professional concern that has little impact upon their own lives. However, they care deeply about such matters as school attendance boundaries, transportation schedules, and the school calendar; those issues touch them very directly.

Develop a Computerized Parent–Community Data Base

The next component in the school-based program is the development of a computerized data base that will provide needed information to the leadership team and teachers about parent and community resources. Every parent should be asked to complete a form similar to the one shown in Figure 13-4, in addition to the usual student registration form. Notice that this form does not ask for a great deal of information about the family; parents would be justifiably concerned if the school tried to store in a computer too much information about the family. It requests only information that will enable the teachers to keep the parents informed and enable the school to use the services of available parents.

The other component of the computerized data base is a community resource file. Such a file can be developed by notifying the local media and all community organizations about the school's interest in using community talent. A form similar to the one shown in Figure 13-5 can be used to collect the needed information. Two master files can be developed from the information provided— one file by the name of the individual, and one by area of expertise.

Because of the potential problems likely to result from the use of ineffective or insensitive people from the community, two kinds of quality control are needed. First, teachers should be cautioned to interview anyone whom they do not know before making a commitment to use that individual. Second, teachers should be asked to submit a brief written evaluation of anyone who does make a presentation to a student group. These confidential evaluations should then be added as part of the file information.

Given those controls, such a resource file can have several uses in the middle schools. People from the community can present assembly programs, provide expertise in career education programs, speak to student clubs and activity groups, and make presentations in the classrooms.

Keep in Touch with Parents

Regardless of the level of parent involvement in making policy and serving the school, all middle schools should develop effective means for communicating with and listening to parents. Many studies indicate, however, that most middle schools do not communicate effectively; they rely on the parent–teacher organization, which typically is not a representative group, and on evening parent meetings, which are often poorly attended. A survey of the literature and discussions with middle-school principals suggest that the following guidelines and practices are much more effective.

Go to the parents—don't always expect them to come to the school. Middle schools serving large geographic areas have found it necessary to decentralize their parent meetings. Many principals have found it useful to meet with small groups of parents over coffee in homes or community centers. While such meetings are time-consuming, they are very effective means of communicating with parents who are unable or reluctant to attend meetings at the school. Such meetings are more successful if they are set up and held with the cooperation of neighborhood organizations.

Personalize and individualize communication. Instead of relying on report cards and printed messages, many middle schools find it more effective to personalize communication. Many, of course, use parent conferences as a means of reporting pupil progress; some middle-school principals recommend the practice of distributing report cards in evening meetings with parents. Several also report great success in sending home what one principal calls "happygrams"—personal letters to parents about the accomplishments of their children.

Use direct mail to get important information to parents. Since young adolescents are notorious for losing or discarding notices from the school and many parents do not attend parent meetings, the schools must rely upon other methods. A parent newsletter, published quarterly in cooperation with the parent organization and mailed to the home, is perhaps the most effective means of communicating directly to the parents. The newsletter can provide a means of surveying parents for the several types of information discussed in this and previous chapters. It can also include such diversified content as the following: faculty notes, activity program news, student accomplishments, calendar of school and community activities, curriculum developments, parent activities.

Decentralize parent representation. Many middle schools supplement the standard parent organization with other decentralized approaches. Several have found it helpful to have each group of parents whose children are in the same homeroom elect a parent homeroom representative who is the chief medium for a two-way communication flow. Some middle schools serving larger regions have organized local neighborhood parent groups, primarily as a means of communicating with parents who are less likely to be represented by the central parent organization. And some have found that activity-related groups are more active than the usual parent organization: Such groups as the "band parents" and "football parents" are more likely to participate because they and their children share a common interest.

Taken together, all these measures are likely to add up to an effective parent–community program that reflects the special nature of each individual school.

Several schools with effective community relations programs are listed in Appendix G.

Notes

1. Joan Lipsitz, *Successful Schools for Young Adolescents* (New Brunswick, NJ: Transaction, 1984).

2. W. B. Brookover, J. H. Schweitzer, J. M. Schneider, C. H. Beady, D. K. Flood, and J. M. Wisenbaker, "Elementary School Climate and School Achievement," *American Educational Research Journal* 15 (1978), 301–18.

3. Joan Lipsitz, *Successful Schools for Young Adolescents* (New Brunswick, NJ: Transaction, 1984).

4. Steven T. Bossert, David Dwyer, Brian Rowan, and Ginny V. Lee, *The Instructional Management Role of the Principal: A Preliminary Review and Conceptualization* (San Francisco, CA: Far West Regional Laboratory, 1981).

FIGURE 13-1.   General guidelines for developing community relationships

1. The school emphasizes quality education for its students as its primary means of gaining public support.

2. The school is responsive to its special social and political milieu, staying within the limits of community tolerance.

3. The school attempts to keep parents and the community fully and accurately informed about students, programs, and faculty.

continued

FIGURE 13-1. (cont.)

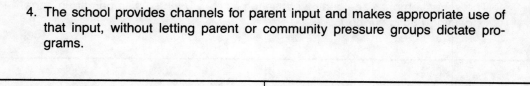

4. The school provides channels for parent input and makes appropriate use of that input, without letting parent or community pressure groups dictate programs.

5. The school makes appropriate use of parent and community resources as a means of extending its program, broadening the educational program, and enriching the educational experiences of its students.

6. The school provides appropriate services to the community.

FIGURE 13-2. Steps for effective parent conferences

THE GOAL

A satisfied parent who trusts the school even when a child is having trouble.

SCHEDULING PARENT CONFERENCES

1. Regular parent–teacher conference days are scheduled each semester. You should supplement these regular conferences with a special conference any time you feel one is necessary.

2. If you want to schedule a special conference, the easiest way is to send the form letter, "Request for Conference." Make a copy for the principal, just to keep him or her informed.

3. If a parent requests a conference, inform the principal in writing about the reason for the conference and the time and date of the conference. Doing so enables the principal to stay on top of parent relationships.

4. In scheduling conferences, be sensitive to the fact that most of our parents have full-time jobs. Try to schedule conferences so that they cause minimal inconvenience for you and the parent.

continued

FIGURE 13-2. (cont.)

HOLDING THE PARENT CONFERENCE

1. Begin by welcoming and thanking the parent for coming—even if the parent has requested the conference.

2. If the parent comes with a complaint, try to listen attentively and respond calmly. Avoid becoming defensive or counter-attacking. Most angry parents simply want a chance to be heard.

3. Never discuss other students or their families; keep the focus on the parent and the child.

4. Give the parent full and specific information in an objective manner. Avoid making sweeping judgments or labeling the student's behavior with psychological jargon. Don't say, "Billy is lazy." Say instead, "In math class Billy seems satisfied to meet only the minimum requirements."

5. Even when you have bad news to deliver, try to find something positive to say about the student.

6. Never blame the family. Even if you suspect that family problems may be causing part of the school problem, don't offer such judgments. Report your observations and let the parents interpret them.

7. Parents are entitled to have information about their children's aptitude and achievement. Give such information freely, but also help the parent understand that single test scores need to be interpreted carefully.

ENDING THE CONFERENCE

1. Try to end on a positive note, even if there has been disagreement. Be sure that all parents understand that they can speak with the principal if they are not satisfied with the results of your conference.

2. Make a note for your own records of the time of the conference, the names of the individuals present, and your summary of the conference. If the conference was in any way unpleasant or ended with issues unresolved, give a summary to the principal.

FIGURE 13-3. Survey on parent involvement.

Directions: Listed below in the left-hand column you will find several aspects of our educational program about which parents might have some involvement. Across the top you will find listed several degrees of involvement. For each aspect, indicate with an "X" in the appropriate column the extent of parent involvement you consider desirable.

ASPECT OF EDUCATIONAL PROGRAM	PARENTS DETERMINE ALONE	PARENTS DETERMINE WITH TEACHERS	PARENTS RECOMMENDED	PARENTS HAVE INPUT	PARENTS ARE INFORMED
School goals and their priorities					
Content and priorities of a particular subject					
Elective subjects offered					
Textbooks used					
Qualities of good middle-school teaching					
School activities offered					
Policies and rules governing school activities					
Types of guidance services offered					
Schedule and content of programs for parents					
Pupil grading and reporting system					
School discipline policies and rules					
Programs offered for less able and more gifted pupils					
Student-grouping practices					

FIGURE 13-4.   Questionnaire for parent data base

1. Student's name_____

2. Student's address_____

3. Phone number in emergencies_____

4. Phone number for routine calls_____

5. Father's name_____

6. Father's address, if different from student's_____

7. Mother's name_____

8. Mother's address, if different from student's_____

9. If parents are not living together, which parent should be the primary contact for school purposes?_____

10. Best time for parent conferences:

    Day of week_____ Hours_____

11. Father's occupation_____

12. Mother's occupation_____

13. Parents' availability as educational resources: If either or both parents are available to assist the school, please place an "X" next to the type of service, in the appropriate column:

SERVICE	MOTHER	FATHER
Tutoring	_____	_____
Supervising field trips	_____	_____
Homeroom representative	_____	_____
Career information	_____	_____
Lunchroom playground aide	_____	_____
Classroom aide	_____	_____
Other_____	_____	_____

FIGURE 13-5. Community resource survey

Our middle school is interested in developing a community resource file. We are interested in locating adults from the community who can enrich the educational experiences of our students. There are several ways that you might be able to help: discuss your career, make a presentation about your hobby or special interest, describe your travels, or explain your area of expertise to a class. If you think you can help, please provide us with the following information.

1. Name _____

2. Address _____

3. Telephone number _____

4. Please describe briefly your area of expertise or the type of program you might present. Use the back of this sheet.

5. Please summarize briefly your qualifications as they relate to your area of expertise or the program described.

   _____

   _____

   _____

6. Availability: Please list the days of the week and the hours when you would be available to assist students.

   _____

   _____

   _____

7. References: Please list the name and address of two persons in the community who can be contacted as references.

   _____

   _____

   _____

   _____

PART FIVE

ACHIEVING EXCELLENCE
IN
MIDDLE SCHOOLS

14

Using Evaluation
as the Basis
for Improvement

**Assessment and Evaluation of Programs
in an Effective Middle School**

1. There is a continuing assessment of all the major
   components of the school's program, in order to provide
   administrators and teachers with the data needed for
   systematic school improvement.

2. Particular attention is given to the evaluation and
   monitoring of the curriculum, to ensure that curricular goals
   are being achieved.

One of the hallmarks of effective schools is their use of evaluative data for continued improvement. Consequently, evaluation has been emphasized throughout this book, primarily as a means of establishing a focus for such improvement. This chapter expands on those suggestions and describes a comprehensive approach to school assessment that includes three distinct components—diagnosis, monitoring, and summative evaluation.

NATIONAL AND SCHOOL-BASED ASSESSMENT PROGRAMS

School evaluation is too often reduced to a somewhat cursory analysis of student performance on achievement tests. Although such data are somewhat useful indicators of general accomplishment, educational excellence requires a more comprehensive and systematic approach.

National Assessment Programs

Before we describe in detail how a school-based assessment program can be developed, it might be useful to examine briefly two currently available national assessment programs for middle schools.

The National Study of School Evaluation (NSSE). The National Study of School Evaluation, a professional association concerned primarily with fostering school evaluation for purposes of accreditation, publishes the *Middle School/Junior High School Evaluative Criteria* and assists schools in using these evaluative criteria.[1] The NSSE criteria relate to eleven areas: school and community; philosophy and goals; major educational priorities; design of curriculum; learning areas; individual faculty data; school staff and administration; student activities program; learning media services; student personnel services; school plant and facilities. Most schools using the NSSE materials begin with a year of self-study, during which faculty committees use the criteria in making their own assessments and recommendations. Then, during the following year, an external committee reviews the self-study materials and makes a three-day visit to the school, interviewing, observing, and gathering additional data in preparation for making its own recommendations. Many school administrators who have used the NSSE approach feel that it is much too time-consuming and tedious, although it does produce useful results.

The Middle Grades Assessment Program (MGAP). The Middle Grades Assessment Program, developed and published by the Center for Early Adolescence, is a more recent and perhaps more intensive evaluation program designed expressly for the purposes of school improvement.[2] The MGAP is a self-assessment process ordinarily implemented by a team of six to eighteen staff and parent members who work through a systematic process that involves several steps: reviewing the research on effective middle schools; developing a consensus on the purpose of self-assessment; sharpening their observing and interviewing skills; using the forms to compile interview and observational data; interpreting findings; and developing a plan of action for school improvement. The MGAP is based on nine criteria derived from the research on public expectations for schools, school effectiveness, and early adolescent development. These are the nine criteria:

1. Is the school safe?
2. Is the school academically effective?
3. Is the school responsive to students' needs for diversity?
4. Is the school responsive to students' needs for competence and achievement?
5. Is the school responsive to students' needs for structure and clear limits?
6. Is the school responsive to students' needs for meaningful participation in their school and community?
7. Is the school responsive to students' needs for self-exploration and self-definition?
8. Is the school responsive to students' needs for positive social interaction with both peers and adults?
9. Is the school responsive to students' needs for physical activity?

The MGAP has much to recommend it. It is based on a sound conceptual framework and is supported by reliable research. It emphasizes the importance of using good observational and interview data, not relying solely on the reported perceptions of faculty and students. And it stresses self-evaluation as a keystone of school improvement. However, as one critic has observed, MGAP is "labor-intensive"; this critic has determined that the process will require 400 to 500 person hours of team time over a four-month period.[3]

Both the NSSE and the MGAP self-study approaches can be very useful to middle schools that have the interest and the resources to complete a comprehensive evaluation and want to use materials that have been carefully developed and rigorously evaluated. Other schools that have fewer resources and prefer "home-grown" approaches can develop their own school-based assessment program, making their own decisions about what will be assessed and what assessment approach will be used.

School-Based Assessment Programs

A school-based assessment program makes sense for several reasons. First, a school-based program is more likely to reflect the special needs of that school. Second, a school-based program is more likely to be supported by the faculty, since they will have had an active part in developing it. Finally, a school-based assessment program should be more feasible to implement successfully, as it will have been developed by those who have a realistic sense of the resources available.

An effective and efficient school-based assessment program should include three complementary approaches to assessment:

- *Diagnosis* is a preliminary assessment process concerned primarily with identifying areas for intervention. Undertaken at the outset of projects or instructional interactions, it attempts to answer the question "What should we do?"

- *Monitoring* is a formative assessment process concerned essentially with checking on the current health of the organization. Performed periodically throughout the assessment period, it attempts to answer the question "How are things going?"

- *Summative evaluation*, as the term is used here, is the assessment process concerned with establishing the effectiveness of a program or of an individual. Implemented at some end point, it answers the question "How effective is this?" Summative evaluations are typically undertaken to assist in organizational decision making: "Should this program be continued?" "Should this teacher be granted tenure?"

Although these three approaches can be usefully delineated for examination here, in practice there is much overlapping; a survey of teachers' perceptions about the organizational climate, while diagnostic in intent, can also be seen as an act of monitoring.

How can these three complementary approaches be combined into an effective and efficient assessment program? It seems appropriate to answer this key question by describing each approach in greater detail and then suggesting a process for organizing those components into a comprehensive program.

DIAGNOSING FOR SCHOOL IMPROVEMENT

Throughout this book we have urged the use of several diagnostic processes in order to determine the focus and direction of school improvement efforts. It might therefore be useful at this juncture to summarize those processes and comment on their implementation. As indicated in Figure 14-1, all the diagnostic processes are generally similar in methods used and outcomes intended. The diagnostic process usually encompasses this sequence of steps:

1. Determine which program or programs will be diagnosed.
2. Develop for each program to be evaluated an appropriate set of criteria. The criteria should be derived from the best available theory and research.
3. Use the criteria as the basis for gathering diagnostic data—through observations, interviews, surveys, and document analyses.
4. Analyze the diagnostic data to detrmine improvements needed.

Diagnosis Should Be Ongoing

Even though each school will determine its own approach in implementing these steps, a review of the literature on school improvement does suggest certain guidelines that should be followed. First, the diagnostic efforts should be part of an ongoing concern for organizational renewal, not a series of *ad hoc* measures undertaken in an emergency. Excellent middle schools are committed to such renewal as part of their culture; they have developed an emotional and intellectual disposition toward improvement. Instead of adopting an innovation simply because it seems attractive and is widely publicized, these schools continually assess their programs and develop their own solutions to problems identified by the assessment data.

Diagnosis Should Involve Those Affected

Second, the diagnoses should involve either directly or indirectly all those who will be affected by the changes. Although the members of the small leadership team may play the most active role in initiating and directing the diagnostic efforts, they should have the advice of all the teachers and have suitable input from parents and students. Educational changes are most enduring when those changes are supported by a well-organized constituency—and the constituency should be built from the outset, when the diagnosis begins.

Diagnosis Should Be Part of a Comprehensive Plan

Third, the diagnoses should be undertaken as part of a systematic and comprehensive plan for school improvement. The leadership team should decide which components should be diagnosed and in what priority, being careful not to overburden the system with too much assessment or too many changes. Teachers will become impatient with too many questionnaires and confused by too many changes.

Diagnosis Should Be Communicated to All Involved Parties

Next, there should be full communication about those plans. Teachers especially should be completely informed about which components will be diagnosed, how the diagnosis will be performed, and what use will be made of the diagnostic data. Finally, of course, the diagnostic data should be used. Even if the data indicate that no serious problem exists with a given component, the information should be analyzed to determine the probable factors contributing to its success.

These guidelines provide some tentative answers for those responsible for the diagnostic part of the assessment program. Along with the recommendations offered in previous chapters, they suggest a diagnostic system with the following features:

1. The school curriculum should be diagnosed perhaps once every four years to assess the fit between curricular goals and curricular offerings. This major undertaking should be performed by a representative team whose members have access to sufficient resources to do the job effectively.

2. All teachers receiving clinical supervision should be diagnosed throughout the supervisory cycle, in order to determine which skills should be emphasized. The diagnosis should be performed by those providing the clinical supervision.

3. The other five components of middle-school excellence—the activity program, the guidance program, school climate, the organizational structure—should be diagnosed periodically, either as called for by a predetermined schedule or as suggested by an analysis of school needs. Experience suggests that no more than two components should be diagnosed in a given year. The diagnosis should be directed by the leadership team, with significant involvement of all those affected.

These features should be embodied in the school's comprehensive assessment plan.

MONITORING THE ORGANIZATION'S HEALTH

Monitoring is an important assessment process that is often disparaged by educators who impugn its intent and question its usefulness. They speak derisively of "snooper-vision," conjuring up the image of a distrustful administrator watching the side doors, clocking the time when teachers arrive and leave; and they argue somewhat naïvely that it lacks any value in a healthy organization. Such disparagement is unwarranted. Monitoring can be carried out in an atmosphere of trust and openness by a leader who can explain and exemplify the difference between watchfulness and suspicion. And its usefulness is well documented: Most of the studies on school effectiveness note the importance of monitoring as a function of instructional leadership.[4] The principal who does not monitor is like the engineer who never checks the pressure gauges.

MONITORING FOR SCHOOL IMPROVEMENT

Monitoring will be most effective if, again, certain guidelines are followed. First, as noted previously, the monitoring should be conducted in an open atmosphere of trust. Those doing the monitoring should communicate fully with the faculty about the foci, purposes, and methods of the monitoring component. Second, because monitoring connotes a managerial review, it should probably be considered an administrative function, not a teacher's responsibility. Teachers should be fully involved in the process but should not have primary responsibility for the implementation of the process. Third, monitoring should be carried out on an ongoing basis, not performed sporadically or periodically; it is designed to provide current information for decision makers. Finally, because it should be a continuing function of administration and will therefore consume considerable administrative time, the monitoring process should focus on a few priority areas.

These guidelines and the recommendations offered in previous chapters suggest that the following features should be embodied in the monitoring program:

1. The curriculum should be monitored closely and intensively through the processes described here. The purpose of curriculum monitoring is to determine if the written curriculum is actually being implemented.

2. Instruction should also be carefully monitored, using the processes described in Chapter 8. You will remember that those processes involve brief, unannounced classroom visits carried out on a systematic basis by an administrator. The chief purpose of instructional monitoring is to ensure that teachers are satisfactorily carrying out their instructional assignments.

3. The school climate should also be monitored on a continuing basis, as it is subject to frequent change and is an important indicator of overall organizational health. The purpose of climate monitoring is to be preactive rather than reactive—to stay on top of organizational problems. The processes for monitoring school climate are explained briefly in the following section.

4. The other components—the activity program, the guidance program, the organizational structures, and the community program—should be monitored only if administrators perceive a critical need for close attention. These components are important and from time to time may need close attention, but they should not require the close surveillance given to curriculum, instruction, and climate. A realistic monitoring program should not overtax administrative resources.

How should the monitoring be carried out? The answer depends upon what is being monitored. Curriculum monitoring and climate monitoring are both very different processes.

Curriculum Monitoring to Ensure Consistency in Meeting Mastery Objectives

Curriculum monitoring is a process of determining to what extent the teachers are actually teaching the objectives specified in the written curriculum guides. Its purpose is to improve learning by ensuring consistency throughout the curriculum. Many teachers object to curriculum monitoring, complaining that it inhibits their creativity and reduces their autonomy. The mastery curriculum approach, as explained in Chapter 5, seems to invalidate such complaints. The mastery curriculum concept gives teachers complete freedom with methods they use and grants them autonomy in the enrichment content. If you use the mastery curriculum system, then you monitor only to be sure that the mastery objectives are taught.

How can the curriculum be monitored? Several different approaches are possible.

Monitor by observing. An administrator or supervisor visits each class and checks on the content taught. Although this method yields the most reliable data, it is simply not feasible; there are just not enough administrators and supervisors to monitor every class.

Monitor by surveying students. An administrator or supervisor surveys the students periodically to ask them what they were taught in a particular class. This method does not yield very reliable data, as most students do not remember what they were taught.

Monitor by checking daily lesson plans. Some principals require that all teachers submit at the end of the week their lesson plans for the coming week; the principal reviews the plans and makes appropriate comments. Some teachers value such checking; they believe it indicates that the principal cares about teaching. Most teachers question its value and resent the fact that they must submit detailed written plans. The checking of lesson plans has two other drawbacks as a monitoring device: It does not yield reliable data, as there are often major discrepancies between the written plan and the delivered plan; and it requires a great deal of teacher and administrator time.

Monitor by reviewing long-term plans. The teachers submit unit or semester plans that are checked by an administrator or supervisor for content coverage. This review of unit or semester plans has two advantages over the checking of daily plans: It takes less time, and it encourages teachers to master the skills of long-term planning. The long-term planning helps teachers think about the matter of time allocation, a critical factor in student learning.

One variation of this long-term review involves a system that relates yearly and marking-period plans. First, each department develops from its mastery curriculum guide a complete list of general mastery concepts and skills for each grade level. At the start of the year, each teacher indicates when he or she plans to teach the concepts and skills listed and also notes any intention to omit specific content. This annual checklist is then reviewed by an administrator or supervisor, who has an opportunity to discuss with the teacher any issues raised by the annual plan. The teacher then uses the approved annual plan to develop a quarterly or marking-period plan, which indicates tentative time allocations. Figures 14-2 and 14-3 illustrate how such plans might be reported.

The main drawback to the long-term report is that it also lacks reliability; there is no assurance that the teacher taught what he or she planned to teach.

Monitor by reviewing teacher reports of what was taught. The teacher submits a report of what he or she taught during the previous week, marking period, or term. Many school systems use this approach to curriculum monitoring, again using a checklist format to simplify reporting. Besides lacking reliability, this retrospective report does not give instructional leaders an opportunity to have input into plans; they can criticize only after the fact.

Monitor by administering examinations. Each department prepares a comprehensive examination based upon the curriculum; the examination results are used both to check on student progress and to monitor the curriculum. This monitoring system seems to be increasingly used by school districts concerned with curriculum accountability. It is appealing because it fulfills a two-fold purpose: The test scores are indicators of student achievement and yield some measure of curriculum coverage. The chief drawback with using examinations lies in the difficulty of developing valid and reliable examinations. In general, examinations produced at the district level are not of high quality; for example, some sample materials distributed by one large urban school district included four items in which the "correct" answer was either wrong or debatable.

Obviously, there is no perfect system for monitoring the curriculum. The leadership team, therefore, should either adopt one that seems most acceptable to the teachers or give teams an option. If the latter choice seems preferable, the leaders should review the six methods just described, decide which ones seem most appropriate for that school, and then let each team choose from the approved list the monitoring system it will implement.

Climate Monitoring to Indicate Possible Trouble Ahead

Climate monitoring is also important because changes in the school climate often act as an "early warning system"—preliminary indicators of more serious trouble ahead. It is therefore important for one of the administrators to assume responsibility for monitoring the school climate. These are the systems that can be used to accomplish this task:

Keep a barometer of student and teacher attendance. Sharp declines in attendance suggest that some serious problems might be developing.

Keep records of student tardiness. A certain amount of lateness is both predictable and unavoidable; marked increases may be a symptom of problems in student motivation and attitude.

Maintain careful records of discipline referrals. Many schools now computerize all discipline referrals, noting identifying information about the student, the staff member referring the problem, the day, the time, the place, and the discipline problem. Administrators are thus able to analyze the data both to note general trends and to understand some of the root causes. For example, a sharp increase in the number of referrals from the lunchroom on Mondays may be the result of some weekend confrontations in the community.

Check closely on utilization of support services. The number of students seeing the nurse, guidance counselor, or school psychologist is a general indicator of student well-being. The data, of course, need to be probed carefully; a large number of students visiting the health suite may indicate one of several things—virus attacks, examination fever, or school fatigue.

Monitor the appearance of the building. Vandalism and graffiti may be only the result of adolescent mischief-making—or may be an expression of some deep-seated hostility toward the school and its staff.

The best monitoring system will track all these data, giving the administrators a rich "weather report" of how things are going at the school.

SUMMATIVE EVALUATIONS FOR SCHOOL IMPROVEMENT

The final aspect of the assessment program is summative evaluation—making summative judgments for purposes of administrative decision making. A review of the evaluation literature and the previous chapters in this book suggest the following evaluation guidelines.

First, those performing the summative evaluation should be clear about the purposes for conducting the evaluation and the uses to be made of the evaluation data. No evaluation should be carried out unless there is a specific plan for using the results. Second, those affected by the evaluation should play an active role in determining the criteria to be used, the data to be gathered, and the analyses to be performed. Evaluation has such long-lasting impact that full involvement here is essential, not simply desirable. Next, any criteria used in making summative evaluations should be derived by a careful analysis of that which is to be evaluated and by a review of the pertinent literature. Using inappropriate criteria will result in invalid evaluations.

Fourth, any judgments made with respect to each criterion should be based upon and supported with objective data—and multiple data sources should be used wherever possible. Evaluation can never be fully free of a subjective element, but the use of multiple sources of objective data will make the final judgments fairer and more valid.

Finally, because summative evaluations should be made only when some administrative decision is likely to be made, it makes sense to evaluate only those components where such decisions are anticipated. Making rigorous evaluations is a time-consuming process, and administrators should focus their evaluation efforts on areas of priority need.

FEATURES OF A SCHOOL-BASED
ASSESSMENT PROGRAM

These guidelines suggest that the following features would be desirable in a school-based assessment program:

1. The curriculum should be evaluated carefully on a regular cycle, in order to decide if important modifications should be made. A process for evaluating the curriculum is described here.
2. Instruction should be evaluated in order to make personnel decisions—retain, dismiss, promote, grant tenure, and so on. The procedures used here will be those mandated by the state and required by the school district.
3. The activity program and the guidance program should be evaluated perhaps every three or four years in order to determine if major changes are needed in content and structure. (Note that the programs, not the personnel, should be evaluated; the personnel will be evaluated as part of the system's standard procedures for personnel assessment.) The criteria used should be derived from the goals allocated to those programs and from an analysis of the relevant literature.
4. School climate, organizational structure, and the community program should be evaluated only if major changes are contemplated. Although these components should undergo continuing diagnosis and periodic monitoring, summative evaluations are less likely to be needed here.

These features should be reflected in the school's comprehensive evaluation program.

Curriculum Evaluation in a School-Based Assessment Program

Curriculum evaluation is such an important and complex process that it probably needs separate attention here. The following process has been used successfully in several evaluations.

Evaluate all major subject areas. The process begins by developing a regular schedule for evaluating all the major subject areas in the school's curriculum. Because effective curriculum evaluation takes considerable time, perhaps no more than one academic subject area should be evaluated each year. The order should, of course, reflect the leadership's team perceptions of need. Here is what a typical schedule might look like:

1986–87: English language arts
1987–88: mathematics
1988–89: science

1989–90: social studies

1990–91: any other curriculum area where a need is evident

Determine the scope of curriculum evaluation. The next step in the process is to determine the scope of the curriculum evaluation. Which components of that curriculum should be evaluated? A very comprehensive curriculum evaluation could measure all these components: curricular goals; the scope and sequence of level objectives; the written course guides; time allocations; the taught curriculum; the tested curriculum; the learned curriculum; and the instructional materials. Too often those who evaluate the curriculum limit their attention to the written course guides and the learned curriculum—and by doing so, ignore those other vital components.

However, few schools can evaluate every component. Priorities have to be determined and decisions made based upon the resources available. Perhaps the most efficient way of assessing priorities is to use a survey form similar to that shown in Figure 14-4. It lists all the components of the curriculum and for each identifies several criteria. The form is distributed to all who have a stake in the process: district administrators, school administrators, teachers, and representative parents. Each person is asked to report his or her evaluation priorities by rating each criterion—highly important to me, moderatley important to me, less important to me. The ratings given to each criterion are collated, and those responsible for the evaluation determine which of the top-rated criteria will be used in the evaluation process, given the resources available.

This step in the process ensures that the evaluation will focus on those elements considered most important by the stakeholders. It avoids the trap of being too narrow—but does not overtax the resources of the institution.

For each criterion thus identified, the evaluators then determine the data sources to be used and the standards to be applied. Here is an example of how this might be done:

COMPONENT: Goals
CRITERION: Are the goals understood and accepted by classroom
  teachers?
DATA SOURCES: Survey of all teachers who teach that subject
STANDARDS:
    1.75 percent of those surveyed will correctly identify 75 percent
      of the goals of that curriculum, as stated in the district curricu-
      lum guide.
    2.75 percent of those surveyed will indicate acceptance of those
      goals.

Those statements thus constitute a set of specifications for the curriculum evaluation. The evaluators then proceed to use those specifications in conducting the evaluation. The results of the evaluation are then shared with all those involved and used in making decisions as to how that curriculum should be modified.

Developing the School-Based Assessment Program

The suggestions given in the previous section about diagnosing, monitoring, and evaluating should assist the leadership team in developing a comprehensive and systematic school-based assessment program. Most schools will find that a three-year evaluation plan is useful; it provides sufficient time for long-range planning without making commitments too far into the future. For each aspect of evaluation, the leaders should answer certain specific questions, as follows:

DIAGNOSIS

1. Which components will be diagnosed during each of the next three years?
2. Which diagnostic measures will be used?
3. Who will be responsible for conducting each diagnosis?
4. What use will be made of diagnostic data?

MONITORING

1. How will the curriculum be monitored—and who will be responsible in each area?
2. Will all teachers receive instructional monitoring—or only those who have not opted for other forms of supervision? Which administrator will be responsible for the monitoring?
3. Who will be responsible for monitoring the school climate? Which measures will be used?
4. During the next three years, is it anticipated that any other component will be monitored? If so, which? When? By whom? How?

SUMMATIVE EVALUATION

1. During the next three years, which curricula will be evaluated? Who will be responsible?
2. Who will be responsible for personnel evaluation?
3. Will the guidance or the activity program be evaluated? If so, when, by whom, and how?
4. Will any other component be evaluated? If so, which? When? By whom? How?

These answers should, of course, be reviewed by district administrators and by the teachers, with suitable revisions to reflect the input received.

Notes

1. National Study of School Evaluation, *Middle School/Junior High School Evaluative Criteria: A Guide for School Improvement* (Arlington, VA, 1979).

2. Gayle Dorman, "Making Schools Work for Young Adolescents," *Educational Horizons* 61 (1983), 175–82.

3. Ross Zerchykov, "The Middle Grades Assessment Program in Action," *Citizens Action in Education*, 10 (1984), 1, 8.

4. K. A. Leithwood and D. J. Montgomery, "The Role of the Elementary School Principal in School Improvement," *Review of Educational Research*, 52 (1982), 309–39.

FIGURE 14-1.   Summary of diagnostic assessments

SCHOOL COMPONENT	DIAGNOSTIC ASSESSMENTS
Curriculum	Compare curricular goals with curricula to determine where and how curricula can be strengthened.
Teaching	Use diagnostic observations to determine which teaching skills should be improved.
Activity Program	Evaluate program against criteria of effectiveness to determine improvements needed.
Guidance Program	Use assessment data to determine how guidance services can be improved.
School Climate	Use criteria of desirable climate to determine which climate aspects should be modified.
Organizational Structure	Use criteria of effective organizational structure to effect organic improvements.
Community	Assess parent and community relationships to determine focus of improvement efforts.

FIGURE 14-2. Annual monitoring plan

Teacher: *Joe Williamson*   Class: *8th grade, level 1*

	MARKING PERIODS			
GENERAL MASTERY CONCEPTS	1	2	3	4
Grammar				
1. Participial phrase	x			
2. Adjective clause		x		
3. Adverb clause		x		
4. Complex sentence			x	
Composition				
1. Sentence combining	x	x	x	x
2. Expository essay	x			
3. Persuasive essay		x		
4. Personal narrative			x	
5. Library paper				x

Request approval not to teach following general mastery concepts:
Literature: do not plan to teach "theme" in the novel; seems too difficult for my eighth-graders.

FIGURE 14-3. Quarterly monitoring plan

Teacher: *Joe Williamson*   Class: *8th grade, level 1*   Marking period: *2*

GENERAL MASTERY CONCEPTS TO BE TAUGHT	TIME ALLOCATED
1. Participial phrase	1 week
2. Sentence combining	1 week
3. Expository essay	1 week
4. Short story: plot, setting	2 weeks
4. Interviewing	1 week
5. Mass media: evaluating documentaries	2 weeks

ENRICHMENT	TIME ALLOCATED
1. Language change	1 week

FIGURE 14-4.   Criteria for curriculum evaluation

Directions: What questions should we try to answer in evaluating our _____ curriculum? We would like your opinion about this matter. Below you will find the major aspects of a curriculum evaluation identified. For each aspect several questions are listed. Read each question and tell us how important you consider it in evaluating this curriculum. Give us your opinion by writing one of these letters next to each question:

> *H—I consider this question **highly important**.*
> *M—I consider this question **moderately important**.*
> *L—I consider this question **less important**.*

ASPECT AND QUESTION	YOUR RATING

GOALS

1. Are the goals of this discipline, subject, or field of study clearly and explicitly stated and readily accessible to those who need to refer to them?

2. Are the goals consonant with the general goals of the school district?

3. Are the goals in accord with the recommendations of experts in the field?

4. Are the goals in accord with the state guidelines and requirements?

5. Are the goals understood and supported by parents?

6. Are the goals understood and supported by school administrators?

7. Are the goals understood and supported by classroom teachers?

8. Are the goals understood and supported by students?

continued

FIGURE 14-4. (cont.)

ASPECT AND QUESTION	YOUR RATING

SCOPE AND SEQUENCE OF LEVEL OBJECTIVES

1. Have the goals been analyzed into a set of grade-level (or achievement-level) objectives that identify the important concepts, skills, and attitudes?

2. Are those level objectives sufficiently comprehensive that they adequately respond to the goals of the curriculum?

3. Do the objectives seem attainable, given the nature of the learner for whom they are intended?

4. Are those level objectives clearly displayed in some form that makes them readily understood and easily used by administrators and teachers?

5. Are the grade-level objectives in accord with the recommendations of experts in the field?

6. Does the grade placement of objectives reflect the best current knowledge of child development?

7. Does the grade placement of objectives provide for sufficient reinforcement without undue repetition?

8. Are the objectives appropriately distributed over the grades so that there is adequate balance between the grades?

9. Does the grade placement of particular level objectives suggest adequate growth and development in complexity?

WRITTEN COURSE GUIDES

1. Are there written course guides that are readily available to administrators, parents, and teachers?

2. Does the format of the guides facilitate modification, amplification, and revision?

3. Do the guides clearly specify grade-level objectives in a format that teachers can readily understand and easily use?

4. Do the guides distinguish between essential skills and concepts and enrichment content?

5. Do the guides distinguish between objectives that require planning, instruction, and assessment—and those that can be developed incidentally and informally?

continued

FIGURE 14-4. (cont.)

ASPECT AND QUESTION	YOUR RATING

6. Do the guides indicate clearly the relative importance of the objectives so that teachers can make appropriate planning decisions?

7. Do the guides suggest ways of organizing objectives into learning units, without requiring a particular unit organization?

8. Do the guides suggest teaching/learning activities, without requiring that a particular model of teaching and learning be used?

9. Does it seem likely that the teaching and learning activities suggested will lead to the achievement of the objectives for which they were specified?

10. Do the teaching and learning activities suggested reflect the best current knowledge about teaching and learning?

11. Do the guides suggest evaluation processes that provide for appropriate assessment of achievement?

12. Do the guides recommend appropriate instructional materials and resources?

TIME ALLOCATIONS

1. Has the school district clearly specified the time that will be allocated to this field of study?

2. Does the time allocated to this field of study seem appropriate in relation to the district's goals, the goals of this field of study, and the recommendations of experts?

3. Does the school's schedule or administrative guidelines about the use of time adequately respond to the district's time allocations?

4. Are teachers given guidelines about allocating time within that field of study, so that classroom time allocations reflect curricular priorities?

THE TAUGHT CURRICULUM

1. Do the teachers allocate time to this field of study in accordance with district and school guidelines?

2. Do the teachers allocate time within the field in a way that reflects curricular priorities?

continued

FIGURE 14-4. (cont.)

ASPECT AND QUESTION	YOUR RATING

3. Do the teachers teach for the objectives specified for that grade level?

4. Do the teaching activities used reflect the best current knowledge about teaching and learning in that field of study?

THE TESTED CURRICULUM

1. Does the district provide curriculum-based tests that help administrators and teachers assess pupil mastery?

2. Do those tests adequately reflect and correspond to the written course guides?

3. Does the district make use of standardized tests that provide comparative data on achievement in this field of study?

4. Do the standardized tests adequately reflect and correspond to the written course guides?

THE LEARNED CURRICULUM

1. Do pupils believe that what they are learning is useful, meaningful, and interesting?

2. Do pupils achieve the specified objectives at a satisfactory level?

THE INSTRUCTIONAL MATERIALS

1. Do the textbooks and other materials in use adequately reflect and correspond to the written course guides?

2. Can pupils understand the textbooks and other materials in use?

3. Are the textbooks and other materials sufficiently responsive to teachers' needs and requirements?

15

Making Staff Development Work

Staff Development in an Effective Middle School

1. There is a systematic and continuing staff development program in which the principal and the teachers work together to improve the school and solve emerging school problems.

2. The staff development program helps administrators and teachers respond effectively to the special developing needs of young adolescents.

Staff development has become one of the most thoroughly researched topics in the field of education. That body of research provides both a rationale for emphasizing staff development and specific guidelines for developing programs. The rationale can be presented quite simply: according to several research reviews, effective staff development is essential for the successful implementation of any new program or for the systematic improvement of existing programs.[1] The principle undergirding its importance seems clear enough: New or improved programs require changes in teacher behavior—and effective staff development is the best way to change such behavior.

Note that throughout this book we have emphasized the importance of staff development in helping teachers acquire specific knowledge and skills. This chapter deals with a general staff development strategy that embodies four related steps: developing the ideal program based upon the research; modifying the ideal by analyzing the constraints; assessing needs and preferences; planning the program.

DEVELOPING THE IDEAL PROGRAM

The first step in the process is to develop an ideal program based upon your knowledge of the research. This step gives you a view of what could be done if all conditions were right and resources were unlimited; it enables you to conceptualize an ideal goal that you can then modify to fit the real world you know.

What would be the characteristics of an ideal staff development program? Here the research is especially useful in offering specific guidelines about duration, management, content, learning activities, site, and instructors. These guidelines are summarized in Figure 15-1 and discussed briefly here.

Timing Is Critical in Staff Development

To be effective, staff development programs should be ongoing ones that provide ample opportunity for complex skill development at the time those skills are most needed. Consider first the matter of duration. In too many school systems, when staff development is offered, it consists of a one-day workshop or two or three after-school meetings. Such "one shot" approaches are a waste of time and resources. Joyce and Showers report their own rule of thumb, which is that teachers learning a new instructional strategy require fifteen to twenty demonstrations and at least a dozen opportunities to practice the skill.[2] The ideal program should last at least several months on a continuing basis.

And the ideal program should be timely. It should deal with skills that teachers need now, not at some distant point in the future. Suppose, for example, that your faculty members decide in April that they will implement cooperative learning in selected classrooms during the succeeding fall term. They will need an orientation session in April or May to understand the basic principles and perhaps a summer workshop to develop new learning materials; however, they will feel the most urgent need for training in the fall, when the new program is implemented and problems develop.

Planning and Management Must Work Hand in Hand

Ideal staff development programs require collaborative planning and management. The principal should participate in the program as a means of both demonstrating support and developing professional skills—but should not dominate the planning or implementation. The teachers need to feel ownership of the program, and too much control by the principal will militate against this goal. Teachers should play an active role in setting the agenda, in determining the structure of the program, and in directing the learning activities. The program should be continually monitored, with adjustments made in response to changing needs; such monitoring is best accomplished by a small team of participants who have the trust and respect of the others.

Ensure Meaningful Content in Skill Development Programs

The content of the program will vary from school to school, but the research offers some general principles that can be useful here. First, the staff development program should emphasize the skills that teachers believe they need in meeting new demands of their professional roles. Administrators, of course, will frequently have to provide leadership in creating an awareness of that need, but they should not require that teachers suffer through sessions dealing with skills or knowledge that the participants consider irrelevant.

Those new skills should not be presented simply as a bag of tricks without a knowledge base. Instead, those skills should be grounded in appropriate theory, as the theoretical foundation will ensure better retention and transfer of the skills. The theoretical grounding is also essential in developing "executive control"— understanding the purpose of the skill, knowing how to adapt it for particular students and subject matter, and learning how to integrate it with other skills. It is a complex mental ability that governs the effective use of the skill in unpredictable settings. And the research suggests that this executive control requires an intellectual understanding of the skill being mastered.

Suppose, for example, that you want all teachers to use writing as a way of learning in all the disciplines. Before they try to develop strategies for using writing in their disciplines, they should understand the theory: Writing is a way of knowing; it can be used in several ways at different points in the learning process. Knowing that theory helps them see the skill in broad terms and gives them some flexibility in knowing when and how to use it.

Note also that the program should aim to help teachers master those skills to a high degree, not simply acquire a superficial understanding. Too often trainers explain a new skill, demonstrate it once or twice, and then lead teachers in a discussion of its use. The result of such an approach is predictable: Teachers never use the skill because they really have not mastered it; they have only observed and talked about it. To promote mastery, the program's content should emphasize the need for transfer of training: The goal is to be able to use this complex skill in the classroom, not just talk about it. Teachers should understand that transfer is the goal—but should also be cautioned about the problems involved in transferring any new skill to a complex environment like the classroom.

Finally, in considering matters of content, keep in mind, of course, the indicator mentioned at the start of this chapter: Middle-school staff development programs should give continuing attention to the needs of young adolescents.

Use Learning Activities to Help Teachers
Share Their Strengths

The typical staff development session uses the lecture-discussion approach: The consultant presents information and leads the teachers in discussing it. Such an approach, the research suggests, is entirely ineffective in changing behavior or developing new skills. The ideal program makes extensive use of active learning strategies: Teachers demonstrate the skill to one another, role play situations requiring the use of the skill, and produce and share teaching/learning materials related to the skill. The staff development session thus becomes a training laboratory in which new skills can be tried out in a safe and supportive environment. But the learning doesn't stop with the training session itself; each participant tries out the skill in his or her own classroom, getting feedback from a colleague who has also participated in the training. This colleagial coaching model, strongly advocated by Joyce and Showers as the optimal method of acquiring new teaching skills, is obviously quite compatible with the cooperative professional development model of supervision recommended in Chapter 8.

Use Local Sites and Local Instructors:
Home-Grown Works Best

The local school, rather than the university, seems to be a better site for staff development, according to the research, and local teachers, not outside consultants, should compose the instructional staff. The expert consultant can be brought in from time to time to present a different perspective or provide current information—but should not play the chief instructional role. Teachers distrust the visiting expert; they trust only other teachers who live in their same world.

Those, then, are the features that would characterize the ideal staff development program. If you had all the resources and freedom you needed, that is the kind of program you would plan.

MODIFYING THE IDEAL BY ASSESSING
THE CONSTRAINTS WITHIN WHICH
YOU MUST WORK

Now you have to modify that ideal to suit the real conditions you face. You do that by assessing the constraints and making appropriate modifications.

Assess Your Constraints Realistically

You assess the constraints by determining realistically the boundaries within which you must work. Those boundaries are determined by several factors.

The first factor is the expectations of district administrators. Even though the research indicates the importance of responding to needs the teachers identify, the superintendent may have decreed, for example, that all teachers should learn how to work with handicapped children. The second factor is the limits imposed by the teachers' contract or by district policies. Even though you are aware that longer sessions are needed for the development of complex skills, the teachers' contract or district policies might require after-school sessions to end one hour after dismissal.

A third factor that must be considered is the resources available. The ideal program assumes that time, money, space, and people are all available. In the real world of your school, all those resources are in short supply. Finally, you must confront the limitations inherent in the participants themselves: Your teachers may not be interested in extensive staff development programs; they are too busy with graduate courses, second jobs, or family responsibilities.

All these factors will limit what you can do and will require that you make some modifications. Let's examine next their nature.

Modify the Duration and Timing of the Program

Even though the research is clear about the need for ongoing programs of suitable length, most school systems find it difficult to achieve this ideal. In some cases the teachers' contract stands in the way, restricting the length and frequency of after-school sessions and specifying the compensation to be paid to participants. In other cases, the school system lacks the resources to support extensive programs. In still others, teachers feel too busy and prefer briefer programs, even though they know that such programs will probably be ineffective.

Successful middle schools have used several different strategies for coping with these constraints.

Enlist volunteers. Offering the program only to volunteers has several advantages: It may avoid contract constraints; it requires fewer resources because smaller numbers are enrolled; and it excuses those who feel too busy. The voluntary program, however, also has two major drawbacks: It does not reach those who may most need the training; it can create a sense of elitism and separateness among those who experience the training.

Pool resources. The problem of insufficient resources can often be dealt with by cooperating with other schools or districts in a joint staff development program. Such cooperative programs cost less for each participating system, but they run the risk of becoming too general in their approach and fail to deal with the specific problems of the participating schools.

Combine time. School districts ordinarily have four types of staff development schedules: summer workshops, inservice days, faculty meetings, and after-school sessions. When time is a problem, one solution is to combine two or more of these options, rather than relying solely on one. Thus, a school might decide on a three-part strategy: Use an inservice day to get the new program off to a fast start; hold four longer after-school sessions to develop the skill in depth; and use faculty meetings to reinforce the skill.

And, of course, the timing may have to be modified. Although the best time is at the moment of greatest need, you may have to compromise here. If your district will support a summer workshop but not a continuing program during the school year, you should use the summer workshop to accomplish all you can and then deal on an *ad hoc* basis with problems that emerge during the school year.

Be Flexible in Managing the Program

Although the research supports a cooperative management model, some middle schools by choice or necessity have successfully used other approaches. In schools where there is a high level of trust between the principal and the teachers, the principal can play a more active role in organizing and conducting the staff development without being seen as manipulative and without the teachers' feeling disenfranchised. In smaller schools where the leadership team is in close touch with the teachers, formal involvement of all teachers in identifying the agenda and the structure may be unnecessary.

Adapt the Program's Content as Necessary

The research suggests an ambitious agenda: complex skills supported by theory and taught to a high degree of accomplishment. Each of these may require some modification, depending upon local resources and needs. First, you may see fit to teach only a few simpler skills. For example, rather than trying to train teachers in the more complicated task of using cooperative groups, you might decide to emphasize only one aspect, such as organizing and monitoring small-group performance. Also, you may see fit to reduce or increase the theoretical component, depending upon the nature of the group. Less mature teachers seem impatient with theory; highly intelligent leaders who think abstractly become impatient with "tricks of the trade" and want more theory.

And, of course, you may have to be satisfied with less than high accomplishment, although it is one place where compromise is rather undesirable. Suppose, for example, that you want all teachers to emphasize critical thinking in their disciplines. You may decide, because of time limitations, just to introduce the skill to all teachers in the staff development sessions, hoping that a few will become sufficiently interested to pursue the topic on their own.

Vary the Learning Activities to Suit the Situation

It will not always be feasible or desirable for staff development programs to embody all the learning approaches supported by the research. Some teachers may actually prefer discussion to the more active materials development, role playing, and demonstration. A sensitive leader will make the necessary accommodations by using some of the individualization strategies suggested here. And in some schools, the conditions for classroom follow-up and colleagial feedback may not be present. These colleagial coaching approaches seem to require adequate time during the school day, a climate of trust and openness among all members of the faculty, a willingness on the part of teachers, and a supportive administration. If one or more of these conditions is absent, the leader may wisely decide to limit development efforts to the workshop sessions, rather than extending them into the classroom.

Use Consultants Where Necessary

Although the research supports "home-grown" staff development programs, both site and instructors may be suitably modified. Site seems less important; as long as there are convenient facilities and a welcoming environment, teachers may not care too much about the actual location. The staffing of the program, however, seems more crucial: Wherever possible, local classroom teachers should be used to instruct. If, however, it is not possible to find local classroom teachers competent to lead the sessions, then there are two options that can work. Some middle schools have used staff development teams composed of one or two consultants and one or two teachers: The consultants bring the theory and the professional expertise; the teachers, the knowledge of the classroom and the students. And in some cases consultants have been used to train a school-based leadership team that then takes over and does the actual teaching.

By this process, you now have established the general features of the best feasible program—you began with an ideal and you made only the essential compromises. You might find it useful to summarize the decisions you might make by using a chart like the one shown in Figure 15-2.

ASSESSING TEACHERS' NEEDS
AND PREFERENCES

By this process, you have developed the general features of the staff development program. Now you need to assess teachers' needs and their preferences for structure.

Teachers' Needs Assessment

Needs assessment is not a simple process of asking teachers what they want to do on inservice day. It is instead a more complex process that involves three related tasks—analyzing demands, determining priorities, and surveying preferences. Although the leadership team plays a key role in completing these tasks, they should involve teachers throughout the process, thus creating an awareness of need through continuing dialogue.

The leadership team must first analyze the new demands that teachers are confronting in their professional roles. Those new demands emerge from several sources: a new technology, like the computer; changes in the student population, such as the influx of a large number of immigrant children; changes in the curriculum, such as a new humanities course; a new instructional approach, such as the use of cooperative learning; or a new organizational structure, like a block-of-time schedule. In a sense, the leaders ask themselves this question: "What new skills do our teachers most need in order to function successfully in a changed environment?" In analyzing these new demands, the leaders should get input from the teachers themselves by holding informal discussions in faculty and team meetings.

This analysis of demands should result in a rather comprehensive list of possible staff development foci. Here is an example of such a comprehensive list drawn from the improvement strategies described in previous chapters:

- Understanding the nature of young adolescents and using that knowledge in the classroom
- Developing the mastery curriculum
- Teaching for mastery
- Strengthening our activity program
- Improving the guidance function
- Communicating high expectations
- Making team planning and assessing more effective
- Holding more effective parent conferences
- Developing and using curriculum based tests

This list, of course, is only representative. The school's leadership team should develop its own comprehensive list of possible program topics.

The second task is determining the school's priorities. Because the school most likely lacks the resources to implement all those programs effectively, some prioritizing is essential. The prioritizing process attempts to identify three or four areas of critical need. Which problems faced by the school are considered most acute? Which program will most likely bring about the greatest improvement? Here again, the leadership team should take the initiative in their own deliberations but should also get continued input from teachers. At this stage, teacher input can be secured either through faculty discussions or surveys; open discussions in small groups are probably preferable, as they provide more of an opportunity to hear multiple viewpoints and to reflect together about these key issues.

The third task is to assess preferences. If the foregoing process has been followed, the leadership team with significant teacher input has been able to identify three or four possible areas of staff development. The process itself has created an awareness and deepened understanding. Now a survey can produce meaningful results, not superficial responses. The leaders can use a form similar to the one shown in Figure 15-3 to assess teacher preferences for content.

Teachers' Preferences for Program Structure

The final step before actually planning the program is to assess teachers' preferences about the structure of the program. Even though the research indicates which structures are generally more effective, teachers vary considerably in their readiness to learn from particular structures. For example, although the research suggests that active learning is more effective than passive listening, many teachers prefer to learn from listening to presentations and are impatient with "kindergarten activities." One researcher concludes that these preferences actually reflect differences in teachers' conceptual development.[3] Those at a lower level of conceptual maturity prefer highly structured programs that emphasize practical ideas; they like to listen to authorities who can tell them what to do and show them how to do it. Those at a higher level of conceptual development prefer more open-ended programs with group discussion; they want to raise questions, explore issues, and listen to conflicting points of view.

One easy way to survey preferences for structure is to use a form like the one shown in Figure 15-4. The thirteen items, which focus on the critical issues of structure, can elicit useful information that can help you determine the structure of your staff development program.

If the survey reveals some marked differences among the teachers, you have three options. The simplest, of course, is use the structures that most teachers prefer. If you have sufficient resources, you can offer two programs that embody different structures. One program, for example, might emphasize the theoretical issues, with teachers leading small-group discussions; the other program would have a consultant make a brief presentation, followed by classroom teachers demonstrating some practical applications. The third option would be to offer a program that reflects the preferences of most of the teachers, with some options to provide for their differences. For example, the general session for all teachers might begin with a brief presentation by a consultant explaining the theoretical aspects; following that presentation, teachers could either attend small-group discussion sessions to explore the issues or could participate in a hands-on workshop.

PLANNING THE STAFF
DEVELOPMENT PROGRAM

The planning process involves three closely related steps: identify the parameters; specify the objectives; plan the sessions.

Identify the Parameters

When you identify the parameters, you determine the basic format of the program: general focus; participants; site; number of sessions and length of each session; leadership and staffing. In making these determinations, you will, of course, use all the data you have generated in the previous phases discussed in the foregoing section.

Specify the Objectives

The second step of specifying the objectives is a very important one. Specifying the objectives will help you plan a more effective schedule and clarify for the teachers what outcomes are expected. The process also gives you a chance to model an important instructional behavior. Too often, principals who admonish their teachers to specify learning objectives in classroom planning do not specify the objectives of staff development programs.

How do you determine the objectives of the program? The process that usually works best is to identify the general goal of the program and then analyze that general goal into its specific components. You attempt to answer this question: What specific knowledge and skills will the teachers need in order to achieve this general outcome? Suppose, for example, that you have decided to offer a program on writing across the curriculum. You begin by identifying this general goal: "The teachers will use writing as a means of facilitating learning in the subjects they teach."

By reviewing the literature in the field, by conferring with experts, and by talking with your teachers, you should then be able to analyze that general goal into these specific objectives:

- Understand the theory that links writing and learning.
- Understand the composing process and its uses in the classroom.
- Know how to write good essay-test questions.
- Know how to use a learning journal in the classroom.
- Know how to help students take useful notes from class presentations and discussions.
- Know how to help students use writing to share their knowledge with classmates.
- Know how to respond to students' writing.

Plan the Sessions Thoroughly

That list of objectives will help you take the final step in the planning process—planning the individual sessions. You begin by putting the objectives into the best sequence. You then determine how much time you will allocate to each objective. Finally, you decide which activities will be planned to enable teachers to achieve those objectives. A form similar to the one shown in Figure 15-5 may help you with this detailed planning. Note that for each objective, it asks you to identify the presentation-discussion content, the hands-on activities, and the follow-up experiences.

Obviously, the process of planning effective staff development for excellent middle schools is a complex one. But the time and effort are worth it: Good staff development programs are a powerful means of moving a school forward.

Notes

1. P. Berman and M. McLaughlin, *Federal Programs Supporting Educational Change, Vol. 8: Implementing and Sustaining Innovation* (Santa Monica, CA: Rand Corp., 1978).

2. Bruce R. Joyce and Beverly Showers, *Power in Staff Development through Research on Training* (Alexandria, VA: Association for Supervision and Curriculum Development, 1983).

3. Toni E. Santmire, *Developmental Differences in Adult Learners: Implications for Staff Development* (Lincoln, NE: University of Nebraska, 1979).

FIGURE 15-1.   Characteristics of an ideal staff development program

TIME

• The program should be ongoing and continuous, providing sufficient opportunity for the development of complex skills.

• The program should be timely, developing the skills when teachers most sense the need for them.

MANAGEMENT

• The principal should participate but not dominate.

• Teachers should play an active role in setting the agenda, determining the structure, and directing the learning.

• A small team of participants should monitor the program and suggest modifications as needed.

CONTENT

• The program should emphasize skills that teachers feel they need to meet new demands of their professional roles.

• The program should provide a theoretical grounding for those skills to ensure retention, facilitate transfer, and lead to executive control.

• The program should aim to develop those skills to a high degree of mastery.

• The program for middle schools should give continuing attention to the special needs of young adolescents.

continued

FIGURE 15-1. (cont.)

LEARNING ACTIVITIES

- The program should make extensive use of such active learning as role playing, demonstrating, and producing materials.

- The program should provide ample opportunities for those new skills to be tried out in a supportive environment.

- The program should enable teachers to apply the skills in their classrooms, receiving feedback and support from a fellow participant.

SITE

- The program should be held at the local school, not at a university.

INSTRUCTORS

- Local teachers, not visiting consultants, should be the instructors.

(SOURCES: P. Berman and M. McLaughlin, Federal Programs Supporting Educational Change, Vol. 8: Implementing and Sustaining Innovation *(Santa Monica, CA: Rand, 1978); Bruce R. Joyce and Beverly Showers,* Power in Staff Development through Research on Training *(Alexandria, VA: Association for Supervision and Curriculum Development, 1983); and Gordon Lawrence,* Patterns of Effective Inservice Education *(Tallahassee, FL: Florida Department of Education, 1974).*

FIGURE 15-2. Comparing the ideal program with the best feasible one

	THE IDEAL	YOUR BEST FEASIBLE ONE
Time	Ongoing for several months	_____
	Timely, when most needed	_____
Management	Principal participates but does not dominate	_____
	Teachers set agenda and determine structure and learning	_____
	Team of participants monitor and modify	_____
Content	Emphasizes skills that teachers feel they need	_____
	Theoretical grounding	_____
	High degree of mastery	_____
	Emphasizes adolescent needs	_____
Learning	Much use of active learning	_____
	New skills tried in supportive environment	_____
	New skills applied in class with colleague feedback	_____
Site	Local school	_____
Instructors	Local teachers	_____

FIGURE 15-3. Assessing teacher preferences for content

To the teachers: As you are aware, we have been discussing during the past several weeks some possible topics for next year's staff development program. Listed below are the four topics that seem to have the highest priority. Consider your own needs and preferences and tell us what your priorities are. Rate each one by giving the number 4 to the topic that for you has the highest priority and the number 1 to the lowest.

TOPIC	*YOUR PRIORITY*
1. Teaching critical thinking	_____
2. Developing the mastery curriculum	_____
3. Developing and using curriculum-based tests	_____
4. Making team planning more effective	_____

FIGURE 15-4. Assessing preferences for structure

Directions: Listed below are the features that might characterize our staff development program. Indicate your preference for each feature by circling the appropriate letter:

     P—prefer this structure be used
     N—prefer this structure not be used
     I—indifferent as to whether or not this structure is used

FEATURE: THE STAFF DEVELOPMENT PROGRAM...	*YOUR RESPONSE*		
1. Follows a regular schedule with a well-organized agenda for each meeting.	P	N	I
2. Emphasizes practical skills you can use in your teaching.	P	N	I
3. Uses consultants considered experts in the field.	P	N	I
4. Gives appropriate attention to theory and research.	P	N	I
5. Enables participants to develop and share classroom materials.	P	N	I
6. Makes use of lectures followed by discussions.	P	N	I
7. Gives participants an option about what they learn and how they learn.	P	N	I
8. Emphasizes hands-on activites.	P	N	I
9. Uses our own teachers as instructors.	P	N	I
10. Provides participants with opportunity to see skills demonstrated and practice skills.	P	N	I
11. Provides opportunities for observing other classes and schools.	P	N	I
12. Provides opportunities for participants to try out skills in their classrooms and get feedback from colleagues.	P	N	I

FIGURE 15-5.   Planning the staff development sessions

General goal of program: _____
_____

Participants: _____
_____

Location: _____   Hours: _____

DATE	OBJECTIVES	PRESENTA-TIONI DISCUSSION	HANDS-ON ACTIVITIES	CLASSROOM ACTIVITIES	FOLLOW-UP

16

Developing the Leadership Team

Leadership in an Effective Middle School

There is a strong and active leadership team, headed by the principal, that focuses on the improvement of instruction.

Most of the current literature on leadership in the schools focuses on the principal as the instructional leader. Although we believe that the principal needs to play a key role in the move toward excellence, we argue in this chapter for a team approach to instructional leadership—one that draws from the special contributions of several individuals.

RATIONALE FOR A TEAM APPROACH TO LEADERSHIP

The Arguments Against the Team Approach

To understand best the nature of and rationale for a team approach to instructional leadership, it might be useful to summarize first the proposals of those who argue that the principal must be the instructional leader. Their case goes something like this:

> In several studies of effective schools, the principal plays the role of instructional leader. He or she emphasizes achievement, sets instructional strategies, provides an orderly atmosphere, coordinates the instructional program, and supports the teachers. Therefore, all principals should function in this manner. The effective principal should not be a manager or administrator—but must be an instructional leader.

There is much in this argument that is both plausible and sound, but it is flawed in several ways. First, that model of the principal as a very active leader who works closely with teachers on instructional matters may be a useful for one for small elementary schools, where most of the research on school effectiveness has been conducted, but it is not very helpful in analyzing the role of the principal in most secondary schools. The typical secondary school is a large, complex, loosely coupled organization in which the principal must function more like a manager who coordinates the efforts of several individuals and groups.

Second, that model of the principal as an instructional leader seems to denigrate the importance of the management functions. This point is most cogently stated in a recent critique of the "instructional leadership" literature:

> At best, the role of management in much of the new educational leadership literature is undervalued.... At worst, leadership and management are viewed as two ends of a continuum, with "true leadership" occupying the good and wholesome end and "mere management" activities clustered at the negative and tainted end of the continuum....[1]

The management functions are important. Someone must be sure that the duty roster is made, that the cafeteria is supervised, that the buses are loaded safely.

The third weakness in this model is that it requires all principals, regardless of their talents and their predilections, to perform as instructional leaders. Some principals are highly effective managers without much depth in supervision or curriculum; to insist that they function as instructional leaders is to ignore their strengths and impose unrealistic demands upon their capabilities.

Finally, restricting the leadership functions to the principal is an unwise use of resources. In each school there are many members of the staff who can supervise, assist teachers with instructional approaches, and monitor the curriculum. It makes more sense to use their talents, rather than insist that only the principal should provide those services.

The Arguments for the Leadership Team

The team approach to instructional leadership attempts to respond to all those weaknesses by allocating leadership functions to all those able to serve. In essence it is both a structure and a process. The structure is a small leadership team, led by the principal and composed of both administrators and teachers; the process involves identifying the critical leadership functions and assigning chief responsibility for each function to the individual or individuals who can best discharge those functions. Rather than assume that the principal must be the instructional leader, the team approach enables the principal to perform those functions he or she can best perform—and allocates the other critical functions to those who can most competently perform them.

Such an approach has several advantages. It is a flexible model that can be used in any school, regardless of size or organizational complexity. In a small elementary school, it enables the principal to function as a very active instructional leader; in a large middle school, it enables the principal to serve as a manager, coordinating the services of several colleagues. It recognizes the importance of the management functions and makes them a part of the allocation process. It enables the principal to carve out a role that is tailored to his or her special talents. And it capitalizes upon the strengths of several individuals, making the most of the human talent available in a large school.

ORGANIZING THE LEADERSHIP TEAM

The nature of the leadership team will vary with each middle school, depending upon its size, its staffing, and its organization. Each school should develop a leadership structure that reflects its own special needs. There are, however, some general guidelines drawn from the management literature and from the experience of successful principals that can be of help in developing that structure.

The Team Should Reflect the School's Organizational Priorities

First, structure the team so that it reflects the organizational priorities of the school. To understand this guideline, consider first of all the range of roles that might be represented on such a team: administrators (principal, assistant principal), house leaders, interdisciplinary team leaders, grade-level chairpersons (sixth-grade chairperson, seventh-grade chairperson) and department heads (English department head, science department head). The ones selected and the authority granted them should reflect the school's organizational priorities. If you want to emphasize the importance of the house or the mini-school, then their leaders should be included—and have more authority than the grade chairpersons. If you want to emphasize the importance of the subject-matter departments, then the department heads should serve and have more authority than the team leader.

The Authority Structure Should Be Made Clear

Second, make clear the authority structure. Although we argue for a team approach, the teachers must understand the chain of command. Continuing difficulties develop when this basic principle is ignored. We have consulted with some schools in which the classroom teacher was never sure about the next level of authority. Was it a department head, a team leader, or a grade-level chairperson who approved changes in the daily schedule? If, as we have advocated in this book, middle schools use an interdisciplinary team approach, that team leader must be given enough power to be effective; he or she should not have to compete with a department head for influence over the classroom teachers. Subject-matter expertise can be provided either by district personnel or by teachers in that building designated as "specialists," who serve only in an advisory capacity.

The Team's Size Is Important

Third, keep the group large enough to represent all major organizational units—but small enough to achieve efficiency. Teams of only three or four may be seen as too exclusive and not sufficiently representative. Teams of fourteen or sixteen are probably too large. Some larger schools have solved this problem of team size by the use of a two-tiered system: The school leadership team is composed of the school administrators and the house leaders; house leadership teams are made up of the house leaders and the team leaders.

The "Levels of Command" Should Be Minimal

Fourth, keep the organizational structure as flat as possible; avoid having several "levels of command" that teachers must work their way through. Even in large schools, teachers should feel that they have direct access to the principal when they need special help and that their requests for resources are handled quickly without requiring approval from several layers of the bureaucracy.

The Team Should Be Flexible

Finally, keep the leadership team flexible. Bring in consultants as you need them, rather than add more members. Use more *ad hoc* task groups and fewer standing committees. And appoint second-level leaders for three-year terms, with systematic evaluation of their performance; avoid the difficulties of having to deal with entrenched second-level leaders who feel that they own their jobs until they retire.

THE SPECIAL NATURE OF THE PRINCIPALSHIP

Although we advocate a team approach to leadership, our analysis of the literature on organizational leadership, our reading of the research on effective schools, and our analysis of our own experience all suggest that there are certain responsibilities that the principal must retain and not delegate.

Articulate the Vision of the Ideal School

The principal should be the one who articulates a vision of what the school is trying to become. That vision is the idealized form of what the school is becoming, not a description of its reality. That vision speaks of the mission of the school, its special climate, its belief in the young adolescent, and its view of teaching and learning.

How is this vision articulated? It first of all must be articulated often through the spoken word. In faculty meetings, in parent meetings, in school assemblies, in the morning announcements, in public events, the principal must speak of this vision of the school. On every suitable occasion the words should be spoken again and again until they create a vivid image in the minds of all who listen. The printed word is also important. Through posters in the corridors, through columns and editorials in school and community newspapers, through newsletters and flyers, the message is reinforced.

In these public spoken and written messages, the wise principal will make effective use of slogans and symbols. Slogans are an important means of summing up the vision: "a school where caring counts"; "every child is a winner"; "mastery for all"; "we're a family here." Such slogans are often ridiculed by teachers, but they are needed as a means of epitomizing the belief system that energizes the school. Symbols also count, especially with the young adolescent. The team needs a mascot and a nickname; the class needs class colors and a motto; clubs need special insignia.

Communicate the School's Goals

The principal as the titular leader of the school is also the one who should communicate the goals of the school. As noted in Chapter 2, all the staff should be involved in formulating and prioritizing those goals; but the principal should bear the primary responsibility of communicating those goals to school and community. Through discussions with the faculty, meetings with the students, presentations to the parents, and publications to the larger community, the principal should specify clearly the full range of goals and indicate those that have priority.

Set the Expectations for Teachers and Students

Another important aspect of the symbolic function of leadership is setting expectations for teachers and for students. The essential message is this one: "I believe so much in your potential that I have high expectations for your performance. I expect greatness of you." That message is communicated to the teachers in several ways: through open discussion at faculty meetings, through informal interactions throughout the day, and through the supervision and staff development activities used to improve instruction. Those high expectations must also be communicated to the students. Although teachers must also play an important role here, the principal as the chief authority figure must make clear to all the students that the school has high expectations for them—in their academic work, in their discipline in school, and in their behavior in public.

Visibly Represent the School

The principal must be a highly visible figure in the school and in the community. He or she can delegate many responsibilities, but no one else may act the public role of leader. The students must see the principal in corridors, in the cafeteria, in the classroom, and at special school events. The teachers must see the principal at faculty meetings and in classrooms. An assistant principal may work with individual parents who need help, but the principal must represent the school at parent meetings. And in all major community events, it is the principal who must play this role of official representative. Such responsibilities will make demands on time and energy, but the principal must see these functions as part of the burden of leadership.

ALLOCATING THE LEADERSHIP FUNCTIONS

The process of allocating the leadership functions begins by identifying the important functions—what are the critical tasks that must be done if the middle school is to achieve excellence? Here you will find the list in Figure 16-1 especially useful. It has been developed by reviewing the literature on effective school leadership and by analyzing the processes suggested in the preceding chapters. Some special comments are in order about both its content and its form. First, the list is intended to be comprehensive in content—but also somewhat selective. You will note that it includes every aspect of school leadership, including the important management functions that are often overlooked. Yet it is also selective: It includes only those functions that are both essential and specific. It excludes both trivial duties ("prepare daily bulletin") and global responsibilities ("administer discipline").

The organization of the list follows the organization of this book. You will observe some intentional overlapping with regard to staff development and evaluation activities. First, specific staff development and evaluation activities are listed as specific functions under each category where they pertain, in order to emphasize their importance to that category. Second, they are listed separately in more general terms, as a reminder of the need to develop and implement comprehensive and systematic plans in those areas. Note also that the list has been structured so that it can be readily used for both surveying and informing the staff. You list across the top the leadership roles in the school and then show by a code letter who provides and contributes to leadership. Figure 16-1 has been partially completed to illustrate this point.

The leadership team should review and revise this tentative list, making three kinds of changes: Delete items that are not appropriate; add items that have been omitted; change the wording of any that are unclear or misleading. This revision process is important; the team should feel some ownership of the final list.

Once that refined list of leadership functions has been developed, you then have two choices as to how you can effectively allocate these functions. One way is to begin by surveying the preferences of the leadership team. The individual members of the team should be asked to identify those functions for which they would like to *provide* leadership and those to which they would like to *contribute*. The person providing leadership for a particular function is the one primarily responsible; those contributing assist without assuming chief responsibility. In determining their preferences, members should consider several important issues: the nature of their role; their talents and abilities; and the time they have available.

When those preferences have been collated, the principal should then review the results very critically, keeping these questions in mind:

- If two or more want to provide leadership for a particular function, should they share this leadership—or should one individual be designated?

- Is someone providing leadership for all desired functions? If not, who can be asked to lead here?

- Is there a fair distribution of leadership, in relation to roles and time available? Has anyone asked for too many—or too few—responsibilities?

- Is there an effective distribution of leadership? Are functions well matched with people?

The principal's revisions are then communicated to the leadership team—and then to the faculty—as a plan for leadership.

The other process begins with the faculty's perceptions of the status quo. The refined list of leadership functions—without names or roles attached to them—is presented to the faculty in a survey form, with these instructions:

> Attached is a list of the leadership functions important in our school. At the top of the form are the leadership roles used in our school. Read each

function carefully. Determine for each function which person in the school, from your perception, chiefly *provides* leadership; write the letter "P" under that person's role. Then for each function determine which other persons *contribute* to it; write the letter "C" under the role of each one who contributes. If in your perception no one either provides nor contributes to a given function, then leave the appropriate spaces blank.

The results of that survey are then collated and analyzed by the leadership team. They review both their own and the teachers' perceptions of the status quo from the following perspectives:

- How do we change assignments so that we legitimate the contributions of those actually performing certain functions?
- How do we change assignments so that all functions are adequately provided for?
- How do we change assignments to eliminate undesirable overlapping of responsibilities?
- How do we communicate leadership roles and functions more clearly to the teachers?

You can start with preferences or perceptions. The important goal is to develop an effective allocation system—and then communicate that clearly to the entire faculty. Each member of the team should receive a complete list of those functions for which he or she provides leadership and contributes to it. That list thus functions as a guide to individual performance: This is what you are responsible for. Then the faculty should receive a comprehensive list that shows each person's responsibilities. This list thus functions as a leadership map for the faculty, answering with specific information the perennial organizational question—"Who's in charge here?"

Note

1. Joseph Murphy, Philip Hallinger, and Alex Mitman, "Problems with Research on Educational Leadership: Issues to Be Addressed," *Educational Evaluation and Policy Research*, 3 (1983), 297–305.

FIGURE 16-1. Allocating leadership functions

Code: P = provides leadership for this function
C = contributes to this function

FUNCTION	Principal	Assistant Principal	House Leader	Team Leader
LEADERSHIP ROLES				
Goals				
1. Identify, prioritize goals.	P			C
2. Communicate goals to all groups.	P		C	C
3. Align goals with programs.		P		C
4.				
Curriculum				
1. Align curriculum goals with subjects.				
2. Identify mastery goals for each subject.				
3. Develop for each subject a mastery scope-and-sequence chart.				
4. Develop mastery objectives for each subject.				
5. Monitor mastery curriculum to ensure that mastery objectives are taught.				
6. Develop curricular options as needed.				
7. Assess curriculum articulation between subjects at given grade level.				
8. Assess and improve coordination between grade levels for each subject.				
9. Develop, implement curriculum evaluation system.				

continued

10. Help teachers use evaluative data to improve curriculum.

11.

Guidance Program

1. Communicate guidance goals to all groups.
2. Develop plan for school-wide guidance services to achieve goals.
3. Assess guidance program in relation to goals.
4. Provide staff development to assist teachers with guidance function.
5.

School Climate

1. Assess school climate.
2. Direct faculty in improving school climate.
3. Develop clear policy guidelines for school-wide classroom discipline.
4. Monitor enforcement of discipline policies to ensure consistency and fairness.
5. Provide for disciplinary supervision in cafeteria, corridors, other public spaces.
6. Handle disciplinary referrals from classroom teachers, aides.
7. Monitor faculty, student morale.
8. Develop, implement participatory decision-making structures.
9. Monitor school's reward system, make needed adjustments to improve impact on climate.
10. Provide staff development to help teachers facilitate student cooperation.

FIGURE 16-1. (cont.)

FUNCTION	LEADERSHIP ROLES			
	Principal	Assistant Principal	House Leader	Team Leader
11. Monitor student attendance, punctuality.				
12.				
Organizational Structure				
1. Determine organizational structures in relation to school goals.				
2. Develop, implement organic processes for monitoring, improving structures.				
3. Develop, implement teacher-assignment patterns.				
4. Identify, allocate team responsibilities.				
5. Monitor team planning time for adequacy and effectiveness.				
6. Assess grouping practices, modify as necessary.				
7. Provide staff development to assist teachers in using small-group learning.				
8. Develop a master schedule that reflects school priorities.				
9. Defend academic time against unwarranted intrusions.				
10.				
Community				
1. Represent school in public functions.				
2. Provide for appropriate involvement of parents in decision making.				

240

3. Develop, implement system for keeping community, parents well informed.

4. Identify, make plans for using community resources.

5. Provide staff development to help faculty understand values, power structure of community.

6. _____

Staff Development

1. Develop comprehensive staff development program in relation to school needs.

2. Implement staff development program.

3. Monitor, assess staff development program.

4. _____

Evaluation

1. Develop comprehensive evaluation program.

2. Administer evaluation program.

3. Communicate results to all group.

4. _____

Management

1. Develop budget that reflects school priorities.

2. Supervise nonprofessional personnel and support services.

3. Supervise maintenance of facilities.

4. _____

APPENDICES

A: THE MASTERY CURRICULUM

B: TEACHING AND SUPERVISION

C: THE ACTIVITY PROGRAM

D: GUIDANCE PROGRAMS

E: THE SCHOOL CLIMATE

F: ORGANIZATIONAL STRUCTURE

G: PARENT AND COMMUNITY RELATIONS

Appendix A

The Mastery Curriculum

Bloomington Junior High School
Stroudsburg Middle School
Nipher Middle School
Westbrook Middle School
C. Fred Johnson Middle School
Byrns Middle School
South Spencer Middle School

BLOOMINGTON JUNIOR HIGH SCHOOL

Most schools have goal statements and curriculum guides, but what we urge is the aligning of goals and curriculum as an important step in developing excellent middle schools. Aligning goals and curricula is one process that can remind faculty that they are joined in common pursuits of educating young adolescents. Robert N. Knight, principal of **Bloomington Junior High School,** has achieved the same results through his Mastery Learning Program.

Bloomington Junior High School includes grades 7 and 8. The pupils come from mostly middle-class families. The enrollment for 1983–84 was 850 pupils with an ethnic/racial make-up of 89 percent white, and 10 percent black.

The mastery learning process used at Bloomington Junior High School puts greater emphasis on learning than on grades, and it allows for different learning rates. Teachers must truly believe that all students can learn whatever is being taught, and they must be willing to extend the time and energy required to ensure that learning occurs. Even though the program uses the now familiar pretest–posttest system, the mastery learning process is one in which all kinds of teaching and learning alternatives can be used. Each teacher establishes a class structure that is personally manageable, thus giving it the stamp of individuality. The mastery learning program requires a great deal of adjustment for those teachers who are accustomed to a traditional program—perhaps a couple of years of adjustment and very hard work in preparation and organization. The Bloomington Junior High School teachers feel that the increased, meaningful interactions with students are worth the effort.

For additional information, contact Robert N. Knight, Principal, Bloomington Junior High School, 510 East Washington Street, Bloomington, Illinois 61701.

STROUDSBURG MIDDLE SCHOOL

Stroudsburg Middle School includes grades 5 through 8. The pupils come from mostly working-class families. The enrollment for the 1983–84 school year was 1,000. The ethnic/racial composition was predominantly white.

Stroudsburg Middle School introduced a program to help pupils learn how to learn "study skills." What are study skills? Literally, study is acquiring knowledge or competence; skill is learned abilities that one has for the purpose of acquiring, recording, synthesizing, organizing, remembering, and using information and ideas. These skills are valuable in non-academic settings and indispensable for school success. When one learns a study skill well, one is learning more than a specific series of technical behaviors. Rather, one is learning methods that can be employed in a relevant context. Study skills are transferable processes for learning. Why teach study skills? Parents and teachers are aware that students do not always achieve their potential, and both groups identify the inability to study as the cause. Even though instructional approaches vary and trends in education shift, the nature of the skills at the heart of the educative process has not changed. The importance of learning how to learn never diminishes.

This program was constructed to provide twelve to fifteen lessons that will alternate biweekly with the Physical Education Enrichment Program. Instruction was from 1:45 to 2:30 in the advisory group. Studying in the content area was taught independently by individual academic teachers in the program. The student who develops efficient study skills has, in a true sense, learned how to learn. To acquaint each student with the nature of study skills and his or her own strengths and weaknesses regarding them, a Study Skills Checklist was completed in the initial lesson. This checklist was completed again at the end of the program so that students and teachers could assess improvement. In discovering that studying is not a magical trick but rather a process that can be learned and used effectively, the student is better able to achieve success. Because study skills are naturally integrated with all content areas, this success will be evident throughout the student's school career.

The Study Skills Committee members served as resource persons throughout the year to answer questions and offer suggestions to help teachers implement the program. Suggestions and comments regarding the program were directed to Steve Boston and used to improve the study skills program.

For more information, contact Steve Boston, Assistant Principal, Stroudsburg Middle School, Chippenfield Drive, Stroudsburg, Pennsylvania 18360.

NIPHER MIDDLE SCHOOL

Nipher Middle School includes grades 6 through 8. The pupils come from mostly working-class families. The enrollment for the 1983–84 school year was 558. The ethnic/racial composition was 74 percent white, 25 percent black, and 1 percent Asian.

Nipher Middle School has a very impressive computer education program. With the use of a word processor, Nipher students have the opportunity to become familiar with computers in a variety of ways. All basic skills teams have a computer, and it is used for word processing. The teachers prepare lessons on the machines and teach the students to use them as part of our process writing program. The students write, edit, draft, and publish a book using the computers. This process includes sewing the book pages together and attaching a hard cover. Every student leaves for the year with his or her own hardcover book.

Every student has the opportunity to learn to program a computer using either LOGG, PILOT, or BASIC. The classes include LOGG in our co-curricular. Co-curricular is a program in which teachers, parents, and administrators teach special courses to students for a limited period of time. PILOT is taught in a special seventh-grade class that combines our most academically talented black and white students. The children are identified through our achievement test scores. The purpose is to provide computer-assisted instruction, programming, and interpersonal skills. BASIC is available to the students in grade 8 as an elective; approximately 40 percent of the grade level take the class. Some of the students design and implement teacher utility programs for the staff.

Basic skills instructors (language arts and math) take classes to the computer lab for individual skill work in math and language arts. This program is coordinated with Project Excellence. Project Excellence is our instructional management package, which defines goals, objectives, and assessments for all academic disciplines.

At Nipher Middle School, some of the computers are used as simulation machines. They are moved to the science and social studies classrooms to create situations that are difficult to duplicate. They simulate ponds, airplanes in flight, or a covered wagon traveling to the west coast. Simulations are wonderful for middle-level students because they add an experiential component to all segments of the academic program.

Nipher Middle School is fortunate to have parent volunteers to assist with the computer education program. They do word processing in the library and teach co-curricular after-school open computer lab. Nipher Middle School competes annually in local and state computer contests.

For more information, contact Dr. Dan H. Edwards, Principal, Nipher Middle School, 700 South Kirkwood Road, Kirkwood, Missouri 63122.

WESTBROOK MIDDLE SCHOOL

A major step in improving middle schools is to align the curriculum goals with specific subjects offered in the school. The most important step is to use those goals in developing what we call a mastery curriculum. Both concepts are reflected in the Policy and Curriculum Handbook for **Westbrook Middle School.**

Westbrook Middle School includes grades 6 through 9. The enrollment comes from mostly middle-class white families.

The entire curriculum is organized into semesters and year-long courses and is offered to students from any of the various learning communities. Each course is structured to meet the needs of students. In all cases, courses are designated as sequential or nonsequential. Each course is described through measurable objectives, the coordinated activities, and available resources. In addition, the core of basics is identified with the framework of the curriculum. Students are required to complete the core basics at the designated level of mastery for the curricula offering. Students who do not complete the objectives at the required level of mastery may be scheduled into directed study or recycled through the course for the necessary portion of the course.

The teacher–adviser system is the head of the school's personalized education program. The primary function of the teacher–adviser is to provide an island in the school where students can plan their directed study time and evaluate progress.

For more detailed information, contact Leslie L. Sladek, Principal, Westbrook Middle School, 1312 Robertson Drive, Omaha, Nebraska 68114.

C. FRED JOHNSON MIDDLE SCHOOL

An excellent example of the mastery curriculum is found in C. Johnson City Central School District, where the entire school district has focused its attention on this concept. R. Joseph Meehan, principal of **C. Fred Johnson Middle School**, is operating an effective mastery curriculum in that it conforms to our basic criteria: It is considered essential for all students, and it needs careful structuring.

C. Fred Johnson includes grades 6 through 8. The pupils mainly come from working-class families. The pupil enrollment for the 1983–84 school year was 650.

C. Fred Johnson operates under the rationale that curriculum and instruction are fundamentally intertwined and should not be separated. Curriculum should be organized as to be consistent with the instructional process. The curriculum is focused by the instruction on specified learning objectives and careful assessment of mastery. There is involvement of the entire staff in the mastery learning concepts. Staff development time is provided. There is a structured instructional process. Courses of studies are organized into separate units, each approximately of two weeks' duration. Each unit's desired outcomes are clearly stated. Teachers work in teams but have the freedom to use their teaching styles and methods to achieve the desired outcome.

The staff devlopment program emphasizes the mastery learning assumptions: Almost all students are capable of achieving excellence; the instructional process can be changed to improve learning; an effective instructional process varies the time for learning according to the needs of each student; success influences self-concept, as it in turn influences learning. Staff and pupils share responsibility for successful learning outcomes; and assessment of learning is continuous. For more information, contact R. Joseph Meehan, Principal, C. Fred Johnson Middle School, 100 Albert St., Johnson City, New York 13790.

BYRNS MIDDLE SCHOOL

Byrns Middle School includes grades 6 through 8. The pupils come from mostly middle-class families. The student enrollment for the 1983–84 school year was 1,069. The student body was predominantly white.

Byrns Middle School presents a unique foreign language program. All students in the sixth and seventh grades are given exploratory experiences of about fifteen days in each of three foreign languages: French, German, and Spanish. In the two-year period, each student will have about thirty days in each language, covering such things as the culture and customs of each country in addition to certain vocabulary words, phrases, and sentences.

In the eighth grade, if the student so chooses and his or her reading teacher so recommends, that student may take French I, German I, or Spanish I instead of reading. The student is then eligible to take French II, German II, or Spanish II in the ninth grade.

For additional information, contact Robert H. Berry, Principal, Byrns Middle School, Route 3, Owensboro, Kentucky 42301.

SOUTH SPENCER MIDDLE SCHOOL

South Spencer Middle School includes grades 6 through 8. The pupils come from mostly working-class families. The enrollment for the 1983–84 school year was 425 pupils. The ethnic/racial composition is 99.9 percent white. The school is located in a small rural community.

South Spencer Middle School offers a mini-course program. The mini-courses are required for those students scoring significantly low on their Math Achievement Test. A course may last up to twelve weeks, but students passing a proficiency test are transferred to other classes immediately. The mini-course program is offered during the last period of the day with both required and elective courses being programmed. Sixth-graders are required to take six weeks of shop and home economics and six weeks of geography—map study. Those needing extra help in math take six to twelve weeks of basic math. Eighth-graders are required to take basic reading, composition and/or literature, speech, and basic math, if needed. Many of the mini-courses are open to all students, regardless of grade, which provides an opportunity for the mixing of classes.

For more information, contact Mark Dartt, Principal, South Spencer Middle School, South Fifth Street, Rockport, Indiana 47635.

Appendix B

Teaching and Supervision

J. Cooke Junior High
Andrews Middle School
Albert D. Lawton Intermediate School

J. COOKE JUNIOR HIGH

One of the most effective ways to improve middle-school teaching is through teacher supervision that focuses on the improvement of instruction and classroom management. The differentiated model described in this book is similar to one developed by Norman K. Spencer at **J. Cooke Junior High.**

J. Cooke Junior High includes grades 7 through 9. The enrollment reflects mostly working-class families. The school's enrollment fluctuates from 1,300 to 1,600, with a ethnic/racial makeup of 76 percent black, 20 percent Hispanic, and 3 percent Asian.

J. Cooke Junior High used a supervisory approach called "Supportive Supervision." The plan included the curriculum goals, instructional and classroom management requirements, "mastery learning," staff development, and supervisory options. During the first year, one staff meeting a month was devoted to inservice activities to develop the Support Supervision Plan. This was reinforced with half-day inservice in the following years. One assistant administrator was the instructional coordinator for the school. Staff development in mastery learning/

competency-based education was provided for each department chairperson, who in turn held staff development sessions for the department. Other teachers who had received courses or staff development in mastery learning/competency-based education were made a part of the leadership team. The principal and another administrator taught many demonstration classes for teachers to underscore the supervisory process. Teachers could request the kind of supervision they desired. All teachers were observed, and teachers requesting help received support.

For additional information, contact Norman K. Spencer, Principal, Benjamin Franklin High School, Broad and Green Streets, Philadelphia, Pennsylvania 19130.

ANDREWS MIDDLE SCHOOL

Andrews Middle School includes grades 6 through 8. The pupils come from mostly working-class families. The student enrollment for the 1983–84 school year was 800. The student body's ethnic/racial composition was 62 percent white, 2 percent black, 35 percent Chicano/Hispanic, and 1 percent Asian.

The Andrews Middle School philosophy states that "The educational process should be centered in the child and his needs, and the only true test of the value of this process is what it does to aid the child. The end result should be an individual who is interested in continuing learning." The purpose of the language arts program in Andrews Middle School is to help the students mature, to use languages as a tool for learning, and to help them to evaluate their own ideas and the ideas of others. The program is organized in a series of language arts mini-courses. The mini-courses are of six weeks' duration. All students are required to take six weeks of composition and twelve weeks of grammar. Pupils who need remedial help can take courses in the Reading Center; this is individualized work under the direction of the reading instructor. It includes analysis of individual skills, practice in different types of reading, and development of vocabulary and listening skills. Individualized Reading is a course available to advanced reading students only. The mini-courses are centered on concepts and interest or a book. Some mini-course titles representing concepts and interest include: Mythology, The Sporting Spirit, That's Where It's At, Say It Out Loud, and Heroes of the Old West. Some book titles used in the mini-course offering: The Bible as Literature, Johnny Tremain, and The Diary of Anne Frank.

For additional information, contact Dr. Ervin L. Huddleton, Principal, Andrews Middle School, 405 N.W. 3rd Street, Andrews, Texas 79714.

ALBERT D. LAWTON INTERMEDIATE SCHOOL

The **Albert D. Lawton Intermediate School** includes grades 6 through 8. The pupils come from mostly middle-class families. The student enrollment for the 1983–84 school year was 415. The student body was predominantly white.

The Lawton School has a cognitive-based program that is planned and directed where generalized cognitive skills are transferred to mathematics practice. The inclusion of accountability, objectives, skill analysis, sequencing, eye-space, sample writing, maintenance/reinforcement, ongoing pre–post testing, precursors, practice drill, and evaluation has resulted in an increased level of success among remedial mathematics students in grades 6, 7, and 8.

The research project from which this program evolved has been co-sponsored by the Essex Junction School District and the University of Vermont under the direction of Dr. Charles A. Letteri, Director, Center for Cognitive Studies, and W. James Walford, Mathematics Department, Albert D. Lawton Intermediate School.

For additional information, contact Stanley A. Knapp, Principal, The Albert D. Lawton Intermediate School, 104 Maple Street, Essex Junction, Vermont 05452.

Appendix C

The Activity Program

Francisco Middle School

FRANCISCO MIDDLE SCHOOL

The best middle schools must have strong activity programs. At the middle-school level especially, excellence in education must include the special contributions that a strong activity program can make. The basic argument for a strong activity program is that adolescents have needs that cannot be met solely through the academic component of the school day. Helen M. Hatcher, principal of **Francisco Middle School,** has developed a "Spirit Program" to enhance school activity.

Francisco Middle School includes grades 6 through 8. It is an inner-city school with a population of 915 pupils. Fifty-four percent of the student body come from families that receive federal assistance. The ethnic/racial mix is extremely heterogeneous, with large proportions of black, Asian, and Hispanic children.

The Francisco School Spirit Committee was organized in September 1983 as a unified school-wide program to help students enhance their self-concepts, work for positive social interaction with other students from various ethnic backgrounds, and promote an atmosphere in which students could learn to be more responsible to their school community. The main components of Francisco's Spirit Program are: Service Block Award System, Club Day, 6th Grade Field Day, Auditorium Programs, Student Recognition Bulletin Boards, and School Spirit Days.

Implementing the Spirit Program meant that the staff volunteers serving on the Spirit Committee had to hold numerous meetings to shape up the total program. The program generated a great deal of positive student enthusiasm and activity during its first year. The most successful activities involved the 6th Grade Field Day, Club Day, Auditorium Programs, Award Program, and Bulletin Boards.

For more information, contact Helen M. Hatcher, Principal, Francisco Middle School, 2190 Powell Street, San Francisco, California 94133.

Appendix D

Guidance Programs

Snellville Middle School
Webster Transitional School
South Side Middle School

SNELLVILLE MIDDLE SCHOOL

Snellville Middle School includes grades 6 to 8. The pupils come from mostly middle-class families. The enrollment for the 1983–84 school year was 1,030. The ethnic/racial pupil composition was 99 percent white.

Snellville Middle School has developed Comprehensive Counseling Programs. The counseling department recognizes that it has a multi-faceted role that includes counseling, coordinating, consulting, and program development to deal with very special people—middle-school children. The counselor's job is to understand the unique developmental stage of the early adolescent and to communicate with the children, their parents and their teachers. The counselors have a variety of counseling programs, based on such observed needs as self-awareness, problem solving, decision-making skills, communications, interpersonal relations, and study skills. Although the counseling department continues to offer traditional individual counseling and advisement, it also offers a systematic classroom guidance program at each grade level and guidance group. The work is focused on the developmental and preventive aspects of counseling. The counselors certainly respect and deal with crisis and remediation counseling on a daily basis; they are committed to directly serving all students as they cope and grow through a difficult developmental stage. Some of the Classroom Guidance Programs are: Sixth Grade, "Discovering Myself"; Seventh Grade, "Getting Along With Others"; Eighth Grade, "Making Decisions"; and other individually designed classroom guidance modules as requested by classroom teachers and/or administrators for any grade level. Small-group sessions are based on topics: Students, Parent Study Groups, and Teacher Personal Growth Groups.

For additional information, contact Joseph P. Davis, Counselor, Snellville Middle School, 3155 E. Pate Rd., Snellville, Georgia 30278.

WEBSTER TRANSITIONAL SCHOOL

Young adolescents need the advice and support of caring adults at school who can help them cope with and learn from the special problems of growing up. Thomas R. Pautsch, principal of **Webster Transitional School,** has developed a uniquely successful Teacher–Advisor Program.

Webster Transitional School includes grades 6 through 8, with an enrollment of approximately 700 pupils. The pupils come from mostly middle-class families with only 1.5 percent of them nonwhite.

At Webster, all teachers and counselors serve as advisors. During the second week of school, teachers meet with students and provide information to help pupils know them. Following this, students turn in the names of three teachers they would like to be with. From those ballots the advisor groups are organized. Advisors meet with their advisees in group sessions twice each week (fifteen and fifty minutes), a single longer session once each week, and a shorter follow-up session the next week. Students remain with the same advisor for grades 6 and 7 and move to a different advisor in grade 8. Pupils in grade 8 have special needs in terms of both academic and social development. The grade 8 advisor provides a comprehensive career-exploration program and an ongoing orientation program designed for pupils preparing to move on to high school. Over the years this program has assumed an increasingly important role in the school's overall program. Students, teachers, administrators, and parents view the Teacher–Advisor Program as a school component equal in importance to that of any other subject in the curriculum. As a result, there is a need to ensure high-quality activities in the program.

For additional information, contact Thomas R. Pautsch, Principal, Webster Transitional School, Cedarbury, Wisconsin 53012.

SOUTH SIDE MIDDLE SCHOOL

South Side Middle School includes grades 5 through 8. The pupils come from mostly working-class families. The enrollment for the 1983–84 school year was

435. Racially the South Side Middle School is mostly white, with a few Asian students.

South Side Middle School's guidance program is designed to meet the needs of students in grades 5 through 8. The counselors are available to assist students in regular classes and are available also for individual counseling. Because there is no longer one teacher primarily in contact with the child each day, as in elementary school, the counselors along with the teacher serve the role as the person in the school who watches over the child's total progress and development. In addition to personal counseling, the guidance program provides information concerning occupations, high school curriculum, group counseling, and other concerns. The goal of the guidance department is to provide for the social, emotional, and learning needs of the emerging adolescent child while considering that child as a whole person. Orientation for fifth-grade students introduces the student to South Side Middle School and aids in the transition from elementary school to middle school. Individual orientations and school tours are given to each new entering student in grades other than the fifth. The purpose of the New Student Group is to help students new to South Side and the district make a transition from their old school to the new school and feel comfortable and well-adjusted in their new surroundings.

The Study Skills Program is designed to involve the student in an organized program that allows him or her to have the necessary trial-and-error experience that is needed in learning any type of skill. Students become involved in their learning process and develop their own choices and judgments. Class discussions are held with students about the various types of informational documents they must complete when starting their careers and joining the job market; this culminates in a career day in which professionals come in to talk with students about their job. This class also focuses on the rights and responsibilities of adolescents to know and understand laws regarding juveniles. Students hear speakers from the local police force and the juvenile center. Adolescent Concerns is a mini-course offered to seventh- and eighth-grade students with the permission of their parents. The course addresses the needs of students who are in transition from childhood to adolescence. Prior to the class, a parent meeting is held to discuss course goals. The class is voluntary, and classes are kept small. Student discussion is the primary instruction method.

Adjustments to Changes in the Family is a mini-course offered to interested students who are experiencing some change in their family life through divorce, separation, or death of a parent. The course is designed to help students work through the changes that have occurred in their families and face these changes and adjustments in their lives. The course is offered with parent permission and is voluntary.

For additional information, contact Ronald M. Burger, Principal, South Side Middle School, 720 New Waterford Rd., Columbus, Ohio 44409.

Appendix E

The School Climate

White Brook Middle School
Clarksville Middle School
Steuben Middle School

WHITE BROOK MIDDLE SCHOOL

White Brook Middle School includes grades 5 through 8. The pupils come from mostly working-class families. The enrollment for the 1983–84 school year was 815. The ethnic/racial composition of the student body was predominantly white.

White Brook Middle School has a unique environment and staff. The middle-school learning environment has provided an opportunity for normal social interaction among students. Because of the increased importance of peer relationships, small- and large-group experiences have helped the middle-schooler grow not only in conceptual and factual understanding but also in experiencing and appreciating the democratic process and skills necessary for effective citizenship. Students are involved in some decisions relating to their school life so that they can participate in change. Through this involvement, students acquire abilities that help them adjust to change patterns in schools and later in life.

The staff members at White Brook Middle School are constant models of grown-up life and reflect such attitudes, interests, and behaviors of adulthood as cooperative effort, recognition of leadership roles, manners, participation, caring, and sharing. It is important also that staff members work together to involve students in planning learning experiences and take advantage of opportunities to work individually or in small groups as well as in large classes to maximize interaction among youngsters and adults.

The school also offers an interesting program to "Fill the After School Gap." Because of the decline in funds for extracurricular activities, schools have been hard pressed to find ways of offering youngsters social and recreational opportunities within the school setting at no cost to the taxpayers.

The premise for joining the Student Council is to "help the school, but in reality the youngsters are creating and taking part in activities that offer them something to do while the school program, climate and attitude benefit." Members choose three activities for which they can be called on to serve, ranging from helping the secretary or custodian to editing the school paper. For the ongoing, there's the chance to perform in student-created plays or to decide on assembly programs and guest speakers. Those willing to meet after school can become part of a large group of "officers" who help make other decisions about projects or activities. From this group, top office-holders are elected. Membership changes as the year progresses, and interest rises and falls as children grow and the seasons change. Everyone who feels "in" the group is its strongest supporter, because nobody is ever left out if he or she is interested. It is self-sustaining. In the past, a school might have gotten a teacher to serve as adviser for an annual stipend. There are no stipends as the advisers find great satisfaction in being involved with the students. The student council generates income from sales of stationery, profits on dances, roller-skating trips, and so on. Some youngsters are responsible for recruiting parents to help in these activities. Much of the profit is reinvested in the school to finance assemblies, field trips, and awards, to buy school equipment, or to improve the appearance of the school itself. Finally, the student council also has a governance role, although it is generally unseen. When situations dictate that a school problem be corrected, the members address the issue and make appropriate suggestions. They then become the endorsing agency behind whatever is needed to correct the problem, even though the responsibility still rests with the principal.

For more information, contact William J. Erickson, Principal, White Brook Middle School, 200 Park Street, Easthampton, Massachusetts 01027.

CLARKSVILLE MIDDLE SCHOOL

Clarksville Middle School includes grades 6 through 8. The pupils come from mostly middle-class families. The enrollment for the 1983–84 school year was 470. The ethnic/racial composition of the pupils was predominantly white. The principal considers the school a traditional school with a flair for the unique.

Clarksville Middle School is positively convinced that it has a million-dollar atmosphere. It wants each student to be provided with the best educational experience that is possible so that maximum achievement occurs.

Clarksville Middle School (Junior High School from 1968 to 1971) was first planned in June 1964, when a study was initiated for future construction. In February 1965, the study was concluded, and in March 1967, construction began with a contract to run for 540 calendar days to build a building with much input from the Clarksville educational staff. This building was to be built with flexible ideas and facilities for individual, small-group, and large-group instruction—a school built to let a student develop ethical character and a healthy body and develop technical skills, scientific knowledge, social awareness, civic responsibility, and academic independence.

The first classes to occupy the Clarksville Middle School began on September 5, 1968. This modern 148,000-square-foot facility, built at a cost of $3.5 million, is carpeted and air-conditioned and contains a swimming pool (with a separate diving tank), two gymnasiums, an industrial laboratory, three science laboratories, art and music rooms, home economics areas, and more than twenty-four additional available classrooms. It is a dream come true for this principal, whose administrative career began in an antiquated structure built in the 1890s. In 1977 the library was expanded, and in 1978 a solar project was established to heat the two gymnasiums. The U.S. Department of Energy funded $130,000 of the $282,000 project. It is expected that the local portion of the project will be paid back in approximately 8.8 years in reduction in heating costs. There are 162 solar collectors located on the roofs of the two gyms that heat a combination of water and anti-freeze. This solution is stored in a 10,000-gallon tank behind the school and is pumped through pipes to the unit heaters located in the gymnasiums. Air is forced across the heated pipes by means of blowers to heat the air in the gyms.

All students at the Clarksville Middle School receive daily instruction in English, social studies, math, and science. Sixth-grade students receive reading on a daily basis. Art, music, chorus, home economics, industrial arts, and physical education are offered on a regular basis. In addition, the school houses classes for all moderately mentally handicapped in Clarks County, Indiana, grades 6 through 12. Education is on the move in Clarksville as each year, approximately 325 students, teachers, and administrators participate in tours to Chicago and Washington, D.C. Clarksville educators feel that moving from the theoretical classroom program to the practical field experience expands the student's world. The Chicago and Washington tour groups are made up of sixth- and eighth-grade students from the Clarksville Middle School and from St. Anthony Parochial School.

For additional information, contact John E. Pepper, Principal, Clarksville Middle School, 101 Ettels Lane, Clarksville, Indiana 47130.

STEUBEN MIDDLE SCHOOL

One important aspect of middle-school excellence is the climate of the school. Even if the curriculum is sound and the teaching effective, the school will not achieve excellence unless the climate is supportive. Under the direction of Donald C. Luebke, principal, **Steuben Middle School** has served as a model for other schools that made the transition to a middle-school program.

Steuben Middle School includes grades 7 and 8, with an enrollment of 765 pupils. The pupils come mainly from working-class families, with an ethnic background of 60 percent black, 10 percent Hispanic, and 29 percent white.

Since 1973, Steuben has undergone the process of changing from a traditional course credit system to a more flexible, individualized system designed to be more effective in providing for the transition period between the self-contained, single teacher, elementary school program and the subject-centered high school. In order to meet the needs of early adolescents, Steuben has implemented a unit system. The unit system provides four academic teachers for each group of 120 students. This grouping becomes a "school within a school" and allows teachers to focus on the individual needs of the students. A continual progress instructional program is composed of sequential achievement levels or units of work. The Steuben educational program concerns itself with the total child; the goal is to provide each student with a program that will help him or her reach success and fulfillment as a contributing member of society.

For more information, contact Donald C. Luebke, Principal, Steuben Middle School, 2360 North 52nd Street, Milwaukee, Wisconsin 53210.

Appendix F

Organizational
Structure

Stoughton Middle School
MacDonald Middle School
Jamesville–DeWitt Middle School
Samuel V. Noe Middle School
Thomas J. Rusk Middle School

STOUGHTON MIDDLE SCHOOL

Stoughton Middle School includes grades 6 through 8. The pupils reflect a mixture of working-class and middle-class families. The pupil enrollment for the 1983–84 school year was 657. The school's student body is predominantly white.

Stoughton Middle School relates its success to an organizational structure and curriculum it calls a Block Program. Middle School students are scheduled into teaching team structures called blocks. These blocks are composed of four teachers whose subject areas are mathematics, language arts and reading, social studies, and science. All grade levels spend 63 percent of their school day in these basic subject areas. Incoming sixth-graders stay with their block for two years, thereby creating mixed sixth/seventh-grade blocks. Eighth-graders are in separate blocks. This organization enables teachers to prepare them for the transition into the high school academic and social structure. The block system provides a homebase for students and a structure whereby teachers may truly get to know their students. Academic, emotional, and social needs are provided through the individual attention students require in order to more fully develop their skills.

One important middle-school goal is to help students explore subjects other than the academics. The term for these courses is "related arts" and refers to such courses as physical education, home economics, industrial arts, art/music, and band and/or orchestra.

For additional information, contact Barbara Johnson, Principal, Stoughton Middle School, P.O. Box 189, Stoughton, Wisconsin 53589.

C. E. MacDONALD MIDDLE SCHOOL

C. E. MacDonald Middle School includes grades 6 through 8. The pupils mostly come from middle-class families. The pupil enrollment for the 1983–84 school year was 540; the breakdown was 83 percent white, 7 percent black, 3 percent Chicano/Hispanic, and 6 percent Asian.

At the MacDonald Middle School, interdisciplinary teams of teachers, daily individual planning time, daily team planning time, and a heterogeneous group of students per team are all used to meet the needs of individual pupils. The interdisciplinary teams vary in size. A team may be made up of: (1) four teachers (English, math, science, and social studies) and 100 to 120 students; (2) three teachers (English, math, and science) and 75 to 90 students, with all three teachers sharing responsibility for social studies; or (3) two teachers (English, social studies, and mathematics–science) and 50 to 60 students. Each team meets for a block of time of about four hours, during which teachers schedule students into instructional groups for experiences in the respective disciplines or for an interdisciplinary session. Sometimes small groups are made up of students who are either advanced in an area of study or who need remediation.

At MacDonald Middle School, experiences geared to the individual are not restricted to the four basic subjects but rather extend into special-area subjects.

For more information, contact Sal DiFranco, Ed.D., Principal, C. E. MacDonald Middle School, 1601 Burcham Drive, East Lansing, Michigan 48823.

JAMESVILLE–DeWITT MIDDLE SCHOOL

Over the course of the past few decades, educational reformers have advocated several organizational models. Successful schools for middle-school pupils have used an evolutionary approach developed by the leader and staff, frequently reassessed to find solutions to sets of local conditions. We have found several exemplary schools that have successful school organizations.

One of these is the **Jamesville–DeWitt Middle School,** which includes grades 5 through 8. The pupils mainly come from middle-upper-class families. The pupil enrollment for 1983–84 school year was 830; the breakdown was 90 percent white, 5 percent black, and 5 percent Asian.

At each grade level, there are teams of four teachers who work with approximately ninety students. Each teacher is a subject-area specialist (including those at grades 5 and 6). They represent the areas of language arts, mathematics, science, and social studies. Each teacher teaches his or her specialty area to all of the students on the team. In addition, the four teachers team teach an Integrated Educational Experience (IEE) to the students.

The IEE is a curriculum that focuses on the critical thinking skills and stresses reading and writing. It is an interdisciplinary approach so that students will understand the generalizability of skills rather than associate certain skills only with particular disciplines. The emphasis is on transferability of learning to new and different areas. Sometimes instruction is given to large groups, sometimes to very small groups. Because all the students study a foreign language (French, Spanish, or German), the foreign language teachers also become part of the team when appropriate. This is also true of the special-area teachers: art, music, industrial arts, and home economics. The flexible, modular schedule provides freedom to allow sufficient time for planned activities.

For more information, contact Robert P. Anderson, Principal, Jamesville–DeWitt Middle School, Randall Road, Jamesville, New York 13078.

SAMUEL V. NOE MIDDLE SCHOOL

Samuel V. Noe Middle School includes grades 6 through 8. The pupils come from mostly working-class families. The student body enrollment for the 1983–84 school year was 1,198. The ethnic/racial composition of the student body is 77 percent white and 23 percent black. Noe Middle School is an urban center, an open-space structure, located in downtown Louisville, Kentucky.

Noe Middle School's multi-age teaming consists of approximately 160 students, grades 6 through 8, with seven teachers. Through multi-age teaming, older students serve as models for incoming sixth-graders. Eighth-graders assume positions of leadership as opposed to becoming detached from the middle school as can easily occur at that age. Teachers already know two-thirds of their students as a new year begins. Likewise, most of the students know their teachers, having had them for one or two years. The model does assume a degree of stability in the student population so as to cover the middle-school curriculum over a three-year period. Mainstreaming of students in special-education programs and others functioning below "grade level" can be effectively scheduled so that they are not socially stigmatized.

For more information, contact Dr. James L. Stone, Principal, Samuel V. Noe Middle School, 121 West Lee Street, Louisville, Kentucky 40208.

THOMAS J. RUSK MIDDLE SCHOOL

Thomas J. Rusk Middle School includes grades 6 through 8. The pupils mostly come from working-class families. The pupil enrollment for the 1983–84 school year was 1,350, and the breakdown was 67 percent white, 30 percent black, and 3 percent Hispanic.

The school is organized into instructional blocks or teams of five academic teachers representing each of the basic skill areas of reading, language arts, math, science, and social studies.

Each student receives all of his or her instruction in the basic skills and subjects from members of the same block. Physical education and exploratory subjects are taught by teachers outside the block. This organization allows teachers within a block to make changes in instructional groupings and daily schedules as the situation may demand. It also provides opportunities for a broad range of instructional practices—from traditional departmentalization to interdisciplinary team teaching—and aids the conducting of classroom guidance activities by the block teachers.

The school day for students is divided into seven periods—five periods of basic skills instructions, one period of exploratory, and one period of physical education. Advisor/advisee groups are also scheduled on a weekly basis in place of physical education or the exploratory subjects.

Students are assigned to blocks on the basis of grade, race, and sex. The block assignment of some students is determined by their choice of certain subjects, such as algebra, athletics, band, and performing choir.

For additional information, contact Steve Green, Principal, Thomas J. Rusk Middle School, 411 North Mound, Nacogdoches, Texas 75961.

Appendix G

Parent and Community Relations

Shelbourne Middle School
Keokuk Middle School
Twin Peaks Middle School

SHELBURNE MIDDLE SCHOOL

The best school–community relationship will reflect the specialness of the school and the community it serves. The uniqueness of each school and its setting thus provide a rationale for each school to develop its own parent–community relations program.

Shelburne Middle School includes grades 4 through 8. The pupils represent middle-class families. The pupil enrollment for the 1983–84 school year was 486, predominantly white.

Not all the parents at Shelburne Middle School want the same thing from public education. The Alpha Program is an alternative learning situation within the Shelburne Middle School to meet the needs of pupils and desires of parents. The program comprises all five grade levels, providing learning situations in which individual pupils fulfill their own needs while learning basic academic areas at their own rate. There is no special criterion for enrollment in Alpha. Parents are free to select Alpha or regular classrooms for their children. In either case, they are assured of competent teaching and a range of approaches that will provide their child with sound education. The school hopes that when a child enters the Alpha program the parent will make tentative plans to keep the child in the program for the full five years. They stress the word *tentative* because they understand that circumstances change.

For more information, contact John J. Winton, Principal, Shelburne Middle School, Harbor Road, Shelburne, Vermont 05482.

KEOKUK MIDDLE SCHOOL

Keokuk Middle School includes grade 6 through 8. The pupils mostly come from working-class families. The pupil enrollment for the 1983–84 school year was 615, predominantly white.

The Keokuk Middle School, in response to the diverse needs of the school community, provides an option-filled, flexible environment for learning that provides mutual respect in an informal setting in which people come before programs. The staff, working as a team with parents and students, listens to, encourages, and guides students as they pursue a wide variety of individually derived educational goals. The primary goals are to develop a mastery of the basic skills, an awareness of the world of work, a realistic understanding of self, a sense of social skills and responsibilities, and the self-respect and uniqueness of each individual. The school, as an integral part of the community, is responsive to its needs, problems, and interests. The school's programs are enriched by the community's resources. The community, and particularly parents, is encouraged to participate in and be informed about Keokuk Middle School.

For more information, contact Paul Gaylord, Principal, Keokuk Middle School, 14th & Main, Keokuk, Iowa 52632.

TWIN PEAKS MIDDLE SCHOOL

Twin Peaks Middle School includes grades 6 through 8. The pupils come from mostly middle-class families. The enrollment for the 1983–84 school year was 1,405. The ethnic/racial composition of the student body was predominantly white.

Twin Peaks Middle School participated in a Grandpeople Program that was proven mutually beneficial for pupils, staff, and senior citizens of Poway, California.

You may say that all this sounds great, but what are the difficulties? What is essential in order that a citizen volunteer program succeed? Perhaps the most important feature is the point of view of the administration. The enthusiasm of an administrator can do a great deal to bring about the program's success. Before starting a Grandpeople Program, the administrator has to decide whether there is a sufficient climate of caring and enough respecting human beings to permit a citizen volunteer program to succeed. The program should be introduced gradually, and teachers should not be pressured to take volunteers. As the program develops, teachers have more opportunities to recognize ways to capitalize on the services of another person in the classroom—the volunteer. A vigorous, personalized recruiting program is necessary. Announcements at civic, educational, and religious group meetings in recruiting is necessary. Prior to the two-minute announcements, pass out 3 × 5 cards. An individual who wants to know more about the program jots down his or her name and telephone number. If telephoning an interested person results in his or her wanting to explore more thoroughly the Grandpeople Program, an appointment is made to confer at the school. Teacher needs and the prospective volunteer's interest are discussed. A teacher conference is then arranged after the individual has decided on the assignment that is found most appealing. Continual nurturing is essential to keep a program alive and vigorous. Buffet luncheons or a tea enables the volunteers to become acquainted with one another.

What do these volunteers do? Most of them help, on a one-to-one basis, children who are having difficulty in reading, spelling, or mathematics or in expressing themselves orally and in writing. Sometimes a volunteer works with a cluster (two to five) pupils. Some volunteers are general assistants, answering questions of individual pupils when the teacher is busy with others. These general assistant volunteers often help in keeping records and checking up on homework. The school tries hard to tailor-make an assignment, matching a special ability of the citizen with the school need. For example, a talented senior citizen artist comes to Twin Peaks for a half-day each week to help in two sixth-grade classrooms. After he demonstrates on the chalkboard or easel, the pupils take turns in getting his criticism of their creative efforts. Often, as teachers and pupils become better acquainted with the volunteers, the teachers will capitalize on the volunteers' background by involving them in subjects other than their regular assignments.

For more information, contact Judy Endeman, Principal, Twin Peaks Middle School, 14640 Tierra Bonita Road, Poway, California 92064.

Index

A

Ability, development of nonacademic, 101

Ability grouping by subject, grouping students using, 157, 158–59

Academic ambience, importance of, 4, 10

Academic guidance, need for, 115–16

Academic Preparation for College, 43

Academic subjects:
  goal priorities survey and, 49
  identifying basic, 43

Achievement, adolescents and other-oriented, 30, 36

Activity program(s):
  adolescent development and, 38, 99–100
  athletic programs and, 102
  building support for activities of an, 105
  content emphases of, 104, 112
  diagnosing the, 103–4, 109, 197
  evaluating, 202
  example of an, 253–54
  faculty survey of, 110
  honor societies and, 103
  how individual needs are met through, 100–101
  importance of diversification in, 106
  improving the administrative structure for an, 104–7, 109

improving the learning structure of an, 107–8, 109

interest groups and, 102

monitoring of, 198

parts of an, 101–3

purpose of, 8, 98, 99–100

scheduling of, 105–6

social activities and, 102

student government and, 103

student survey of, 111

talent and, 104, 113

use of awards and, 106–7

Administrative analysis of activity programs, 103, 104

Administrative services of guidance programs, 116

Administrative structure of an activity program, how to improve the, 104–7, 109

Adolescents:
  achievement and, 30, 36
  activity programs and, 38, 98–101
  attachment and, 36
  autonomy and, 29, 36
  characteristics of young, 20–21
  cognitive development of, 23–24, 34
  convention and, 27–28, 35
  developmental differences within same-age groups, 22–23, 33
  formation of intimate groups and, 29–30, 36
  glandular and metabolic imbalances in, 33

E

F

M

N

O

P

Q